PROPHECY

PROPHECY

*Why the Biggest Stock Market
Crash in History Is Still Coming...
and How You Can Prepare
Yourself and Profit from It!*

By Robert T. Kiyosaki with Sharon L. Lechter, C.P.A.

The Authors of *Rich Dad Poor Dad*

Published by Warner Books

An AOL Time Warner Company

Although based on a true story, certain events in the book have been fictionalized for educational content and impact.

Warner Books Edition

Copyright © 2002 by Robert T. Kiyosaki and Sharon L. Lechter
All rights reserved.

Published by Warner Books in association with CASHFLOW Technologies, Inc.

Monopoly® is a registered trademark of Hasbro, Inc.

CASHFLOW is a trademark of CASHFLOW Technologies, Inc.

   are trademarks of
CASHFLOW Technologies, Inc.

 Warner Business Books are published by Warner Books, Inc.,
1271 Avenue of the Americas, New York, NY 10020

Visit our Web site at www.twbookmark.com

 An AOL Time Warner Company

The Warner Business Book logo is a trademark of Warner Books, Inc.

Printed in the United States of America

First Printing: October 2002
10 9 8 7 6 5 4 3 2 1

LCCN: 2002108444
ISBN: 0-446-53086-7

To A Great Teacher

We dedicate this book, *Rich Dad's Prophecy,* to Dave Stephens, a high school teacher in Indianapolis, Indiana. The reason we have dedicated this book to a school teacher is that the cause of the problems revealed in *Rich Dad's Prophecy* is not the ups and downs of the stock market but it is the lack of financial education in the school system.

Not only has Dave Stephens tirelessly worked to bring financial education to his students, he has created a program where his high school students go into elementary schools to become financial mentors to younger students. Dave has also contributed his expertise in educating students to Rich Dad's electronic version of CASHFLOW for Kids, plus curriculum, which will soon be available to schools, free of charge and free of commercial messaging.

We are honored by his support and commend him for his contribution to the field of education.

(Further information about Dave Stephens's programs in the school system is available at the back of this book)

Acknowledgments

We acknowledge and thank the Rich Dad Community. We are humbled by the correspondence we receive from people such as you who have taken control of their financial lives and are teaching others financial literacy.

In June of 2002, almost 250 people gathered in Las Vegas to celebrate financial literacy through playing our game CASHFLOW. They had an idea, shared it on the richdad.com discussion forums, and made it happen on their own. What an incredible group of Rich Dad supporters. Keep learning and teaching!

We thank you!

Contents

Introduction

Noah and the Ark

My rich dad often said, "If you want to be a rich business owner or investor, you need to understand the story of Noah and the Ark." Although rich dad did not see himself as a prophet, he did work diligently on improving his ability to see the future. In training his son and me to be business owners and investors who could also see the future, he would often say, "Do you realize how much faith it took for Noah to go to his family and say, 'God told me there is a great flood coming, so we need to build an ark.'" He would then chuckle and say, "Can you imagine what his wife, kids, and investors must have said to him? They might have said, 'But, Noah, this is a desert we live in. It does not rain here. In fact, we are in the middle of a drought. Are you sure God told you to build an ark? It's going to be tough to raise capital for a boat-building company in the middle of a desert. Wouldn't building a hotel, spa, and golf course make more sense than an ark?'"

For nearly thirty years, starting when we were just nine years old, rich dad trained his son and me to be business owners and investors. Since we were kids, he regularly used very simple teaching tools, such as the game of Monopoly, to teach us the principles of investing. Rich dad also used common everyday fables such as the story of the Three Little Pigs to convey the importance of building financial houses, houses made out of bricks rather than straw or sticks. He also used stories from the Old Testament, stories such as David and Goliath, to teach his son and me the power of leverage, in this case the leverage represented by David's slingshot, as the lesson of how a little guy can beat a big guy. In teaching us the importance of having a vision of the future, rich dad would often say, "Always remember that Noah had vision . . . but more than vision he had the faith and courage to take action on his vision. Many people have vision, but not everyone has the sustainable faith and courage as Noah did . . . the faith and courage to take action on their vision . . . so their vision of the future is the same as their vision of today." In other words, people without faith, courage, and vision often do not see the changes that are coming . . . until it is too late.

My rich dad was very concerned about a 1974 law known as ERISA. He said, "At the time of its passage, most people were not even aware of ERISA. Even today, many people have never even heard of this act passed by Congress and signed into law by President Nixon. The full impact of this law change will not be felt for twenty-five to fifty years . . . long after I am gone. I wish I could tell them to prepare now . . . but how do I tell them about the future?"

In January of 2002, the people of the United States, still reeling from the events of September 11, 2001, began hearing of the bankruptcy of one of the biggest blue chip companies in America. But more than the bankruptcy, the news that sent chills through many people of my generation, the baby-boom generation, the generation born between 1946 and 1964, was the realization that many of the employees of Enron had lost their entire retirement savings. For the first time, millions of baby boomers began to realize that a 401(k), IRA, and other such plans, filled with mutual funds and company stock, were not as safe as they thought or had been told by their financial planner. Millions of baby boomers shared something in common with the thousands of people who worked for Enron. The demise of Enron was sounding a personal alarm, a fear, a realization that their own retirement might not be as secure as they may have once thought. Rich dad's prophecy was coming true.

A local television station called me and asked if I would come in and comment on the impact of the bankruptcy of Enron, a onetime oil and gas industry leader. The attractive young TV commentator asked me, "Is this Enron bankruptcy an isolated event?"

My reply was, "The Enron bankruptcy is an extreme case—but not an isolated case." Continuing, I said, "I am surprised that the media is not mentioning Cisco, Viacom, Motorola, and other giants. Although not as dramatic as Enron, there are many companies similar to Enron where employees have a significant percentage of their retirement tied up in their employer company's stock."

"What do you mean?" asked the TV host.

"I mean this Enron disaster should be a wake-up call for people. A wake-up call letting them know that their 401(k) is not bulletproof . . . that it is possible to lose everything just before you retire . . . that mutual funds are not safe . . . even if you do diversify."

"What do you mean mutual funds are not safe? Even if you diversify?" she asked with a hint of shocked anger. I sensed that I was now stepping on her toes even though she did not work for Enron.

Rather than getting into a debate on mutual funds and diversification, I said, "I retired at the age of forty-seven without a single share of stock or mutual fund. To me, mutual funds and stocks are too risky, even if you do diversify. There are better ways to invest for your retirement."

"Are you saying not to invest in stocks, mutual funds, and to diversify?" she asked.

"No," I replied. "I am not telling anyone to do anything. I am simply saying that I retired early in life without a single share of stock or mutual fund—or diversification within funds. If you want to invest in stocks and mutual funds and diversify, that might be right for you . . . but not for me."

"We need to go to a commercial break," said the young woman. "Thank you for being a guest on our show." She shook my hand and quickly turned to the camera and began talking about the advantages of a new wrinkle cream.

The interview was over earlier than expected. It seemed that when the interview strayed from Enron to the likely personal investment strategies of the TV hostess, wrinkle cream became a more pleasant subject to discuss not only for the TV host but also for the thousands of viewers. The subject of retirement was not a comfortable one.

One of the intended results of ERISA was to encourage individuals to save for their own retirement. This would encourage a three-pronged approach to retirement funding:

1. Social Security
2. A worker's own savings

3. A company pension plan paid out of money the company set aside for a defined pension plan for their employees

On May 5, 2002, an article in the *Washington Post* entitled "Pension Changes Pose Challenges" compared this three-pronged approach to a three-legged stool:

> Last time we looked, the first leg, Social Security, was still standing, though shuddering a bit as its guarantees are pecked away at—ever-increasing taxable income, a raised retirement age, taxation of some benefits and so forth. . . .
>
> All the lettered and numbered savings plans blessed by Congress—the 401(k)s, 403(b)s, IRAs, SEP-IRAs, Keoghs—were arguably intended to bolster the second leg, workers' savings, needed to meet an ever longer and ever more expensive retirement. The corporate tax benefits attached to the company-sponsored plans—made up largely of a worker's own cash—have been nudged over to bolster or even replace the third leg of the stool. Instead of rewarding thrift in employees, they have enabled companies to ditch or severely curtail traditional pension plans.
>
> All of which means: Look, Ma, a three-legged stool with only two legs!

So as a result of ERISA, people suddenly became responsible for their own retirement planning, transferring it from the employer to the employee—without the financial education needed to help the employee plan successfully. Suddenly there were thousands of quickly trained financial planners educating millions of people to "Invest for the long term, buy and hold, diversify." Many of these employees still do not realize that their income during retirement is totally dependent on their ability to invest wisely now. If rich dad's prophecy comes true . . . for millions of people, but not all people, the problem will only get worse over the next twenty-five years. Rich dad's prophecy seems to be coming true.

Gloom and Boom

This is not a gloom and doom book. It is really a gloom and boom book. All through the late 1970s and into the 1980s rich dad reminded his son and me about ERISA. He would say such things as, "Always watch for changes in the law. Every time a law changes, the future changes. If you will prepare to change with the changes in the law you will lead a good life. If you do not pay attention to changes in the law, you may find yourself behaving like the driver of a car who fails to see the sign warning him of a sharp turn in the road up ahead . . . and instead of slowing to prepare to make the turn, reaches over to turn on the radio, fails to make the turn, and drives the car off the road and into the woods."

For those of you who have read my other books, you may recall me mentioning the Tax Reform Act of 1986. This law change was another change in the law rich dad cautioned me to pay attention to. Many people did not pay attention to this change and the price tag for their lack of awareness was measured in the billions of dollars. In my opinion, this 1986 law change was a major contributor to the crash of the savings and loan industry, one of the biggest crashes of the real estate market, and the reason why well-educated professionals such as doctors, lawyers, accountants, and architects cannot use many of the tax law benefits businesspeople like me enjoy. Again, as rich dad said, "Always watch for changes in the law. Every time a law changes, the future changes."

For millions of people because of ERISA, this little known change in the law, will negatively affect their financial lives. For others, this law change will be the best thing that ever happened to them. That is why I state that this is not a doom and gloom book but a gloom and boom book. For those that delude themselves into thinking the future will be the same as today, I am afraid that they may find themselves in the same predicament that many Enron employees found themselves in . . . at the end of their working careers without any money left for retirement. For those that are vigilant and are aware that the future always changes and are prepared for the changes coming, the future is very bright, even if the biggest stock market crash in history does occur, a crash caused by this change in the law.

One of rich dad's main lessons from the story of Noah and the Ark was not that any of us try to become prophets. Instead of training us to have crystal balls and become professional fortune-tellers, rich dad used the story of Noah and the Ark as a lesson in vigilance and preparation. He would say, "Just as a sailor constantly watches for signs of changing weather ahead, a business owner and investor must be vigilant and prepared for anything that lies ahead. Business owners and investors must think like sailors, guiding their tiny boat on a giant ocean . . . prepared for anything."

This book is not written to say that rich dad's prophecy will come true. This book is written to make six main points:

1. To remind all of us to be vigilant and to point out some of the warning signs that rich dad said we needed to pay attention to. In this book you will find out about the flaw in ERISA. In other words, inside this little known law is an even less known flaw . . . a little flaw that rich dad said would trigger the biggest stock market crash in the history of the world.

2. To see the world today with a true financial perspective. Rich dad took his cues from solid facts, facts such as changes in the law and the flaws in the law. He also used statistical realities, realities such as the fact that 75 million baby boomers, 83 million if you count immigrants legal and illegal, are getting older as well, and most will live longer than their parents. He would then ask the question, How many of these baby boomers have enough assets set aside to retire on? Conservative estimates show that less than 40 percent of the baby boomers today have enough.

If the U.S. government must raise taxes to pay for these aging baby boomers' financial and medical needs in old age, what happens to the U.S. economy? Can it sustain its leadership role in the world? Can we afford to remain competitive if the government raises taxes to pay for the aged and continue to pay for a strong military? When taxes are raised, companies may leave in search of countries with lower taxes. And what happens if China passes the United States as the world's largest economy? Can we afford to keep wages high when a Chinese worker will do the same job for less? So rich dad trained his son and me to base our prognostications of the future on today's facts.

3. To ask yourself if you're truly ready for the future. I am not saying that rich dad's prophecy will come true, since rich dad did not see himself as a person with special psychic powers or a crystal ball, or a special connection to God. This point is to ask you the question: "Are you prepared *if* rich dad's prophecy comes true?" In other words, *if* the biggest stock market crash in history does occur, sometime between now and the year 2020, how will you do financially? Will you be better off or worse off? If this market crash does occur, will you be prepared for it or will you be devastated by it?

4. To offer some ideas on what you can do to prepare for the biggest stock market crash in history. Although some of the ideas have been mentioned in my previous books, I will go into greater detail on what you can do *now,* and more importantly why it is essential to take proactive steps *now.*

5. To let you know that you may have up to the year 2010 to become prepared. In fact, in this book you will find out why the chances are pretty good that between now and the year 2010, there will be *another giant stock market boom* . . . the big boom before the big bust. So even if you have nothing today, if you are prepared, you may have one more shot at another bull market much like the great bull market we had between 1995 and 2000.

6. Finally, to let you know that you will probably be better off financially, if you actively *prepare.* In other words, if you plan now, take action and prepare, your financial future may be much brighter even if the biggest stock market crash in the history of the world does *not* occur. Being proactive, educated, and prepared is much better than the financial strategy most people have when it comes to their investments . . . the passive strategy of "Buy, Hold, and Pray" . . . praying that the stock market booms and does not bust. Of course people who believe that the stock market only goes up and never comes down probably also believe in the Easter Bunny.

The story of Noah and the Ark is a great story of a great prophet . . . a prophet with tremendous vision, faith, and courage. This book will not teach you to be a prophet . . . but I believe it will give you great faith that a brighter financial future is available to you and your loved ones, regardless if the biggest stock market crash in history does or does not occur. So this book is not intended to be a crystal ball, but it is intended to teach you to be more of a person who is vigilant and prepared for whatever happens . . . good or bad. In other words, to give you more control over your financial future. As rich dad said, "The point of the story of Noah and the Ark is not that Noah was right, but that Noah had the faith, the courage, and was prepared for anything that happened . . . even a giant flood in the middle of the desert . . . a flood that wiped out the rest of the world."

Note: ERISA helped create the infamous 401(k) plan, as well as other retirement plans in America. Other countries have similar plans. They just go by different names. For example:

1. In Australia they are called Superannuation Plans.
2. In Canada a similar plan is called the RRSP.
3. In Japan the plan is also called 401(k).

Rich Dad's Prophecy

- The fallacy of ERISA.
- How ERISA has allowed our generation's financial problems to be pushed onto the backs of our children's generation.
- A major stock market crash will occur—while hard to pinpoint an exact time, it is inevitable.
- The only way to prepare and profit from the crash is through financial literacy and taking control of your finances.
- Solid financial strategies are explained to help you prepare.

AUDIO DOWNLOAD

In each of our books we like to provide an audio inter-view as a bonus with additional insights. As a thank-you to you for reading this book, you may go to the Web site www.richdad.com/prophecy and download an audio of my discussion with one of my advisors about, "why the rich get richer, and how you can too!"

Thank you for your interest in your financial education.

Is the Fairy Tale Over?

Once upon a time, all a person had to do was go to school, get good grades, find a safe secure job, be a loyal employee, retire, move to a smaller house on a golf course, and live happily ever after.

Today, most of us know that any story beginning with *once upon a time* and ending with *they lived happily ever after* is a fairy tale. The problem is that today there are many modern-day fairy princes and princesses who are hoping the fairy tale is not over . . . hoping that their financial planner's advice of "Invest for the long term, buy and hold, diversify" will keep the fairy tale alive for as long as they live.

Unfortunately, as most professional investors know, fairy tales attached to the stock market do not always have happy endings.

What Is More Important than Becoming a Rich Investor?

When I was a kid in the 1960s, investing was an activity only of the rich or those who wanted to become rich. Today, we all need to invest for something far more important than simply to become rich. Today, how intelligently you invest will determine your future . . . your future standard of living, your future financial security, and maybe even if you live or die. In other words, when medical care is factored in, how intelligently you invest today will ultimately determine how well you live and if you can afford to live . . . and that is far more important than simply investing to become rich.

—Robert Kiyosaki
PBS television special, 2001

Chapter 1

A Change in the Law...
A Change in the Future

Both my rich dad and my poor dad were very concerned about the overall well-being of their employees. My real dad, as the superintendent of education for the State of Hawaii, had tens of thousands of workers who counted on him to take care of them. My real dad, the man I call my poor dad, was so very concerned about his teachers that when he was no longer the superintendent of education he became the leader of HSTA, which stands for the Hawaii State Teachers Association, a teachers union, again negotiating for the well-being of his teachers.

My rich dad was also very concerned about his employees, and in many ways, he was much more concerned about his employees than my dad. The reason he was more concerned was because my poor dad's employees had the financial support of the government and the local and national teachers unions. My rich dad's employees did not have the government support and union protection. He would often say, "I wish I could tell my workers what I know and what I see coming in the future. I wish I could but I am afraid I would frighten them too much. Besides, the main problem is that most of them lack the basic financial education first to understand what I am saying and secondly to be able to take corrective action. How do I tell my loyal hardworking employees that today, being loyal and hardworking is not enough? How do I explain to them that long-term job security does not insure long-term financial security? How do I tell them about a change in a law that has changed their future forever? How do I tell them without frightening or depressing them? How do I tell people about what I think might happen, but I am not certain will happen?"

As I said, both my poor dad and my rich dad were very concerned about their workers. The difference was that my poor dad had the power of the government and the teachers unions to help his workers. My rich dad knew that his workers were at a disadvantage and this concerned him greatly. In 1974 there was a major law change in America that was reportedly designed to help workers who worked for people like my rich dad. While many people thought the intent behind the new law was a great idea, rich dad could see its inherent flaws. He knew that in many ways, most of his workers would not be better off in the long run and he could see a growing threat of financial disaster looming in the future . . . a financial disaster caused by the passage of this act into law.

In 1979, I was thirty-two years old and struggling to keep my business above water. My nylon and Velcro surfer wallet business had taken off faster than expected. In only a few years, we were a big company with a sales force of over 380 independent sales reps in the United States alone. Worldwide, we never really did figure out how many salespeople we had selling for us. The problem was that we had a worldwide product but we were a small-time company with a young incompetent management team. When success and incompetence meet, disaster is not far away.

It has been said "You cannot learn to swim from a textbook." I would also add, "You cannot learn business from a textbook or from business school." My partners and I had limited textbook knowledge and very little real-life business experience. At an early age, we were learning some simple yet tough lessons about business, lessons that can only be learned from front line experience. Besides the lesson that success can kill you, some of the other lessons I was learning were:

1. Friends do not always make good business partners.
2. A company can be profitable and still be in serious financial trouble.
3. It's the little things, like not having enough thread, that can stop the whole business.

4. People do not always pay their bills, which means you cannot always pay your bills. People do not like you when you do not pay them.
5. Patents and trademarks are important aspects of a successful business.
6. Loyalty can be fleeting.
7. It is essential to have accurate financial records and accounting.
8. You need a strong management team and a strong team of professional consultants such as lawyers and accountants.
9. It costs a lot of money to build a business.
10. It's not the lack of money that kills a business. It's more the lack of business experience and lack of personal integrity.

The actual list of lessons is much longer. The experience of worldwide success and worldwide failure was priceless. I went through such experiences not once, but twice. And although I do not want to go through it all again, I am ready to . . . because the lessons are priceless, if you are willing and humble enough to learn from your mistakes. Each business failure showed me what I did not know and what I needed to learn . . . and that learning experience led to the next success.

In 1979, I was up to my ears in learning experiences. I was over my head in mistakes, buried by my own personal incompetence, and I did not want to learn anything more. I had more than enough stupidity to learn from, yet rich dad had more to point out to me. In the spring of 1979, I walked into his office for our regular meeting and showed him my company's financial statement. Looking over the statement, rich dad shook his head and said, "Your company has financial cancer . . . and I'm afraid it's terminal. You boys have mismanaged what could have grown into a rich and powerful company."

Mike, rich dad's son, was not a partner in my business, yet he did sit in on most of the mentoring meetings I had with his dad, the man I call my rich dad. Mike and I had been best friends all through high school, but after I returned from college and the Vietnam War, it was difficult maintaining a close friendship since we were in completely different business and financial leagues. In 1979, Mike was in the process of taking over his father's multi-million-dollar empire and I was in the process of losing a multimillion-dollar business. As Mike looked over my company's financials, I felt shame and embarrassment when Mike also shook his head.

"What is this?" asked rich dad, pointing to a section of my financial statement.

Looking at where he was pointing, I said, "It's the amounts we owe the employees and the government for the employees' payroll and payroll taxes."

"Now look at your cash position, there isn't any money there," said rich dad sternly. "How are you going to make payroll, and pay the taxes?"

I sat there quietly saying nothing. "Well . . ." I began feebly, "well, when we collect on some of our back accounts receivables we'll have enough to pay them."

"Oh come on," said rich dad. "Don't give me that jive. I'm not your college professor. I can see from your financials that much of your accounts receivables are over 120 days delinquent. You and I know that these people you have sold product to are never going to pay you. Tell me the truth. Tell yourself the truth. You're broke. You're broke and now you're about to default on paying your employees and their taxes. You're using your employees' money to keep your company afloat."

"But it is only a short-term credit problem. We have money coming in. We have sales coming in from all over the U.S. and the world," I replied in my defense.

"Yes, but what good are sales if you cannot build product and cannot deliver on those sales? I can see from these financial statements that people owe you money and you owe money. You owe money to the people that supply you the materials to produce your products. What makes you think that your suppliers will give you any more credit?"

"Well—" I began but was cut off again by an angry rich dad.

"Your suppliers won't give you any more credit. Why should they?"

"Well, I'll go talk to them again."

"Good luck," said rich dad. "Look, why don't you face the truth? You and the three clowns you call partners have mismanaged your business . . . you don't know what you're doing . . . you're incompetent . . . and worst of all, you don't have the guts to admit any of this. You guys are pretending to look like businesspeople . . . but when I look at your financials, you boys are either crooks or clowns. I hope you're clowns . . . but if you don't make some changes, you clowns will become crooks." Rich dad said this pursing his lips and slowly moving his head from side to side. "Borrowing money from your employees is bad enough. Just look at the back taxes you owe. How are you going to pay them?"

Rich dad had been my teacher since I was nine years old. He was a very loving and caring man, but when he was angry . . . he was not a polite man. This particularly heated lesson in business management went on for hours. Finally, I agreed to shut the business down, liquidate the remaining assets, and use the money to pay the taxes and the employees.

"There is nothing wrong with admitting you're incompetent," said rich dad. "But there is plenty wrong with lying and pretending you know what you're doing. Lying and pretending you know what you are doing is a bad habit . . . and I want you to stop that habit now. If you want to be rich and successful, you need to learn to tell the truth quicker, ask for help quicker, and be more humble. The world is filled with arrogant poor people, educated and uneducated . . . people who cannot admit they do not know something. The world is filled with people who go through life pretending they are smart . . . and that makes them stupid. If you want to learn quickly, the first step is to admit quickly you do not know something.

"Remember the lesson from Sunday school, the lesson that goes, 'Blessed are the meek for they shall inherit'? The passage does not go blessed are the *weak* or blessed are the *arrogant*, or blessed are the *well educated*. It says blessed are the meek for the meek shall learn and if you learn you shall inherit the abundance of life that God or nature has placed in front of us. You boys are arrogant, conceited, cocky, and ignorant . . . not meek. You think that just because your product is a success you are also a success. You boys are not yet businessmen. You boys got lucky but you do not have the skill and experience to turn your luck into a business. No one becomes a successful businessperson overnight. You have a lot more to learn. And the lesson you must learn today is that if you owe money, pay the bill. People hate people who do not pay their bills. Friends, families, and businesses have broken apart because money owed was not repaid. From your company's financial statements, I can see that you owe money to the government, your suppliers, your landlord, and most importantly to your employees. Pay those bills and pay them now. Don't do anything else until those bills are paid. Don't come back here until you've paid your taxes and *all* your employees. You're becoming a sloppy businessman and sloppy businesspeople do not become rich and successful businesspeople. Now get out of here and don't come back until you have done what I have just told you to do."

As I said, rich dad had chewed me out many times over the years, but this lesson from rich dad was especially memorable. As I closed the door behind me, I could feel this particular lesson sinking into my soul . . . becoming a lesson I would never forget. Although I hurt, I knew that the lesson was an important lesson . . . for if it was not important, rich dad would not have gotten so angry or so brutally forthright. Being thirty-two years old, I was old enough to take this strong, emotionally charged lesson and wise enough to know that I had something important to learn.

Over the years, rich dad had a lesson on truth and honesty he repeatedly taught. He often said to his son and me, "Many people ask young people, 'What do you want to be when you grow up?' When they ask that question, they are usually asking what profession the child wants to pursue. Personally, I don't care what you do when you grow up. I don't care if you become a doctor, movie star, or janitor. But as you grow up, I do care that you grow up to become more and more truthful and more honest. Too many people grow up becoming more polite, but not necessarily more truthful, or worse, they tell lies as kids and become bigger liars as adults." As I walked down the street to where my car was parked, I knew it was again time for me to become more truthful . . . more honest with myself, my partners, and my employees.

Climbing into my car, I could hear rich dad saying, "Any coward can tell a lie. Telling the truth takes courage. As you boys grow up, grow up to become people who have more and more courage to tell the truth quicker . . . even if the truth hurts . . . even if being honest makes you look bad. It is better to look bad telling the truth than to be a good-looking lying coward. The world is filled with good-looking lying cowards." As the engine came to life and I put my car into gear, I felt terrible and I knew that I probably looked as bad as my financial statements. Driving away, I also knew that I had two choices. One was to continue lying to myself and never see rich dad again. The other was to begin finding the courage to face the truth, to clean up the mess I made, and then look forward to seeing rich dad again.

At thirty-two, I realized I still had a lot of growing up to do. I knew that if I wanted to become a richer, more successful person and a better human being, I had to be able to hear a more refined truth, even if it was a little tougher truth. As part of my growing up, I also had to be able to tell the truth better. As I pulled up into my company's parking lot, I knew the time to begin telling that truth was now . . . and it would begin with my partners, the partners rich dad called *clowns*.

Approximately four months later, I returned to rich dad's office with a new set of financial statements in hand. Rich dad and Mike looked them over for what seemed to be an extra long period of silence. Finally rich dad said, "So all your back taxes and your employees are paid?"

"That is correct," I said. "If you notice, I also cleaned up a lot of my old accounts receivables."

"You got them to pay?" asked rich dad.

"Either they paid or I took them off the financial statement and sent a collection agency after them."

"That's good," said Mike. "A customer who does not pay is not a customer. A customer who does not pay is a thief."

"I understand that now," I replied. "But I was doing the same thing."

Rich dad looked up at me . . . paused, and then slowly nodded and quietly said, "Thanks for admitting that."

"It wasn't easy," I replied. "I had this image of myself as a successful person, and in reality, I owed a lot of people a lot of money."

Mike and rich dad sat silently, ever so slightly nodding. Finally rich dad said, "The truth does set you free . . . and hopefully now you are free . . . free to clean up your mess and begin building your next business on more solid ground. So many people attempt to build their financial empire upon a mess of lies . . . and lies never seem to support much of an empire."

Now it was my turn to sit silently and just let the crystal-clear silence fill the room. After a long pause, Mike asked, "So what condition is your company in? Your financial statement is a lot more honest but a financial statement can never tell the whole story."

"The company is finished," I replied. "We still have sales and the actual business is strong, but the four of us who started this business are finished. We'll probably never be partners or friends again. Truthfully, the truth tore us apart."

"So when you returned to your company, you had a heart-to-heart?"

"Well, it started out as a heart-to-heart but it soon became face-to-face. We almost came to blows but thankfully that did not happen. It has not been pleasant at work, but I do give my partners credit for being willing to stick it out and clean up the mess, as you suggested."

"Now what happens?" asked Mike.

"Well, we are turning over the remains of the company to one of our suppliers and we are all going our separate ways. We will soon begin letting our employees go, and they will have all the money we owe them. Our investors will get some but not all of their money back, but we have talked to them and they understand the risk they took. Several have said they would invest with me again. And our taxes are paid."

Mike and rich dad just sat silently. It was like being at a funeral . . . a lot of emotion but little to say. The winding down of a business is like the ending of anything. Good or bad, there are parts of the experience that had forever changed our lives, our future, and who we would become. I was dreading turning out the lights and closing the office door for the last time, even though I was also glad it was going to soon close. Finally rich dad broke the silence and said, "Well, I'm proud of the way you handled the loss of your business. I know it isn't pleasant and I know you could have handled it differently. You could have taken the remaining money and run . . . but you chose a better way of ending things. That will give your next venture a little better ground to start from. Have you learned a lot?"

"Massive learning," I said. "I'm still digesting the lessons."

"You will for years," said rich dad. "But someday this experience and the mistakes and experiences yet to come will become the basis for your success and fortune. Most people avoid mistakes. Most people spend their lives playing it safe . . . avoiding such lessons . . . and that lack of life's experience limits their future financial success. Always remember that business experience can never be gained from a textbook or a classroom. Although painful, because of the way you chose to handle this business failure, this painful short period of time will someday become the basis of your long-term financial wealth. If you had run and lied, your financial future would probably be a coward's future . . . because if you had run you would have been letting the coward in you determine your future."

I simply sat quietly and nodded. There was not much to say. I had heard this talk and this lesson before . . . but on this day, this simple lesson had much more meaning and a deeper impact. Rich dad often said to his son and me that inside each of us is a cast of characters. Inside each of us is a kind person, a mean person, a greedy person, a rich person, a poor person, a coward, a crook, a hero, a liar, a cheapskate, a lover, a loser, and more. He constantly reminded us that growing up was a process of choosing which person we wanted to become . . . which person we wanted to draw out of all the cast of characters available. As stated earlier, when he asked us what we wanted to be when we grew up, he was asking which character we were choosing to become . . . not if we were going to be a doctor, lawyer, or firefighter. To rich dad, a person's choice of *character* was far more important than a person's choice of *profession*.

"When it comes to money, the world is filled with cowards," said rich dad. "Money has a way of bringing out the coward . . . more than the hero . . . and that may be why there are so few truly rich people. Money also has a way of bringing out the cheat and the crook in some people . . . and that is why our jails keep filling up. Money also has a way of bringing out the betrayer . . . the person who will steal from those that love and trust them . . . and when you 'borrowed' from your employees, that is the character you were choosing to become . . . and that is why I was especially tough on you. Crooks and cowards are one thing . . . but becoming a person who betrays those that trust you is one of the most despicable of all characters available to all of us . . . and you were choosing that character."

There was not much for me to say. The internal pain was intense. Truth and honesty are not always pleasant and this dose of truth and honesty was very unpleasant . . . yet necessary. I realized that in my desperation to save my company, I had chosen to betray those that trusted me.

"Have you gotten your lesson?" asked rich dad. "Have you gotten the lesson in character choices?"

I just nodded my head again. I had understood the lesson . . . a deep, painful lesson, a lesson I would always remember. I had always thought of myself as a good, honest person . . . yet under pressure, the character that emerged was the person who betrayed those that trusted me.

"Good," said rich dad. "A lesson in character is far more important than a lesson in reading a financial statement . . . yet the financial statement did reflect your character. Your financial statement told me the story of the betrayer in you taking over your business. That is another lesson in the importance of accounting, accountability, and the importance of being able to read financial statements. The numbers tell me a story . . . a story of which character is in charge of the money. When you and your partners started your business, you started off as gamblers, you got lucky and became clowns thinking your luck was skill, when the money came pouring in you became fools buying Porsches and Mercedes sports cars, and when you got into financial trouble you became people who betrayed your suppliers, your government, and your workers. Your financial statements tell a better story than most novels."

"That's enough, Dad," Mike said as he jumped in to protect me from any more of the lesson. "I think you have made your point."

"Okay," said rich dad. Turning to me he then asked, "Have you got the lesson?"

"Right between the eyes," I replied.

"Good. Let's go get some lunch," said rich dad. "There is a far more important lesson I want you to learn . . . a very important lesson . . . a lesson that begins with the question, 'Why did your employees not know what you were doing with their money?'"

When the elevator finally arrived, we found it crowded with people also going to lunch. Packing into the elevator, rich dad said, "Sometime in the future, long after I am gone, millions of hardworking people will find out that clowns like you and your partners have been playing games with their money . . . their retirement money . . . their financial future . . . their financial security. The government has made changes in the law . . . changes to protect workers, but I do not think this law change will solve the problem. In fact, I think the law change will make things worse for many people. I am afraid something terrible is going to happen."

Chapter 2

The Law That Changed the World

Rich dad, Mike, and I went to one of our favorite Chinese restaurants for lunch. As usual, the place was packed because the food was good, the service fast, and the prices fair. We had to wait a few minutes before a table opened and our favorite waiter cleaned it as we took our seats.

As we sat going through the menu, rich dad said to me, "Most people will not have enough money set aside for their retirement. In fact, I would be willing to bet that most of the people sitting in this restaurant will never be able to retire simply because they have nothing in their retirement plans."

"You mean the workers here?" Mike asked. "People like our waiter and those that cook and wash dishes in the back?"

"Not only the restaurant workers, but many of the executives in suits and ties who are dining here will have nothing . . . or will not have enough money to retire on. Most of the people in this room will never be able to afford retirement."

"Most?" I asked in surprise. "Wouldn't it be more accurate to say *some* rather than *most?*"

"No," said rich dad. "I believe the more accurate word is *most* . . . not *some.*"

"How can that be?" I asked. "Most seem to have good jobs. They dress well and appear to be rather intelligent."

"Do you remember me telling you about ERISA?" asked rich dad.

"Yes, vaguely," I replied. "You've mentioned it on several occasions. I just have not fully understood what you were saying or why this law change was so important."

"Most people don't realize its importance," said rich dad. "It may be years before people begin to wake up to the ripple effects this law change will have in the future."

"What is this law change and why was it passed?" I asked.

"Good question," said rich dad. "First of all, ERISA stands for Employee Retirement Income Security Act. It was the Act that made 401ks possible. I too did not pay much attention to its passage . . . but soon my accountants and my attorneys began advising me on changes I needed to make in my businesses. Once that began to happen, I began asking more in-depth questions."

"And what did you find out?" I asked.

"It seems the act was passed to help protect employees' retirement money from abuse by their business owners," said rich dad.

"What kind of abuse?" I asked.

"There have been many kinds of abuses of retirement plans. Even in some large blue chip companies, pension plans are empty or are under-funded. And many times, a company would buy another company not because of the business, but because they wanted the business's retirement money. Some of these more responsible businesses had tens of millions of dollars in their employee retirement funds and that pool of money was often more valuable than the business. So the raiding company would buy the business and bleed the employee retirement fund."

"They would take over the company just for the retirement money?"

Rich dad nodded his head. "But that was not the only abuse. There were more. It was because of these abuses that ERISA was supposedly passed."

"Why do you say supposedly?" I asked.

"Well, the act was passed as a benefit for employees . . . a way to protect employees from these abuses . . . but as we all know, nothing is only good for only one group of people. The company also benefited from the act . . . but the benefits to the company were not really mentioned in the press."

"So how did it benefit the businesses?" I asked.

"Well now that you've had your first business, let me ask you this question. How expensive is an employee retirement plan to the company?"

"You mean including Social Security payments plus adding money to their retirement plan?" I asked.

Rich dad nodded his head, saying, "Yes . . . how expensive is it?"

"Very expensive," I replied. "I often wished I could pay my workers more but the hidden taxes—taxes the employees are often not even aware of—are so high I could not afford to pay much more. Every time I gave them a raise the government also got a raise."

"So while ERISA was passed as a benefit to employees, it was in many ways more of a benefit to the employer. In many cases the expense of retirement has transferred from the *employer* to the *employee.*"

"But doesn't the employer have to match the amount the employee puts in?" I asked.

"They can if their plan allows it . . . but the key word is match," said Mike. "In other words, the dollar amount the employer had to pay was now significantly reduced. That is like taking the cost of your mortgage payment and cutting it in half. Wouldn't you want to reduce your mortgage payment by half?" Mike was very well versed in this new retirement plan because rich dad put him in charge of understanding it. "And on top of that, many *employees* elect not to contribute anything, so the *employer* has nothing to match."

"So if the employee does not put any money into his or her fund, the employer pays nothing. The cost of that employee's retirement just went to zero. And is that why we're going to have a problem? The problem of people without any retirement savings?" I asked.

"That is one of the problems . . . and it's a very big problem. But in my opinion, it is not the person who has nothing in their retirement plan that will ultimately cause the biggest problem . . . the biggest problem will come from those employees who have diligently put money into their retirement accounts. It is those who have faithfully put money into their retirement plans that will cause the biggest stock market crash in history."

"In history?" I asked skeptically. "And the crash will not be caused by those employees who have nothing . . . it will be caused by those who have set money aside?"

Rich dad nodded his head. "Think about it. Can someone with nothing cause the stock market to crash?"

"I don't really know. I've never really thought about it," I replied.

"The biggest stock market crash of all will be caused by millions of people with their money tied up in mutual funds and other types of shares in the stock market, not by those without any shares or money," Mike added. "It's just common sense."

"This change in the law will bring about many problems and one of the problems, way off in the future, will be this giant stock market crash," said rich dad as our food arrived.

"Why is that? How can you be so sure?" I asked.

"Because the people putting money into the market are not investors. As you already know, most of your workers cannot read a financial statement. So how can you invest if you cannot read a financial statement?" asked rich dad. "The resulting impact started by ERISA is not only leaving millions of people without a retirement plan, it is also forcing people to trust their financial future to the stock market . . . and we all know that all markets go up and all markets go down." Rich dad looked directly at me. "I've been training you and Mike to be investors . . . investors who can make money in an up market and in a down market. But most employees do not have that mental and emotional training . . . and when the big crash begins, I believe they will react as most untrained investors react . . . they will panic and begin selling . . . selling to save their lives . . . selling to protect their future."

"When do you think this will happen?" I asked.

"I don't know," said rich dad. "No one has a crystal ball with 20/20 vision. But between now and the biggest crash of all, I predict there will be smaller but growing booms and busts in the stock market . . . and these smaller booms and busts will come before the biggest of all booms and biggest of all busts."

"So there will be warning signs?" Mike asked.

"Oh yes," smiled rich dad. "There will be plenty of them. The good news is that you boys will have plenty of time to practice gaining experience and skill through these smaller booms and busts. Just as you two practice surfing on the smaller waves of summer, in preparation for the larger waves of winter, I would recommend you do the same with your investing skills. As the booms and busts get bigger and bigger, you'll find it easier to become richer and richer."

"But others will become poorer and poorer," I said quietly.

"Unfortunately that is true. But always remember the story of Noah and the Ark. Noah could not get all the animals on board . . . and I am afraid the same is true for the coming stock market crash."

"So it is survival of the fittest?" I asked.

"It will be survival of the financially fittest and the financially smartest," said rich dad. "It will be survival for those who are prepared . . . just as Noah prepared for the future by building an ark. I have been training you boys to build an ark also."

"We're building arks?" I chuckled. "Where is it? I don't see one."

"The ark I have been helping you to build is inside your head."

"An ark inside my head," I said cynically. "That's a new thought."

"Look," said rich dad as he reached for a serving of food. "If you don't want to prepare, then tell me now. Don't waste my time. Do you think I like scolding you for mismanaging your business and your personal finances? Have I been wasting my time and my faith in you? If I have, tell me now."

"No, no, no," I pleaded. "It's just the ark. I have a hard time with this building an ark concept . . . especially in my head."

"Well, where do you think money, investing, and business take place? They take place in your head. If money is not found in your head it will not be found in your hands," said rich dad angrily.

"Okay, okay, okay," I said apologetically.

"Look," said rich dad. "There may or may not be this giant stock market crash. But I can assure you that there will be booms and busts . . . there always have been booms and busts in the past and there will always be booms and busts in the future. Predicting that booms and busts are coming is not much of a prediction. You boys are in your early thirties. You have a good financial foundation and you're gaining great business experience. You are now old enough to face the real world. Just as you practice surfing nearly every day, riding the ups and downs of the waves, I ask you to practice riding the ups and downs of financial markets and financial cycles. If you do that, your skills will improve."

"So markets boom and bust just like the waves on the ocean," I said.

"Correct," said rich dad. "They're called business cycles."

"And you think that ERISA is like a storm out at sea that will soon be sending waves crashing on shore . . . altering business cycles for a long time," said Mike.

"In surfer terms . . . the answer is yes. That is what I think," rich dad said as he finished his meal. "There have always been booms and busts . . . but I believe this law change will lead to the biggest boom and biggest bust of all."

"But what if you're wrong?" I asked.

"If I am wrong . . . and if you do what I suggest, at a minimum you will get richer and richer. You'll get richer and richer because you will be building your ark . . . a financial ark in your head, and that alone will make you rich in a good economy and in a bad economy."

"Okay," I said. "I'll keep this ark idea in my head and think about it. I'll think about it as preparation and planning for the future, preparing as Noah did for something that might or might not happen. But what makes you think this change in the law will have such a big impact and cause such a large market crash?"

"Because changes in the law change the future," rich dad replied. "For example, if the government changed the speed limit on this small street in front of this restaurant from twenty-five miles per hour to a hundred miles per hour, we would see some immediate changes. Immediately there would be more traffic accidents and more fatalities. That is how law changes change our future, good and bad."

"And this law change, what has it changed? Why can't we see the changes? Why aren't these executives sitting all around us as concerned as you are?"

Rich dad took a fresh paper napkin and wrote the following letters on it:

DB

DC

"The reason the executives around us and the workers who work here are not concerned is because I believe we are now in the transition period between DB pension plans and DC pension plans."

"What?" I asked. "DB to DC plans?"

"DB pension plans to DC pension plans," said Mike. "Most people are like you, unaware of the differences between the two plans . . . and there are massive differences. Most of the executives sitting around us are still thinking in terms of DB pension plans . . . not DC . . . that is why they are not concerned. They are not aware of the changes or the future consequences."

"When will these executives start becoming aware of the differences?" I asked.

"The lag time is pretty long," said rich dad. "I predict that it will take twenty-five to fifty years before people become aware of the full impact of this law change."

"You mean sometime around the year 2000, we should begin to notice the changes?" I asked.

"Oh, you will begin to notice the changes way before that year," said rich dad. "Although people will notice the changes, such as smaller booms and busts in the stock market, I don't think people will be aware of the frightening consequences of this law change until the year 2000 or later . . . maybe too much later."

The bill was paid. As we stood up from the table, our favorite waiter was already wiping it off, getting it ready for the next group of hungry diners. "And what are you doing to be prepared for these coming changes?" I asked rich dad.

"I'm already prepared. I've already built my ark," smiled rich dad as we stepped out on the street. "The problems will not be my problem. But they will be your problem. I will not be around when the real impact of this law change hits. Your dad and I will be gone and buried before the tidal wave hits shore."

"So this law change is almost like your generation passing on your problems to our generation," I said, testing rich dad's receptivity to the idea of intergenerational *passing of the buck* . . . or the passing on of the problem . . . as it is in this case.

"I'd say that is pretty accurate," said rich dad. "It's the World War II generation passing on the problem to the baby-boom generation, and coming generations . . . a problem my generation has benefited from."

"Your generation benefited and now my generation pays for your benefits?" I asked. "That is the legacy we inherit?"

"That is part of the story," said rich dad with a sly smile. "First let me explain the difference between a DB pension plan and a DC pension plan."

Rich dad went on to explain that a DB, or defined benefit, pension plan was a retirement plan that defined the benefit or the dollar amount a retired person would receive. For example, if an employee worked for forty years for a company and retired at sixty-five, a defined benefit might pay that employee, let's say, $1,000 a month for as long as he or she lived. If that employee lived to sixty-six, the company actually did well because the company only had to pay the defined benefit for a year. If the ex-employee lived to 105, the company paid the $1,000 a month for forty years. In this case, the employee was much better off, but at the expense of the company. Social Security is a government DB plan.

Subsequent changes to ERISA may allow companies to switch to DC, or defined contribution, plans. The difference between a DB and DC plan is found in the difference between the definitions of the words *benefit* and *contribution*. A DB plan defines the *benefit* whereas a DC plan is defined by the *contribution*. In other words, a worker's retirement is only as good as the contribution . . . if there is a contribution.

A worker might retire with nothing because he or she contributed nothing. In addition, if a worker retired with $2 million in their plan and that $2 million was gone by age eighty-five either through distribution or by mismanagement or market crash, then at eighty-five this worker was out of retirement funds and out of luck. The worker could not go back to the company and demand more financial benefits.

Simply put, the responsibility, expense, and long-term consequences of retirement will pass from the employer to the employee. Although the difference between the letters DB to DC is small . . . the long-term consequences are, and will continue to be, large. As rich dad said, "It's the World War II generation passing on the problem to the baby-boom generation, and coming generations . . . a problem my generation has benefited from." In other words, they got the benefit and now we get the bill . . . and it will be a very big bill.

Returning to rich dad's office, I gave both of them a hug and thanked them for the lesson. I was starting over again, without any money, without a job, but with a wealth of knowledge and experience. Although a little worried and nervous, I was ready to get back to working, looking for a new business opportunity to begin building a new company.

"I have one more question," I said, looking at rich dad. "Many of those executives in that restaurant are not aware of the difference between a DB and DC pension plan?"

"No. I would say most aren't," said Mike, stepping in for his dad. "And that is going to cause the bigger problems in the future. Because they are not aware, they are not preparing for the future. They still think that after retirement, there will be plenty of money for as long as they live."

"I'm afraid that many of your generation will be forced to live at a lower standard of living, after they retire, than my generation will," said rich dad. "Most of my generation still has DB pension plans. They can retire to the golf course community and play golf and bingo all day. Many of your generation will never be able to retire. Many, in fact I would say most, will work all their lives, some because they want to, but most because they have to."

"I hope they love what they do," I said with a smile.

"That is short-term thinking," said Mike. "I've looked into this and statistics show that 25 percent of all workers are disabled at one time or another after retirement. Some are permanently disabled and some are just temporarily. So that is why just believing that doing what you love is a solution is shortsighted. Our generation and future generations need to think long term, because we will live longer . . . but the question is, Can we afford to live longer and can we afford the rising costs of health care? And what happens if we are one of the 25 percent that is disabled and cannot work, cannot do what we love? Those are more pertinent questions you and I need to ask ourselves, our families, and our workers."

"And right now we are not asking those questions," I said, looking at rich dad.

"No, I am afraid not," rich dad replied, checking his watch. "The problem with most of the executives in that little Chinese restaurant is that most of them think they have the same DB pension plans their parents had. They may think that way because they work for large corporations. But in the near future, large corporations will switch to DC pension plans and most workers, even the executives, will not be aware of the long-term consequences of these changes."

"And working for a large corporation is like working on board a large cruise ship," said Mike, jumping back into the conversation. He had done a lot of research and was very concerned about the future. "In the old days, once a worker was through working, the corporation gave the worker a stateroom in the back of the ship. The retired worker joined the other passengers, enjoying the benefits of working for the good ship SS *Good Corporation*. The retired worker was soon dancing the night away, listening to

Benny Goodman music, sipping champagne, and playing shuffleboard all day. But that was the past. The SS *Good Corporation* may now throw the re-tired worker over the side with a small life preserver known as a defined con-tribution plan."

"And what if there is nothing in the defined contribution plan?" I asked.

"Not the ship's problem," said Mike.

"Try building an ark out of a life preserver," smirked rich dad sarcastically. "Most people are not trained to build arks, so most people will spend their later years of life clinging to tiny little life preservers and handouts from family and the government. That is why I want you two boys to begin building your arks now . . . and if you do, when the changes come, you will have your own large ship . . . your own ark . . . big enough and strong enough, able to with-stand any storm at sea . . . and trust me . . . there is a storm coming, a big one."

Thanking rich dad and Mike for lunch, I turned and headed for the ele-vator. I was thirty-two and I had no money and no job, but this time I was starting over again with a wealth of knowledge and experience. I knew that the building of my next business would be easier and faster. So even though I was out of money, I was filled with excitement about the future, even though I knew there was a very large storm brewing at sea. To me, building an ark made more sense than building a life preserver . . . a life preserver known as a defined contribution plan, or whatever else financial life pre-servers are called in other parts of the world.

Chapter 3

Are You Ready to Face the Real World?

The streets of Waikiki were busy with tourists either going to the beach or returning from the beach. Most were dressed in swimsuits and rubber slippers covered with sand. Most seemed happy just to be taking some time off from their regular lives from wherever they came.

As I crossed the street to get to the bus stop, I glanced up at the waves, breaking a few hundred yards offshore, and wondered if I had time for an evening set with my friends who surfed out there. The breaking waves, the warm water, and the sun gently sinking were calling to me. Before the bus arrived, I stood envious, looking out on the ocean at a way of life I grew up in, surfing until the sun and my energy were gone, and knew today it was best for me to head home. Sadness came over me as I realized that I wasn't a kid anymore and it was time for me to clean up the mess from my past so I could have a better future. The lunch with rich dad and Mike was painful yet beneficial. Going over my financial statements was painful yet truthful. Those simple documents told the story of the lies told up to this point and it was time to change the story. I tucked the brown manila envelope that contained my company's financial statement under my arm as the bus arrived and headed back to a home that I would soon have to give up as well.

Many people ask me today, "How did you start over again?" It seems they are very curious about how one picks up after losing everything and begins again. Many of those that ask have good jobs or established careers and seem to be hesitant at losing what they already established. One young man from Japan asked me, "After you lost everything, did you not feel shame?" Laughingly I said, "I felt many things, and shame was definitely one of the emotions." I then asked him a few more questions and found out that he hated his job, it did not pay enough. But his job was secure and he would rather suffer for the rest of his life than risk shame and disgrace. I reassured him that his feelings were not limited to him. Many people would rather have some money and some happiness than risk shame and embarrassment going for all that life has to offer.

"How did you get started without a job or without any money?" That's another frequently asked question about this period of my life. There is not one solid or convincing answer to those types of questions. Words alone are limiting, so the answers I normally give are, "I did it because I had no place else to go. I had nothing to fall back on." I also say, "I took it one day at a time." I also say, "Those were some of the worst days of my life, I would not want to repeat them, but in retrospect they were some of the best days of my life because they changed the direction of my life. Those days also changed who I became in the process of changing my life."

Occasionally I say, "I had to choose between my past and my future . . . the choice of my past being the same as my future . . . or my future being much better than my past." That puzzling statement crinkles a few brows . . . but what I am saying is that most people afraid of change or risk will wind up doing the same thing tomorrow as they are doing today. For many people, surviving one day at a time is better than risking today for a better future. I understand that strategy for life. Today, I occasionally see my friends who are still beach boys on Waikiki Beach and I envy their life—especially when I'm sitting in a 747 flying from London to New York or Los Angeles to Sydney. I, too, often wonder if I have made the right decisions in life. As I am sitting on a plane, eating airline food, my three friends who have been beach boys now for thirty-five years go to the same spot on Waikiki Beach every day, they rent surfboards, meet young coeds that flatter their aging male egos, and they sing and play Hawaiian songs for tips. Tomorrow they will do the same thing at the same spot . . . as in many ways, so will I. The difference I believe is that we wanted different ends to our lives. I wanted a *different* tomorrow and they want the *same* tomorrow.

I believe most people fall into one of those two categories . . . and that will determine who will take the risk for the best of life or settle for the same life today . . . and the same life tomorrow. I risked everything because I wanted a much better tomorrow . . . that is the best answer I have for explaining how I stood up again, after I lost everything. I risked, lost, and stood up because I still wanted the same thing . . . a better tomorrow. Most people stay where they are, like my beach boy friends, because today is safe and they want tomorrow to be safe. Unfortunately, most of us know that today will eventually come to an end and tomorrow will begin. Even my beach boy friends know that.

Rich dad knew how big a financial hole I had blown in my financial statement and in my personal life. As he said when he looked at my business's financial statement a few months earlier, "Your company has financial cancer." Although he knew I was out of money, had no place to live, and no job to go to, he never offered me a job or any financial support . . . and I did not want or expect any such support. I had been studying with him for over twenty years and I knew what was now expected of me.

My poor dad was very understanding. He offered several times to give me money, but I was aware of his financial position, and he was in very bad financial shape. He was not much better off than me. He had his house but now in his late fifties, he was almost totally dependent upon a small early retirement pension from the teachers union. What little savings he did have, he lost on an ice cream franchise that failed. That was my dad's first foray into the real world of business and the world of business pounded him not for his academic brilliance but his lack of real-world experience. He was also having trouble finding a job because of his age and because of his ego. Having once been the boss—the superintendent of education—I believe he found it tough asking for a job from people much younger than him.

He also got very angry when told that his experience in state government did not transfer over to the business world. He was often told, "You have great work experience, you are definitely successful, but your skills are not what we need. We cannot use what you have spent your lifetime learning." He then did what many men at his age and in his predicament do, he became a consultant. I do not know if anyone hired him, but the title seemed to quell a pain inside of him.

One of the things that really kept me going was a vow I made at that time and the vow was: "I would never let my own ignorance, arrogance, or fear get in the way of the life I know I can have." I saw what age, arrogance, lack of practical real-world skills, lack of financial intelligence, lack of up-to-date information, dependence upon a government handout, was doing to my dad and I vowed I would use his example as a lesson, an example of what I would *not* become. At that moment, I vowed to become a student again and *my* education began with first cleaning up my personal financial statement . . . a statement that reflected the mess my financial ignorance and arrogance had gotten me in. I then vowed to listen to rich dad and begin to study what most people do not study.

Since the age of nine, rich dad had been an important mentor to me. Now at the age of thirty-two, I vowed to learn more from him as an adult . . . relearn the same lessons as a child but now as an adult. I knew that my surfing and rugby days were coming to an end, and as sad as that thought was, I was also looking forward to the future . . . a new and different future . . . a future that gave me more control over the subject of money and the rest of my life. I say this because I did not want to grow up to be like my poor dad, a man who was now a *consultant* still looking for work as he neared his sixties because he realized his pension was inadequate. I did not want to wait till I was sixty to make the changes I was making in my thirties. I did not want to wait till I was sixty to find out that there was not enough money in my retirement plan for me to live on for the rest of my life. My vow at thirty-two was to clean up my financial life, get educated, and take care of my future today—not tomorrow.

As I was preparing to move out of my apartment, which I could no longer afford, and wondering where I was going to live next, a friend called. He was moving to California for four months on a job assignment and asked me if I would care for his house, water his plants, and feed his dog. So that solved my housing problem—at least temporarily. Money seemed to come in different forms. Checks would appear in the mail, just in the nick of time, from overpayments, refunds, and money from the bill collectors who had finally collected some of the money owed the business. But even though the checks came in, they were infrequent and there were days when I could not eat simply because there was not any money. As tough as things were at times, the reason I say this period of time was a good one is because it gave me time to find out who I was and what I was made of.

Another friend called soon after I moved into the temporary house. This friend was a headhunter, someone who looked for management-level employees. "I have a company that is very interested in you. I told them you were the top salesman for Xerox and for the last four years you have run a national and international sales team of hundreds of salespeople. They're looking for someone just like you. The pay is great. Lots of travel, big expense account, generous benefits, and who knows, you could someday be president of the company. You don't have to relocate. They want you to be the bridge between their Asian and California accounts right here in Hawaii. Are you interested?"

Let me tell you, being broke and desperate, that phone call was like a phone call from heaven. I was higher than a kite. The needy and desperate part of me could feel the call of a high paying job, prestige, title, benefits, a car, and the corporate ladder. Most importantly, I felt loved and wanted again. I too knew I was perfect for the job because I was educated in New York and I also understood the culture of the Japanese, being fourth-generation Japanese-American. I accepted immediately.

Four weeks later, I was one of only three remaining out of sixteen candidates the company had selected from résumés. I even purchased a new suit for each interview, trading food money for clothes. On the final days of interviewing, I found myself sitting outside the regional vice president's office, but instead of feeling good, I began to feel bad. Something was wrong. My stomach began to turn as I realized that I was doing the same thing my poor dad was doing, the only difference was I was thirty-two and my dad was fifty-nine and we were both interviewing for jobs. The offer of money, security, title, promotion, benefits had called to me and I found out which character inside of me was responding.

For a very long ten minutes, I sat outside the vice president's office and had a conversation with myself. At the end of the ten minutes, I wrote a note that said, "Thank you for your interest in me. I greatly appreciate your time and consideration. It has been good for my self-esteem, but I must move on with my life and that is why I am removing my name as a candidate as a possible employee with your company. Thank you." I handed the note to the secretary and closed the door behind me. That was the last time I ever applied for a job.

Rich dad was always more interested in what character I chose to become rather than the profession I chose. During this period of time, the two characters I had to choose between were the *wimp* and the *warrior*. After facing the real world with nothing, for about two weeks, the wimp in me was winning. Then one day, the warrior won and I felt good for a whole day . . . then the wimp took over again. By the fourth week, the battle was tied. I was a wimp for half the time and a warrior the other half. That is when things finally began to change. Life began to change once I was comfortable with my status of being a person with no money, no job, and no professional status. In other words, I was becoming comfortable with being a nobody. I was no longer a kid, a student, a ship's officer, a military pilot, or an entrepreneur. I had nothing and I kind of liked it. It wasn't that bad. I was facing nothing with nothing . . . and the more I could do that, the more the warrior inside of me was growing stronger. One of the reasons I turned down the possibility of the job as national sales manager was because I was in the middle of my own personal experiment and I simply wanted to find out which character would win.

Rich dad often asked this question of his son and me: "If you had nothing . . . no money, no work, no food, no shelter . . . what would you do?"

If we answered with, "I'd go find a job to make a few dollars," rich dad would say you boys are programmed to be an employee.

If we answered with, "I'd look for a business opportunity and build or buy a business," rich dad would say that we were programmed to be an entrepreneur.

If we replied with, "I'd find an investment and then look for investors," he would say that we were programmed to be investors and entrepreneurs.

Rich dad also said, "Most people are programmed from birth to go and look for a job. In fact they go to school to reinforce that programming. If you want to be able to respond with the latter two answers, you will need a different form of education, a form of education he called *education for the real world*.

In my quiet time alone, I remembered rich dad's little quiz, and now in my moment of nothingness, I began to choose which answer I wanted to be the answer for the rest of my life.

Rich dad called me about six weeks after our Chinese luncheon and asked if I would join him for lunch. Of course I accepted. This time we met at an expensive downtown Honolulu restaurant, the place where the movers and shakers meet to have lunch. Almost everyone there was in business attire. I arrived by bus dressed in shorts and a bright red Aloha shirt, doing my best to pretend I was a man who was rich and no longer needed to dress like everyone else. I doubt if I fooled anyone or if anyone cared. I was having lunch with rich dad and no one else. A suit would not have impressed rich dad because he knew my financial status. Standing to greet me and shake my hand, rich dad asked, "How are things going?"

"Pretty good," I replied as I took my seat. "I'm getting used to having nothing and being a nobody."

Rich dad chuckled and said, "It's not that bad, is it?"

"No, it isn't," I said. "Things only get bad when the self-doubt creeps in and I begin to beat myself up for all the stupid things I've done. But I am getting stronger. The wimp in me is losing his grip and the warrior is getting stronger. I'm about ready to face the real world."

After I told him about pursuing a high-paying national sales manager's job and then turning it down, a broad smile came across rich dad's face. "That is the best thing I've heard you say in months. You have really decided to change your future. And most importantly, I'm glad you're finding the courage to face the real world."

Puzzled, I squinted and asked, "Doesn't everyone want to face the *real* world?"

"Most think they do," said rich dad, "but if the truth be told, most people today do their best to hide from the real world."

The waiter came, handed us our menus, filled our water glasses, and quickly told us the specials of the day. "People hide from the real world? How do they do that? Is it only by job security?" I asked.

Rich dad handed his menu back to the waiter and said, "The usual." He then looked at me and said, "There are many ways people hide from the real world . . . other than job security. Most people today spend their lives running from sanctuary to sanctuary, sanctuaries that protect them from the real world. For example, many people leave the sanctuary of home, and go to the sanctuary of college. After graduation, many run to the sanctuary of a job or profession. If they get married, they then create a sanctuary for their family, and the process continues with people running from safe sanctuary to safe sanctuary. When people lose their job, they often dust off their résumé and run in search of another sanctuary . . . or if they get divorced, many run in search of another person to create a new home sanctuary with."

"Is there anything wrong with that?" I asked.

"No, not necessarily, and as long as there is always another sanctuary," said rich dad, taking a sip from his glass of water. "But problems do arise when a person leaves one safe sanctuary and then cannot find the next sanctuary. That is what happened to your dad."

"My dad?" I replied with a little surprise.

"Yes, your dad," said rich dad. "Your dad is facing the real world today just as you are facing the real world today . . . and I wonder which of the two of you will do better. The difference is your dad began facing the real world after he was fifty and you are only in your thirties. Both of you are out of work. I find it all interesting to observe."

"Explain to me the real world you see my dad facing today."

"Your dad left the sanctuary of his parents' home, went to a good school, got a good job, and climbed the ladder to success. Is that correct?"

"Yes," I replied.

"So your dad went from safe sanctuary to safe sanctuary until he reached the position and title of superintendent of education. He left home and went to school, got married, and never left the school system. Isn't that correct?"

I nodded my head, saying, "He was a great student so he stayed in a system, or a sanctuary, as you say, that fed his ego and allowed him to achieve. Are you saying he should have left the sanctuary of higher education?"

"Why should he?" said rich dad. "He was smart, a great student, class president, soon head of the system, so he should have just stayed in a system that he did well in. If I were in his shoes, I would probably have done the same thing. But then he chose to leave the system at age fifty, and the world outside the school system is the real world. When it came to finances, your dad was not mentally or emotionally ready for the real world."

"You mean when he decided to run for lieutenant governor of Hawaii?" I asked.

"Yes . . . your dad being an honest man runs against a corrupt political system . . . and finds that honesty is not the best policy . . . he runs into the real world when he runs for lieutenant governor and loses. After the loss, he then finds himself outside the system he grew up in, the system he did well in, the only real system he knows, and suddenly he must face the real world—and he is not surviving well. On top of that, as soon as he lost his job, your mom dies of an early heart attack. I suspect that she could not stand the embarrassment that comes with any loss or the fact that your dad was now out of work, because the two of them were now outside of the system that once protected them."

"My mom did take it harder than my dad. Many of her phony government socialite friends stopped calling her or going to lunch with her once my dad lost the election. That included many of her closest friends. The world can be very cruel to people they perceive as losers. They love you when you're on top and forget you when you're down. I believe my mom took my dad's fall from the top harder than anyone else . . . and I believe that is why she died before she was fifty."

Rich dad sat silently as I talked about my mom. He could tell I missed her very much. After an appropriate length of time, he continued, saying, "After your dad finishes his grieving, he marries again, of course to a schoolteacher. Then he purchases that ice cream franchise and loses his life savings. He then gets divorced because I think the pressure of no sanctuary . . . no safe harbor, is terribly stressful on couples, young or old. So today, your dad is like an orphan. His parents are gone, his wives are gone, his kids can't support him, and the sanctuary he grew up in, the educational system, won't let him back in. Now he takes odd jobs trying to stay alive . . . trying to find the door to the next sanctuary so he can find protection from the real world."

"If not for his teacher's pension, the real world would crush him," I said. "He might even be homeless."

Rich dad agreed. "You kids might have to take him in, which many kids do . . . so the sanctuary of last resort is family . . . if the family can afford him," rich dad said, looking directly at me. "You can't afford to take care of him right now—can you?"

"It would be tough but I would find a way," I replied. "But why are we discussing this real-world versus sanctuary stuff?"

"Because your lessons continue," said rich dad with a smile. "Just because you are in your thirties does not mean you can't learn more. The financial situation you are in is a horrible situation . . . but thank God you face it at age thirty-two. Now . . . you can choose to make this bad experience an even worse situation, which is what losers do, or you can turn this bad situation into the best situation of your life so far. Millions of people are stuck in offices, on farms, in sales jobs, in professions, living in terror of what you are facing today. Many would sneer at you and treat you like a pariah. A few might envy you . . . envy you because at least you've gone through the pain of losing it all."

"That sounds ridiculous," I said. "Why would anyone envy me having nothing?"

"Because a few people out there do have vision . . . vision that others do not have or do not want to see," said rich dad. "Some people are beginning to realize that the challenges facing your generation are greater than the challenges facing my generation. After the year 2000, many of your generation will realize that they will be facing the same financial situation you are facing today. A few of those people with vision would envy you, because you are facing nothing, facing the real world, a world without sanctuaries, today, not tomorrow. Just because your peers have money and success today, does not mean they will have money and success tomorrow. Those who realize it will envy you."

"I'm still not totally clear why they would envy me," I said.

"Because you're halfway through the process . . . Most people are clinging to a false sense of security, knowing there is less and less job and financial security today," said rich dad. "So you've screwed up early and now you have time to clean it up and grow from the experience. Are you willing to go forward rather than go backward?"

"I may as well," I replied. "I'm in the middle of this mess. I'm already facing what you call the real world and it's not that bad."

"Good," smiled rich dad. "You see, the best thing that happened to me was I faced the real world when I was thirteen years old."

"When your dad died and left you in charge of the business and the family?"

Rich dad explained: "At thirteen, while your dad was in school learning about the ABCs of job security, I was facing the real world—the world he faces today. As a young teenager, I had no education, no money, a broken-hearted and sick mother, a family to take care of, a failing business, and no one to fall back on. In retrospect, it was the best thing that could have ever happened to me. The reason I have so much money today is because I had no sanctuary to hide in . . . and that is why I won't give you a hand right now. If I gave you a hand, offered you sanctuary, I would be delaying the inevitable. If you were of my generation, I would give you a job . . . because for my generation, job security was all you needed. Your generation needs financial security more than job security. Your generation has lots of jobs . . . the fast food restaurants are always looking for help. Your generation lacks the financial education required to achieve true financial security . . . and that lack of education will be the cause of the inevitable."

"The inevitable?" I asked.

"Yes, the inevitable," said rich dad. "The chances are, your generation will *not* have the safe sanctuary of Social Security or Medicare, or enough of it, to fall back on, as your dad and I do. Millions of people in your generation will not have any or sufficient retirement money to fall back on. Millions of your generation will not have a DB pension plan or a union pension plan to protect them from the real world. So what you are facing today, is what millions of your generation will begin facing sometime after the year 2010 . . . as I said, long after I am gone."

I sat there silently as the waiter placed our meals in front of us. I was beginning to understand why both my dads had been such advocates of their employee retirement plans. After the waiter had gone, I said, "So your generation has DB pension plans and my generation may not. And to you, that is a big difference."

"A monstrous difference," said rich dad. "You see, the employees who worked for your dad have the government and the unions backing their retirement. My employees only have themselves backing them . . . and most of my employees are not putting any money into their retirement plans. They do not know what they are. Some think they are the same as DB pension plans, the same plans their parents have. Because of this false sense of DB security, most of my employees do not have any savings. They have nice homes, nice cars, and nice TV sets, but nothing else. That worries me. I talk to them about investing, but nice cars and nice TVs mean more to them than a mutual fund or savings in the bank. Besides, they do not know the difference between saving and investing. They think they are the same thing. That is why I am worried for you and your generation. Most of my generation has some protection from the real world. Most of your generation will eventually face the real world, a world that they are not prepared to face and many will be too old to face. There is this massive problem brewing and no one seems to worry about it."

"So millions of my generation will someday have to face what I am facing today . . . facing the real world with nothing?"

"Yes . . . exactly what I am saying," rich dad said sternly. "That is precisely what I am saying. The difference is you are facing the real world in 1979 at the age of thirty-two and many of your peers will face the real world after 2010, when they turn sixty-two, or seventy-two, or eighty-two, or, heavens forbid, older . . . but they will face the real world."

"So my generation's pension plan could run out of money, if they do not contribute enough money to it."

"More than that," said rich dad. "Your generation's pension plan could run out of money, *even* if a person puts a lot of money into it, because your generation's pension plans can be wiped out by a massive stock market crash . . . a crash I predict is coming."

"So a DB pension plan has protection from a stock market crash and a DC plan does not?" I asked.

Rich dad nodded. "In most cases, but even DB plans have been known to crash due to mismanagement. But the risks are greater for DC pension plans. So the problems are brewing and soon the moment of truth will arrive. Soon your generation will find out if this new DC plan works or not. The problem is, your generation will only find out if the plan worked after they retire."

"You mean my classmates may find out at age sixty-five that their DC plan was inadequate . . . or insufficient?" I asked. "The only way they are going to know is after they retire, when it might be too late to work and replenish it . . . make up the shortfall?"

Rich dad nodded and continued, saying, "Not only are many of your generation not contributing anything to their plans, many who are contributing are not contributing enough, and very few are aware of how risky stocks and mutual funds are. Mutual funds can fall all the way to zero in a market crash. And it will happen, not to all companies or mutual funds, but sometime in the future, your generation will get the wake-up call that their DC retirement is not safe and their retirement sanctuary is at risk. Once your generation realizes that, they will begin to get out of the market . . . a panic will set in and the market will crash . . . and if the panic is large, the crash will be the biggest in the world. The problem is, too many amateur investors are entering the market . . . and it is these amateur investors that are the problem . . . a problem far greater than the flaws in pension reform. That is why I predict most of your generation will face the real world . . . the real world you are facing today. The only question is, how old will they be when they face it?"

"Most of my generation?" I asked, questioning the statement.

"Yes . . . most of your generation. I would say at least 80 percent of your generation will not have enough money to retire on. And millions will be out of money and out of support after the year 2020, after this massive stock market crash occurs. The U.S. government will not be able to afford over 150 million people needing government support just for financial and medical survival."

"Over 150 million people?" I said again, questioning rich dad's numbers. "There are only 75 million baby boomers."

"Yes, the number will be well over 150 million because there will be members from my generation still alive and still needing support, as well as millions of immigrants who will add to the numbers, as well as the millions of poor people who already exist. By the year 2030, simply because of medical breakthroughs that extend life, half the U.S. population could be requiring more and more government support because they are not prepared financially to face their old age."

"And that does not include the millions of federal and state employees who will also be expecting the government to take care of them . . . as promised," I added. "Lifelong government employees just like my dad."

"That's correct," rich dad nodded. "Too many people have been taught to expect the government to take care of them . . . to be the safe sanctuary that protects them from the real world, and that is why this problem will only grow."

"So many of the kids of the baby boomers will have to support their parents," I said.

"More than their parents," said rich dad. "The kids of the baby boomers, those born after 1970, may be asked to support double families. In other words, if a young couple has two kids, through various taxes, they may have to support an additional four people who cannot afford to support themselves."

"You mean a family of four is really a family of eight?" I asked.

"It's possible. It could lead to a battle for money and life support between the different generations . . . young and old . . . and if the old control the government, the young will definitely be taxed to pay for the old," rich dad suggested. "If the young win in politics, there will be millions of old people, your baby-boom generation, complaining that young people no longer respect their elders." Rich dad chuckled at that thought.

"Why do you chuckle?" I asked.

Still chuckling, rich dad said, "Respect for elders is an idea whose time has passed. I think the coming generations will have less respect for their elders . . . not more. But I could be wrong. Maybe the children of the baby boomers will be glad to open their wallets and give their elders all the money they want. Who knows? Stranger things have happened."

We spent the next few minutes eating . . . not really saying much. I sat there thinking about the bus trip home, wondering if I should walk or splurge on a bus ride. I dared not ask rich dad for a ride. Besides, I did not want to waste this opportunity to face the real world and face it with nothing . . . or in this case very little. I had begun to feel lucky about facing the real world at thirty-two instead of at seventy-two, eighty-two, or ninety-two years of age.

As the bill came and rich dad picked it up, I asked him, "How did we get into this mess? How come we have so many millions of people who need a safe sanctuary from the real world?"

Security Versus Freedom

"Good question," responded rich dad as he handed the waiter his credit card. "I think the big difference came when people began seeking security instead of freedom."

"Don't we all have freedom?" I asked. "After all, this is America, land of the free and home of the brave."

"Yes, it is America and that is an old song," smirked rich dad. The problem is, most people think security and freedom are the same word. They are not. In fact, in many ways, *security* and *freedom* mean exactly the opposite things."

"Security and freedom mean the opposite things?" I asked. "Explain that."

"Look, in 1773, the year of the infamous Boston Tea Party, what were the American rebels protesting?" asked rich dad.

"Taxes," I replied. "We wanted freedom from taxes. Those brave men risked jail or prison by performing a criminal act against Mother England."

"Good," said rich dad. "So they did not throw the tea overboard in the name of greater job security?"

"No, they were willing to fight for freedom, not job security."

"And what do we teach in school today?" asked rich dad. "What is the main reason parents and teachers fearfully insist their kids study hard and get good grades? Is it for freedom?"

"No," I said quietly. "Parents and teachers want their kids to get good grades for job security . . . hopefully a high paying job."

"And what happened to our founding fathers' focus on freedom . . . the freedom brave men and women fought for hundreds of years ago? It's been shoved aside for a focus on job security . . . the fear of not having enough money to put food on the table has replaced freedom as a priority in our society.

"So school is not really about freedom . . . it's about job security and DB pension plans. That is what teachers have . . . but their students will not," said rich dad. "That is only one reason why there is less and less relevance between school and the real world. Most of the real world will not have DB pension plans . . . but schoolteachers do.

"Yes," rich dad went on. "And what did you fight for in Vietnam, even though you did not have to go . . . even though you were draft-exempt? Didn't you fight for freedom?"

"Yes . . . but that is because both you and my dad explained that it was a son's duty to fight for his country. I do not know if I would have gone if the two of you had not insisted I go."

"Right . . . and what did most of your friends' parents do? Didn't they insist their boys stay in school to avoid the draft? Didn't most of your friends not go to Vietnam because they were smart enough to get into college and receive a college deferment from military service?"

"Yes," I replied.

"Do you see how much this country has changed? We were a country founded on the ideal of freedom but now security is far more important than freedom. And security and freedom are not the same ideal and people who seek security are very, very different from those who seek freedom. And that difference—the difference in people—will also lead to the biggest stock market crash in the history of the world. Millions of people are now putting money into their defined contribution plans, into mutual funds, and other investments that they hope will ensure their security. Boy . . . are they in for a rude awakening in the future.

"That is why I am so concerned about ERISA. We are no longer the same people we were when the Boston Tea Party took place. As a people we no longer fight for freedom . . . instead, we are a people who now fight desperately for security. Millions of unwilling and financially unsophisticated people will be pushed into the stock market and, as you know, the stock market is not a place for people who are lovers of security. The stock market is a place for those who want their freedom. I am afraid that those who love freedom will win and those that love security will lose . . . and when they lose, they will face the real world . . . unfortunately at an old age. And that is my prediction."

"So freedom is not the same as security?" I asked, still not sure that there was a difference.

"Not only are they not the same, they are exactly the opposite. The more security you seek, the less freedom you have."

"Explain that to me," I said. "How can more security mean less freedom?"

"That job you turned down may have given you a lot of security, but was it not at the price of your freedom? Did it not hinder what you could earn, when and where you worked, and even when you took a vacation?"

"Yes, job security would have limited my freedom. For many people, their job security even tells them what time they can eat lunch," I added. "But don't most people want security more than freedom?"

"Exactly," said rich dad. "That is their choice. But always remember that the more you have of one, the less you have of the other. In fact, the more security you have, the more trapped you become. Just look at the people in the world who have the most security. They're called prison inmates. They have a house, food, free time, exercise yard . . . they have maximum security, but they have no freedom." Rich dad paused for a while, letting the idea of maximum security settle in. He then said, "Look at people who depend primarily on Social Security. They have a little financial security but at the cost of their freedom . . . the freedom of lifestyle. People who depend upon Social Security are some of the poorest people in America and with the least freedom."

"So you want me to choose between security and freedom. Freedom takes courage and strength and if you lack courage and strength you lose your freedom," I said. "So freedom is not free," I added.

"No way," said rich dad. "Do you remember coming home from Vietnam and having people spit on you and call you 'baby-killer'?"

"Well people spit *at* me, but no one spit on me. But I do understand what you mean. We fought for the right for them to have the freedom to do that . . . even though we did not like it."

"That is why the song goes, 'Land of the free and home of the brave.' Freedom takes courage . . . it takes bravery . . . and you are in the middle of facing that test of courage and bravery inside of you right now. If your courage wins, even when you have nothing . . . you will find a freedom few people ever know . . . even if they live in the land of the free . . . they are not free. The need for security robs them of their freedom."

We were soon on the sidewalk, rich dad waiting for the valet to bring his car. "Want a ride?" he asked.

"No thanks," I said with a very big smile. The warrior character in me was feeling pretty good, even though I still had no money and did not want a job. I wanted to face the real world with nothing for as long as I could and let the stronger person inside of me get stronger. I wanted freedom, freedom from the tyranny of needing a job or a lifestyle dictated by how much money I had. The talk with rich dad had given me a greater insight into what it took to live in his world, the real world he had to face when he was thirteen. "I kind of like the real world and I want to make it as real as possible," I said to rich dad with a smile as the valet brought him his car. "I want to face the real world today rather than tomorrow." Rich dad smiled, waved, and drove off with the valets envying his car.

During this period of facing the real world with nothing, I had the free time to reflect back on my life and recall some very important lessons I had forgotten. One cool morning, while I sat on Waikiki Beach, watching the waves, my mind drifted back a few years, to a day my Marine Corps squadron was preparing to go into battle. Early, before the sun was to rise, our commanding officer stood before all the pilots flying that day and said, "Remember that the lives of our men are an integral part of this mission. Great leaders and great pilots bring their men home alive. If you take care of your men, your men will take care of you."

On another day during this period of having nothing and facing the real world, my mind drifted back over twenty-five years, back to Sunday school and hearing my teacher asking the question, "Are we not our brothers' keepers?" It seemed that I had forgotten that lesson also.

So 1979 was a turning point for me. I realized that in my desperation to

become rich, I had forgotten many lessons from my youth. Now in my thirties, not only was I not rich, I had become someone I was not proud to be. It
was time to make some changes. So while the truth hurt, the benefit is that
I learned some priceless lessons, not only about myself, but also about the
future. It was time to change my future.

The Rich Don't Work for Money

About six months into my experiment, the person who had taken over the
remains of the nylon and Velcro wallet business called. He said, "This business is a bigger mess than I had expected. Will you come back and give me
a hand?"

Thinking for a moment, I agreed and went back to the business as his
partner, the agreement being that if I did not improve the business I would
not be paid. In other words, I was true to rich dad's number one rule, the
number one rule from the book *Rich Dad Poor Dad*: The rich don't work for
money. I was now a partner with equity, building a business . . . and if the
business did not become profitable, I did not get paid.

By this time, I had several other business ventures going that were profitable. One of the business ventures I was in was a joint venture with a local
radio station doing promotions and product sales. The venture would eventually become one of the most successful radio retail merchandising promotions in the history of U.S. radio. I was able to move into my own place and
afford a car again—but most importantly, I began to repay the investors who
had trusted me and loaned me money. Many refused to take the money,
since they had already written the losses off, and instead asked me to call
them for my next business venture.

In 1981, I merged the growing nylon and Velcro wallet company with my
success in rock and roll radio. In 1981, the rock band Pink Floyd called and
my nylon and Velcro wallet company began building licensed logo products
for the band. Bands and performers such as Van Halen, Boy George, Judas
Priest, the Police, and Duran Duran asked us to manufacture similar products for them and soon the wreckage of the first company turned out to be
bigger and stronger than the first company I started. In 1982, MTV hit in a big
way and we were off to the stars again. This time I was a lot less foolish, had
more business savvy, had better advisors, and I was more honest and far less

afraid of failing again and facing the real world. By this time I knew that if I failed, I could stand up again . . . and stand up taller and faster.

I know the real world can still knock me down. I am wise enough to realize that stock markets go up and stock markets go down. I also know that mutual funds are not safe. Even though I know a massive stock market crash could potentially also wipe me out—even if I have limited stocks and mutual funds—the difference is that although I do not want that to happen again, I am not as afraid of it happening again. I have already gone through the embarrassment of losing everything. I have enjoyed the process of getting it back and more. Today, having already faced the real world with nothing, I know I will learn even more if I am knocked down. I know I will bounce back even faster, and I am preparing daily for the biggest stock market crash in history.

Unfortunately, my real dad never recovered, and the older he got, the less able he was to take on the harshness of the real world. In 1982 he was sixty-three years old. At that age, there were no more job offers for him, except jobs as a security guard or at a hamburger joint. He lived in the glory of his past successes, which allowed him to continue to call himself a consultant, but if not for his teacher's pension, Social Security, and Medicare the real world would have crushed him. The kids helped him a little . . . but he often rejected that financial help because he was too proud. He had been well prepared and well educated for the world of government education, but outside that world, that sanctuary, he found he was not prepared at all for the real world . . . a world millions of my generation will soon face, prepared or not.

Personally, I have no plans on following my poor dad's plan. I am not counting on lifelong job security, my retirement plan, mutual funds, stocks, Social Security, Medicare, and other forms of government charity to keep me alive in the future. But unfortunately millions of my peers are following in their parents' footsteps, some only now beginning to realize that there is a difference between a DB pension plan and a DC pension plan.

Most are hoping and praying the stock market will always go up and that mutual funds and a diversified portfolio will save them from the real world. I am afraid such simple unsophisticated investor strategies will not work for most people. A major stock market crash will wipe out most mutual funds even if they are well diversified. As we have seen, the stock market is not a place for people who seek security. The stock market is a place for those that seek freedom . . . and unfortunately, many people who seek security do not know the difference.

ERISA may have been signed into law with good intentions. The problem is the act and subsequent amendments to the act had flaws. But the flaws are nothing in comparison to the panic that will occur when the people who spent their lives seeking security find out the real-world stock market can take that security away. That is a flaw the law did not take into consideration—the flaw that when people who have spent their lives seeking security suddenly find out their security is gone.

The point of this book is to give you some ideas on how to be prepared and do well, regardless if the real-world stock market goes up or the real-world market comes crashing down. The point is to be prepared for whatever happens in the real world of the stock market . . . the real world outside the sanctuaries of home, school, and business. Just as Noah built an ark in the desert, it may be time for you to begin building an ark in your mind while you have the time to build it.

(Appendix 1 has a complete listing of when ERISA was enacted and the major acts which have amended the various title of ERISA since 1974.)

Chapter 4

The Nightmare Begins

The front page of the "Money" section of the November 30, 2001, issue of *USA Today* had a large color photograph of a fifty-eight-year-old man. His hair is gray, his arms are crossed, he is intelligent and distinguished-looking. Although he could pass as the CEO of a large corporation, he isn't. Instead he is a loyal employee of Enron, a company where the CEO and other top executives may have personally made millions of dollars but the company is now bankrupt.

The reason this man is on the cover and *not* the CEO is because this loyal employee's 401(k) has been devastated due to the stock market crash, a down economy, and the downfall of the company he spent a lifetime working for. At one time his company's stock was worth nearly $100 per share. This loyal employee felt rich and bought more and more shares of the company he worked for and put those shares into his retirement plan. On November 30, 2001, that same company's stock was worth less than 35 cents per share and falling. At one time, his 401(k) was worth $317,000 and today he estimates its worth to be about $100,000. It is beginning to dawn on him that he may never be able to retire. He is nearly out of his most important asset, time. Some twenty-five years after the original passage of ERISA, rich dad's prophecy is starting to come true.

The December 2, 2001, edition of the *Miami Herald* ran a headline calling for government reform in 401(k) retirement plans. The journalist who wrote the piece argued that we have laws requiring people to wear seat belts in cars but we don't have laws requiring investors to invest wisely. I say, why not tell our school systems that?

Soon thereafter, every newspaper, and television and radio station, was shouting words of outrage. "How could the government let this happen?" one local broadcaster insisted over the radio. "Why didn't the accounting firm of Arthur Andersen warn the shareholders?" "Employees who are ready for retirement can now never retire." "How can the senior management of Enron run off with hundreds of millions of dollars and leave the employees with nothing?" Other stations went on to compare Enron to a disaster like the attack on the World Trade Center on September 11, 2001. I finally heard a voice of reason say on television, "While Enron is an *extreme* case, it is not an *isolated* case. What about all the millions of employees who have lost billions of dollars in their retirement plans? What about the employees working for hundreds of other companies who may not have lost everything, but have lost years of retirement savings in the stock market? How do they feel now knowing that their dreams of retirement may never come true? Do they feel more trust of the stock market or less trust today? The lack of confidence among investors is growing and is the bigger problem. There is more to this problem than simply Enron and questionable accounting."

In response, a few stations had financial planners repeat the standard company line of, "This problem would not have happened if the employees had diversified." Another famous mutual fund manager with his John Kennedy good looks and Boston accent came on and said, "We have always advised our clients to diversify. Why didn't the management of Enron advise their employees to diversify their portfolios? If they had diversified, they would not have the problems they are having today."

If rich dad were asked, he too would agree that Enron was an extreme case, extreme because of the magnitude of greed and apparent corruption involved. But he would also know that it is not an isolated case. In the last few years, not only did Enron employees take sizable losses, but so did employees of Ford, Cisco, Coca-Cola, Xerox, Lucent, Maytag, Polaroid, Rite Aid, United Airlines . . . and on and on. If rich dad were asked to comment on the plight of the Enron employees and all employees who have money in the stock market, he might say, "The problem is not the lack of diversification. The problem is a lack of financial education and financial sophistication . . . flaws that simple diversification alone cannot solve."

Two thousand one was a year of sensational news . . . the unimaginable attack on the World Trade Center and the Pentagon. Just as we were coming to grips with that tragedy and pain, news of Enron and the questionable accounting of Arthur Andersen burst into the headlines. Even the war in Afghanistan had taken a back seat to Enron, at one time reportedly the seventh largest company in America, and today the biggest bankruptcy in U.S. history . . . so far.

During all this media sensationalism, the public often misses the more important points . . . because the real problems are not front-page news. During this meltdown period of Enron and then WorldCom, one of the many flaws in the pension reform was brought to light in that same December 2, 2001, edition of the *Miami Herald*. To me, more important than the Enron fiasco is the simple question that this retiree asks of a certified financial planner who regularly contributes to the paper.

> QUESTION: I am 70 years old and retired, hoping that my IRA would sustain me when the time came. Since I *have* to begin withdrawing next year, I would appreciate your advice. I was advised several years ago to invest my IRA in mutual funds. For a while it was great, but along with so many other people, I have lost a great deal in the last two years. Should I take my losses and reinvest in a secure savings even though the interest rates are low?
>
> ANSWER: If ever there was a time to stick with the plan, it's now. The ups and downs of the market are to be expected, and if you've been an investor for more than a few years, you've ridden a few waves yourself; mostly up markets, just no down markets this long and nasty. I feel your pain, but 2 percent CD's and no growth aren't going to cut it.
>
> Check your mutual funds and make sure they're solid and leaning more to the conservative growth and growth income funds. Aggressive funds tend to be more volatile. Instruct your custodian to send you your *required* minimum distribution *monthly by selling* shares of your funds. This is called a systematic withdrawal and it works like a charm.

Did you pick up one of the flaws in the law? Did you notice the statement by the seventy-year-old retiree who wrote, "Since I *have* to begin withdrawing next year, I would appreciate your advice." Did you notice the response from the financial planner? "Instruct your custodian to send you your *required* minimum distribution *monthly by selling* shares of your funds."

More Sellers than Buyers

As I said, while most of the world was sipping their coffee and reading about Enron and thinking Enron's problems were not their problems, this retiree's simple question points out how Enron is everyone's problem. One of the flaws that rich dad noticed twenty years earlier was the requirement that the retiree must begin withdrawing from the market, by selling shares monthly, at age seventy and a half. Now that may not sound like a big deal, but as most of us know, it's the little things that make big things big . . . or small.

In other words, as the years go on, more and more people will, by law, be required to withdraw by selling shares while younger workers are required to buy shares. Now, it does not take a rocket scientist to see the flaw in this plan . . . a flaw that will get bigger and bigger as more and more people get older. In other words, how does the price of a stock go up when more people are selling than buying?

The question is more important simply because of the numbers of people involved. While the ripple effect of the Enron disaster will affect hundreds of thousands of people, in one way or another, this seventy-year-old retiree's question will affect tens of millions of people, maybe hundreds of millions, in one way or another . . . just because of its ripple effect.

Speaking of large ripple effects, Japan, once a financial powerhouse, a nation with hardworking, diligently saving people, is on the brink of financial ruin. Is it the fault of the Japanese people or the fault of the leaders of their country? In other words, if America, the richest country in the world, falters and Japan, the second largest economy in the world, goes down, the ripples may soon turn to tidal waves, waves big enough to cause the need for an ark in the desert.

When the December 2, 2001, issue of the *Miami Herald* ran, the retiree's question has little impact simply because at the present time, only a relatively few people are over seventy and less than half have DC pension plans. Most still have DB pensions, which operate via different rules. Also, many of those born before 1946 had good paying jobs, made money on their home they sold at a high price to a baby boomer, and many actually had savings. So the question this retiree asks is shoved to a back page . . . yet it is a most important question to be asking.

The question is, what happens when millions of baby boomers are required to begin withdrawing money from the stock market? Will the stock market still go up by 10 percent, 20 percent, or 30 percent per year as it did in the 1990s? If you were born after 1946, and have a DC pension plan filled with stocks, bonds, and mutual funds, for your sake, I hope the market keeps going up and never stops . . . but history is against that fantasy.

Because there are so few people over seventy with DC plans, this flaw has had very little effect on the market. But by the year 2016, when the first of the 75 million baby boomers begin to turn seventy years of age, many of them will have DC pension plans . . . and each year, more and more will be added to that list. When rich dad made his prophecy, he was not using Tarot cards or tea leaves to look at the future. He was using the change in the law, time, market experience, and the fact that people do get older. In other words, he was not guessing . . . he was just using facts, history, and realities.

Supply and Demand

The price of shares of stocks or mutual funds, or bonds, or anything for that matter, goes up as long as there are more buyers than sellers. Between 1990 and the year 2000, the stock market boomed because there were so many thirty- to fifty-year-old baby boomers entering the stock market, saving for their retirement in their DC pension plans . . . so there was a stock market boom. There was a similar boom in the 1970s when baby boomers left home, left college, and began buying their first home. If you are old enough to remember those years, you may remember the mania over real estate . . . a mania that was also followed by a panic and a bust when interest rates went over 20 percent. Interest rates were raised in order to slow down inflation . . . inflation caused partially because 75 million baby boomers had entered the job market and now had money to burn. In other words, 75 million people buying anything will cause a boom. The reverse is also true. Seventy-five million people selling anything will cause a bust. It is the basic law of economics, *the law of supply and demand.*

Within the next few years, but most certainly by 2016, if they haven't already figured it out, people will begin to understand that stock markets do not always go up by 20 percent per year as they did in the 1990s. Unfortunately, millions of employees will not exit their 401(k) or IRA plans or may only exit after it is too late. Millions of baby boomers may not sell early even though they know the market is crashing because of government-imposed tax penalties for early withdrawal. So instead of withdrawing, they will stay in the market, diversifying, moving money from one mutual fund to another looking for the next hyped safe sanctuary. Most people already realize that they are in financial trouble but still do not realize the full impact of the many flaws of the law. When this realization hits critical mass, a panic will occur as people fight desperately to save their retirement and their lives. Unfortunately, all the diversification in the world will not save them from a crash of that magnitude.

Warren Buffett, reportedly America's richest and smartest investor, has this to say about diversification. He says:

> "Diversification is a protection against ignorance. It makes
> very little sense for those that know what they're doing."

I point out that Warren Buffett is not saying to not diversify. He has repeatedly said that he does not diversify . . . but he is not advising you or anyone else to not diversify. He is simply saying that diversification is protection against ignorance. In other words, if you don't want to diversify, get educated. If you're not financially educated and have no plans on becoming financially educated . . . then diversify, diversify, diversify.

Rich dad, being more blunt, would have said, "If you're financially ignorant, diversify." He did say to me way back in 1979, "One of the many flaws is that the law has failed to advise people to get financially educated. President Ford and Congress changed the law but failed to tell the educational system to provide for the proper financial education . . . the financial literacy required for people who have DC pension plans. Instead, the politicians have left the job of financial education up to the people of Wall Street."

On a more sarcastic note, rich dad later said, "Asking Wall Street to provide financial education is the same as asking a fox to raise your chickens. If the fox is smart, the fox will be patient and raise very fat chickens. The fox works hard to gain the chickens' trust . . . so he cares for them by providing slick brochures, branch offices, and good-looking salespeople who have been trained to sound like investors. The salespeople are all trained to use the same intelligent-sounding financial jargon disguised as advice, such as, 'Invest for the long term, have a plan, choose a family of funds, sector funds, small cap growth funds, tax free municipal bonds, 20 percent in cash, REITs, Roth IRAs, rollovers, tech stocks, blue chips, the new economy, and of course, diversify, diversify, diversify.'" As rich dad pointed out to me, "Pension reform will change the vocabulary we use, but most people will not have a clue what the new words mean." Meanwhile, the fox smiles and knows the chickens are happy. They feel safe in their new sanctuary. They have a safe secure job and they have their money safely entrusted to financially astute people. Then they see the stock market go up and up in the 1990s and they feel even more intelligent and well advised. They know their financial planner is looking after them, will make them rich and protect them from the harsh cruel world outside the chicken coop.

But in March of 2000 the world began to change. The tech bubble burst and the stock market began to deflate. TV commentators began to say, "The recovery will come in the next quarter." But the next quarter came and went . . . and the TV commentators again said, "The recovery will come in the next quarter." Financial planners began to say, "Be patient . . . invest for the long term . . . diversify." The chickens began to feel a little more secure. They knew they were doing the financially intelligent thing. They were in it for the long term, they were diversified, and they knew the recovery was right around the corner.

September 11 dropped the market but the market bounced right back. Again the chickens felt more confident as the market began to climb. Then Enron hit and suddenly many very fat chickens from all over America began to cluck loudly from the sanctuary of their securely wired chicken coops. Although they clucked and cackled loudly, the foxes again said, "Be patient. Invest for the long term. Diversify." One of the reasons the biggest stock market crash in the history of the world did not take place right after the Enron collapse is because the foxes aren't ready for their chicken dinner yet. They know that these chickens have a few more years to get a little fatter and they know that by law . . . the chickens will have to keep coming to the stock market, buying more mutual funds and diversifying. The problem is, some of the chickens are getting nervous and are beginning to ask questions . . . questions such as the one the seventy-year-old retiree in Miami asked . . . and got the standard financial-planner-disguised-as-investor, preprogrammed sales answer . . . "Don't worry, be happy, buy more, and diversify."

Now I want to go on to restate that the advice of "Invest for the long term, be patient, and diversify" is solid advice for those who have limited financial education and investment experience. The point I want to reinforce is the idea that you as an individual have three basic choices. They are, (1) do nothing, (2) follow the same old financial planning advice of diversify, or (3) get financially educated. The choice is yours. Obviously, I recommend long-term financial education . . . and today, many other people are joining the chorus.

In February of 2002, Alan Greenspan, the head of the Federal Reserve Bank, concerned about the loss of confidence in the stock market and in the accounting profession, went before the nation and spoke about the need for financial literacy to be taught to our school kids. He knows that if people lose confidence in the stock market, capitalism as we know it is in trouble. Without investor money, the economy begins to implode. Due to that concern, he addressed Congress and said that this country needed to financially educate its children. As related in an Associated Press article on February 6:

> Schools should teach basic financial concepts better in elementary and secondary schools. A good foundation in math, Greenspan said, would improve financial literacy and "help prevent younger people from making poor financial decisions that can take years to overcome.
>
> "It has been my experience that competency in mathematics, both in numerical manipulation and in understanding its conceptual foundations, enhances a person's ability to handle the more ambiguous and qualitative relationships that dominate our day-to-day financial decision-making," he said.

Immediately after the live telecast of his speech to Congress, the financial news television station on which I was watching Mr. Greenspan's speech asked the head of a large and famous mutual fund to comment on Greenspan's remarks. Immediately, this famous mutual fund manager said, "I agree with Alan Greenspan. I agree we need to teach financial literacy . . . and financial literacy means diversify, diversify, diversify."

"Thank you for your wonderful words of advice," said the TV host to the famous mutual fund CEO. "If we are going to teach our kids financial literacy, we must teach them to diversify."

If rich dad were alive, he would say, "Alan Greenspan did not say 'diversify.' Alan Greenspan called for the need for financial literacy to be taught in our schools. Greenspan stated that for our nation to make progress and evolve, financial education is essential for a First World nation to remain a First World power." Rich dad might have also said, "Financial literacy does not mean diversify. The definitions are not even close. Saying that financial literacy means diversification is just another example of the fox teaching the chickens."

Now all of us who are in business want customers who buy our products or services forever. The same is true with mutual fund managers and owners of financial television stations. You do not have to be a genius to see that the primary advertisers of this financial news TV station are mutual funds. So naturally they would have a mutual fund manager comment on Alan Greenspan's call for financial literacy rather than Warren Buffett . . . a man who does not advertise with that TV station simply because he does not have to. Warren Buffett's own mutual fund, Berkshire Hathaway, is possibly the most expensive fund in America simply because it is so well managed and successful. His fund is so successful and expensive that he has been known to tell his investors *not* to invest in it because he believes the price of his fund is too expensive. If he is telling people to *not* invest in his fund, he obviously does not need to advertise on any financial news television station . . . which is why he probably was not asked to comment on Greenspan's comment. The station invites someone who pays them ad revenues . . . a paying customer . . . and naturally that mutual fund manager will say what is best for his mutual fund.

If rich dad were alive, he would probably say this: "A mutual fund manager advising you to diversify is like a used car salesman saying, 'Don't buy one car . . . buy many cars. You never know when the car you are driving may break down and you may not get to work. So instead of risking buying just one car, diversify that risk, buy six cars and pay me for them every month for forty years until you stop working and retire." I ask you, what businessperson would not want millions of customers like that? The reason most of us do not buy the line of needing to diversify to six cars to protect us from car trouble is because most of us are better educated than that. But when it comes to financial vehicles, vehicles such as stocks, bonds, and mutual funds, most people are clueless as to the differences between different financial vehicles. That is why rich dad saw the lack of financial education as one of the major flaws in pension reform.

Because of this reform, one of the fastest growing professions is a group known as financial planners. Schoolteachers, housewives, ex–real estate agents, insurance salespeople, retirees, plumbers, firefighters et al. are taking a three-day to three-week to six-month course and suddenly they are qualified to advise you on the security of your financial future.

The problem with the financial planning industry, as rich dad noted, is that not all financial planners are equal. While many financial planners are well educated and dedicated professionals, many planners lack the proper training and financial education to be dishing out financial advice . . . advice that will affect a person's financial future and financial security. The profession of financial planning is very confusing because of this huge variance of expertise, not to mention varying methods of compensation. When your financial planner gets paid on selling you something, do you really feel comfortable that it is the right buy for you? So let the buyer beware. Just because someone says they are a financial planner does not mean they know anything about financial planning, much less investing. It is this lack of professional training that rich dad saw as one of the flaws . . . a very big flaw in pension reform because millions of people are now taking financial advice from people who are often poorer and less educated than they are.

The May 5, 2002, "Business" section of the *Washington Post* discussed this very issue in an article titled "When Hiring a Planner Know the Bottom Line," with the subtitle "Financial Planners Proliferating in Largely Unregulated Market." In it the following observations were made:

> Experience points to a growing issue in financial planning, where many different types of professionals now offer services in a largely unregulated marketplace. And even more players will presumably be attracted to the planning field as the big boomer generation continues its inexorable march to retirement and beyond. . . .
>
> Full-fledged financial planners come in several versions, CFPs, 39,500 strong, being one. CFP certification entails testing, continuing education and course work. CFPs charge fees (as an hourly rate, a flat

rate or percentage of assets under management), commission or a combination of the two.

Another group's members charge only on a fee basis . . . the 16-year-old National Association of Personal Financial Advisors (NAPFA). . . ."

The article went on to recommend two Web sites as references to finding a financial planner, *www.napfa.org*, sponsored by NAPFA, and *www.fpanet.org/plannersearch*, sponsored by the Financial Planning Association.

This growth in the financial planning field is in response to a demand for investment education and advice. To repeat because it is important to repeat: One of the biggest flaws in pension reform is that it failed to tell the educational system that financial education was no longer an option . . . it is now mandatory.

This flaw truly shocked rich dad. To him, Congress not requiring the schools to teach basic financial literacy after the law was changed bordered on criminal negligence . . . a crime far more serious than the crimes allegedly committed in the Enron scandal. When Congress passed that law and left the job of financial education up to the people who work in the financial markets, rich dad smelled a very big rat. Not a fox . . . a rat. When that law was passed, rich dad realized that many people in Congress knew exactly what they were doing. Many of our leaders knew that they had just made it mandatory for millions of workers to turn trillions of their hard-earned dollars over to those who run the financial markets.

Let me be clear again. Rich dad was not against investing money in the stock market . . . or against investing becoming more or less mandatory. Rich dad was angry at men like my real dad, the schoolteacher, who had absolutely no idea what was going on in Congress. Rich dad was against the sleight-of-hand and the lack of formal financial education. To him, leaving financial education up to those that profited from financial ignorance was criminal.

There are now thousands of professional financial planners, stockbrokers, real estate agents, insurance agents, accountants, and attorneys all handing out investment advice for money. Rich dad's concern was that most of these people are not investors. They do not live off their income from their investments, which a true investor does. He constantly reminded his son and me that the majority of people dishing out investment advice are salespeople, working for commissions, salary, or a fee. It is these salespeople who do the financial education for the financial institutions and, obviously, most will say what the institution tells them to say and promote, or they lose their job. Then we wonder why we have millions of people who grow more and more worried about their future financial security. They grow insecure because instead of receiving unbiased financial education, they receive a sales pitch disguised as financial education from a salesperson. As rich dad often said, "The reason salespeople are often called brokers is because they are often broker than you are."

Warren Buffett has this to say about financial advice from Wall Street. He says:

> "Wall Street is the only place that people ride to in a Rolls-Royce
> to get advice from those that take the subway."

Again, I must clarify something. I love the salespeople who sell me financial services and investments. Some of them are my best friends. Some of these salespeople have made me very rich . . . which means I like them even better. In other words, I need them as much as they need me. I pay my commissions because I want the people who sell me investments to prosper. If they prosper they bring me more deals and they often bring me the best investments first. Investors who hate paying commissions always get the worst investments . . . as they should because they are cheap. In fact, I have friends who will tip their waiter 20 percent for a burger and fries and then refuse to pay the commission on an investment that could make them rich. Talk about being wired up with a poor person's financial value system. You tip those who make you poor and hesitate to tip those who can make you rich. I have several friends like that. The point is, as an investor, you may want to become better educated and find advisors you can trust. If you are not educated, then one financial salesperson is just as good as another.

Again quoting Warren Buffett:

> "The market, like the Lord, helps those who help themselves."

In other words, if you want to do well in the future, do not leave *your* financial education up to someone else.

Two Flaws

In closing, let's review the two flaws in pension reform. The first is that the law requires participants to begin selling once they hit seventy and a half years of age. Within the next few years we will see the panic begin. When the first of 75 million, 83 million if you count immigrants, of the baby-boom generation reach the age of seventy, simply put, more and more money will begin to come out rather than go in. While the year 2016 is bandied around as when this occurs in a major way, beware that the financial impact may begin much earlier. You do not need advanced math to figure out that it's tough to keep prices going higher when, each year, more and more people are selling.

The second flaw rich dad saw was that financial education was left up to those that made more money if the investor was less educated. Hence financial education today is really a sales pitch.

In the next chapter, I will go into the third flaw in the system . . . and again that flaw was glaringly obvious in the letter from the seventy-year-old retiree who wrote the newspaper asking for advice. As I said, while most people were sipping their coffee reading about Enron and Arthur Andersen, glad that they were not affected by the scandal, many of these people were missing the important facts, facts hidden in the back pages of the newspaper—flaws in a system that will affect them today and tomorrow.

Chapter 5

What Are Your Financial Assumptions?

Professional negotiators know that one of the most important watchwords in any negotiation is the word *assume*. When I was just beginning my business career, and was actually negotiating for real money, rich dad would always remind me to watch my assumptions . . . as well as tune into the other person's assumptions. To rich dad, the word *assumption* was not a word to be taken lightly. He often would accentuate the word *assume* in this way: ass-u-me. In business today, this punctuation tells a fairly common story of warning and if you have not yet heard what ass-u-me means, then ask around. I am certain someone close to you knows exactly what ass-u-me means.

Dr. R. Buckminster Fuller, one of America's most accomplished citizens, having many patents in his name, had this to say about the word *assume*. He said, "You cannot question an assumption you do not know you have made." As a student of his, it took me a while to begin to understand how profound that statement is. In business and investing, I have noticed many people lose and lose badly because they did not know they had made certain assumptions. In other words, it was their unconscious assumptions that cost them dearly . . . assumptions they did not even realize they had. For example, an attorney friend of mine told me of a couple who lost everything because they bought their dream piece of land and assumed it was clean. Three years from retirement and after holding the land for fifteen years, they found out the land was once used as a toxic waste site and the people who had owned the land were long gone. The couple was sued by the federal government and ordered to pay for its cleanup . . . at a cost of millions of dollars. Naturally they fought the lawsuit in court and even won a few concessions, but the legal battle cost them everything they had saved. My attorney friend said, "The couple later said, 'When we looked at this beautiful piece of wooded land, we just assumed it had never been used for anything or by anyone.'"

When I lived in San Diego, I read about a local couple who decided to take the family to Disneyland. Due to conflicting work schedules, the husband and wife agreed to travel separately in two cars. When the couple met at the hotel, neither parent had brought the children. They had both assumed the other would be driving with the kids. Since it was an assumption they did not know they had made, they never bothered to ask if the other was going to bring the children. That is why Dr. Fuller emphasized the need to ask ourselves what assumptions we have made that we do not know we have made.

In business today, I often ask my attorney and my accountant to check the contracts. I never used to do this, but today, I realize I need to have other eyes look over my agreements to check for anything I may have missed. I often ask them to question my assumptions or lack of assumptions in the process. I have learned a lot about myself by questioning my assumptions . . . especially those assumptions I do not know I have made.

I have found that many legal fights are not over the main point of the contract but often rest upon simple assumptions no one realized were made. Recently I was in a disagreement with a holiday lighting company who put up some holiday lights on my property. The owners, a couple, came over in early December and gave me a quote for putting the lights up, and then put them up a few days later. Once the lights were up, I paid the bill in full. We shook hands and I was very happy with the great job they did . . . a far better job than I could ever do.

After the holidays, when I called to ask them to take the lights down, the owner said, "We said we would put them up. We never said we would take them down." Because I did not have a written agreement, the discussion became a heated disagreement on what was said and who said what. Finally, I hired someone else to take the lights down. Needless to say, I doubt if I will use that company again even though they did do a good job of putting the lights up. I assumed that any company that put lights up would also take lights down . . . but obviously I made an assumption I did not know I had made. You can be certain that with the next company I hire, I will have a written contract stating that the price includes taking the lights down as well as putting them up. That is another case of ass-u-me.

As you can see from these examples, assumptions are very important in many different facets of life, but rich dad was especially cautious of assumptions when it came to money, business, and investing. He said, "More money has been lost, more friendships have been destroyed, more people have been hurt, more accidents have happened, and more people have gone to court because someone failed to question their assumptions." So the question is, how does the word *assume* apply to retirement, the coming stock market crash, and the advice people are receiving?

To answer that question, all we need do is go back to the question asked by the seventy-year-old retiree in the December 2, 2001, issue of the *Miami Herald*. The retiree was seeking advice, but was the advice wise?

> Check your mutual funds and make sure they're solid and leaning more to the conservative growth and growth income funds. Aggressive funds tend to be more volatile. Instruct your custodian to send you your *required* minimum distribution *monthly by selling* shares of your funds. This is called a systematic withdrawal and it works like a charm.

So here are some test questions. From the financial planner's answer, how many different assumptions can you pick up? How many assumptions can you *not* pick up? How can the assumptions be right and how can the assumptions be wrong? What happens if this retiree follows the financial planner's advice but the advice is based upon faulty assumptions? What assumptions need to be questioned? What assumptions has the financial planner made in handing out this advice? What other questions does the financial planner need to ask before handing out any financial advice?

Before I give you my answers, I would suggest you sit around with some of your friends and have a discussion on the number of assumptions found in this answer. Just take the planner's answer, read it out loud or give everyone a copy of it and then ask your group to find as many assumptions as possible. I think you will find the process enlightening, educational, and possibly frightening. It may even inspire you to ask yourself about your own personal financial assumptions. All you have to do is question the assumptions found in the answer and you might greatly improve your financial IQ.

The first assumption I would question would be "If ever there was a time to stick with the plan, it's now." Obviously, the planner assumes this retiree has a plan or knows what the plan is. While many people do have plans, most are ignorant of the laws behind the plan.

The response of, "I feel your pain, but 2 percent CD's and no growth aren't going to cut it," I find interesting. The financial planner assumes this retiree knows nothing about investing and is most likely thinking about putting money in 2 percent CDs . . . which the retiree never said he was considering. I suspect that the reason the planner mentioned the option of 2 percent CDs is because that is all the planner knows. For all he knows, this seventy-year-old retiree could be the best hedge fund trader in the world, capable of taking his retirement and gaining a 100 percent leveraged return every thirty days in the futures markets. I realize this is doubtful, but the point is that the planner assumes this person knows nothing . . . even less than the planner.

If I were the planner I would ask, "What is your investment experience? Do you have a portfolio of assets outside your retirement plan? Have you invested in other assets and done well? What investments do you feel comfortable and confident investing in? In other words, I would first ask questions before handing out advice based upon the assumption that this retiree knows nothing about investing . . . which many financial planners assume.

After assuming the retiree knows nothing, the planner then swings the advice around to this statement saying, "Check your mutual funds and make sure they're solid and leaning more to the conservative growth and growth income funds." First, the planner assumes this retiree knows nothing but then he assumes this retiree is savvy enough to know how to check out mutual funds to make sure they're solid. The question I raise is how does anyone know what mutual funds are solid? I sure don't. Besides, a mutual fund may be good one year and bad the next year. If you check the facts, many of the mutual funds people thought were solid turned out to be disasters during that last downturn. In 1999, there was one famous and well-promoted fund that was the darling of many financial advisors. It was definitely considered a solid mutual fund and it still is. But by 2001, this fund family had lost nearly 60 percent of its value. It will take years for this fund to return to its 1999 level.

The facts are that, today, there are more mutual funds than there are public companies whose shares the mutual funds buy. If this retiree could tell which of the approximately twelve thousand mutual funds was the most solid, and what's the next winner, then maybe he should come out of retirement and make a fortune advising the millions of people who are today wondering which mutual funds are solid. I find it absurd that this planner first assumes this retiree knows nothing about investing and in the next sentence assumes this retiree is far more financially sophisticated than most people in the market.

There are many more assumptions and contradictions I could get into from this financial planner's advice. My point is this: I do not know how anyone can offer any kind of financial advice knowing so little about the special conditions of the person seeking answers. Yet the facts are, millions upon millions of people are being given what rich dad would call "white bread financial advice." He called it that because it was financial advice for the masses. It was financial advice that followed a formula . . . a formula repeated by tens of thousands of financial advisors who are simply repeating sales pitches they are taught to say by the company selling the financial products.

Rich dad also called it "fast food financial planning." When you look at the health problems of millions of people today, many are suffering because they are eating fast food that tastes good, is extensively advertised, well packaged, and easy to buy. Rich dad's concern was that the Western world would not only have a health problem, a health problem caused by too much fast junk food, but we would also have a wealth problem, a problem caused by too much fast junk investments.

He said, "Any food or investment that is too easy to buy, overly advertised, wrapped in convenient attractive packages, with sales offices and salespeople on every corner, is probably not good for you." Rich dad went on to say, "Just as some of the best-tasting, healthiest, and best-value food I have found has been in tiny out-of-the-way restaurants, some of the best investments I have found have been in tiny obscure places run by true artists and gifted geniuses . . . not big corporations." He would remind his son and me of this saying, "Great food and great investments are found in similar places in every part of the world. The trouble is, bad food and bad investments can also be found in such places. If you want to find great food and great investments you first have to know what great food and great investments are. Just because something is convenient, looks good, sounds good, is affordable, and everyone else is buying it, does not mean it is good for you."

Obviously, I could go on finding and challenging more of the assumptions found in the financial planner's answer. That is not the point of this chapter. And in defense of the financial planner, the people in that profession have a massive job with millions of people to serve, so many times, all they can do is give fast, quick, prepackaged words of advice. I have several friends who are financial planners and they often say, "If a person does not have at least $250,000 in cash to invest, I cannot afford to spend much time with them." In other words, if you don't have much money, most financial planners cannot afford the time to give you much advice. They too need to earn money so they can feed their family and invest for *their* retirement.

The primary assumption in the newspaper article I challenge is the statement that goes, "This is called a systematic withdrawal and it works like a charm." The reason I challenge this assumption is because it is the underlying assumption of much of the financial planning industry. So in this case, I am not going after the financial planner; rather, I am questioning the assumption of the industry. Much but not all of the financial planning industry runs on the assumption that the stock market always goes up. So when this financial planner said, "it works like a charm," a more accurate statement would be, "it works like a charm as long as the stock market goes up, if you have chosen the right funds, and if you have enough money in your portfolio." To me, that would have been a more truthful and accurate answer.

Any professional investor who has taken the time to study the history of markets knows that all markets go up and all markets go down. A true professional investor would never bet their future on the assumption that markets only go up . . . yet that is what millions of people are doing.

In book number three of the Rich Dad series of books, *Rich Dad's Guide to Investing*, I included charts of different market booms and busts. The following chart is the chart of the 1929 stock market crash on Wall Street.

Applying the assumption of the financial planner's statement, "This is called a systematic withdrawal and it works like a charm," to the actual numbers following the 1929 crash, this is what working like a charm would look like.

These numbers are provided by Ibbotson Associates and these are the assumptions applied to the following numbers. Let's say you follow your

DJIA 1921–32

"systematic withdrawal" advice and you take out 8 percent of the balance of your account per year, leaving the rest to grow "so you'll never be poor." By the way, that's another part of the financial planning industry assumption.

Let's say that at age sixty-five, you have $1,000,000 and you stay invested in the S&P 500 Index—a group of large, stable companies. The market behaves exactly like the market did in 1929. The following is what would have happened to your DC retirement nest egg, adjusted for inflation, in the years following the 1929 crash:

Year End	Value Change (in dollars)	Ending Value (in dollars)	Cash to Live On (in dollars)
1929	just retired	1,000,000	80,000
1930	(461,840)	487,719	39,017

Before going on, I thought I might explain the meaning of these numbers, just in case they may be confusing. The 1930 numbers reflect a loss of

$461,840 (parentheses around a number in accounting means it is a loss, not a gain), which means the remaining balance in the account is $487,719, down from the starting 1929 value of $1,000,000. This means that this person has $39,017 (8 percent of $487,719) to live on in 1931.

1931	(294,797)	169,976	13,598
1932	(10,946)	162,166	12,973
1933	63,407	211,441	16,915
1934	(3,307)	187,389	14,991
1935	98,267	262,941	21,035
1936	145,144	382,564	30,607
1937	(291,789)	58,391	4,671
1938	25,678	81,632	6,531
1939	(601)	74,884	5,991
1940	(13,503)	54,826	4,386
1941	(10,592)	36,334	3,242
1942	10,864	40,530	2,935
1943	18,644	54,205	4,336
1944	23,887	72,196	5,776
1945	70,339	133,795	10,704
1946	(39,389)	70,858	5,669

Summarizing these numbers, if a baby boomer with a DC plan has $1,000,000 at age sixty-five, and the market follows the exact path the market followed after 1929, this baby boomer would have lost over 90 percent of the $1,000,000 by age eighty-two. Instead of living on $80,000 annually, by age eighty-two this baby boomer would be trying to live on $5,669 per year, which would be tough to do.

That is why, when the financial planner said, "This is called a systematic withdrawal and it works like a charm," it will only work like a charm if the assumptions hold true (meaning that the market keeps going up). But what if the assumptions do not hold true? What if the market does not respond according to predetermined assumptions? Then what would you say to that retiree in ten to twenty years?

Many of the financial planning formulas assume that things will work out—based on the assumption that the market continues to go up. For the sake of millions of people, I hope these assumptions hold true. Yet most professional investors know that in the real world, markets move in three basic directions. Markets move up, which is called a bull market. Markets move down, which is called a bear market. And markets move sideways, which is called a channeling market.

The problem with most retirement portfolios is that they are based upon the assumption that markets ultimately move up in the long run. That is why they always say "Invest for the long term." To compensate for market volatility, that is, the up, down, and sideways movements of markets, financial planners advise *diversification* as the solution. Again, this could work if the investor does invest for the long term and the investor does not happen to retire just at a market peak, leading to a market crash. If that happens, as you can see by the tables, all assumptions are off.

You may notice from the first table above that the market was very high in 1936, even higher than the 1929 peak. Yet, if the retiree had followed the law and continued to withdraw each month, the retiree would have had far less money with which to take advantage of the boom in 1936. This points out an unintended flaw in the law . . . the flaw being that the retiree has unlimited downside protection, and due to systematic withdrawals has only limited upside potential when the market does happen to move up. As a professional investor, that scenario is far too risky to the downside and far too limiting to the upside.

Since markets move in three different directions, and most portfolios are filled with investments that do well only in up markets, that means that most portfolios of the average investor will only do well in one out of three market directions. Rich dad once said to me, "Most of us have heard of Russian roulette. That is where a person takes a revolver with six chambers and puts one bullet in one of the chambers. They then spin the cylinder, put the gun to their head, and pull the trigger, hoping that the hammer lands on one of the five empty chambers. In other words, the odds are five to one in their favor. With most retirement plans loaded with mutual funds, a person is spinning a cylinder with only three chambers and two out of three chambers are loaded. In other words, your chances of losing are two out of three. Talk about risky.

The truth is, diversification will not necessarily protect you from a flawed system—a system with unlimited downside risk and limited upside potential. That means your retirement plan may not deliver what you need to live on, if things do not go as planned . . . or assumed.

While it is true that the market did eventually rally and come back up after 1929, the facts are that the market was for all practical purposes down for nearly twenty-five years. While that may be a short period of time in the overall history of the markets, bear in mind that when the market plunged from 1929 to 1932, it wiped out 80 percent of most people's portfolios. Losing 80 percent of everything you spent a lifetime saving would have made those two years into two very long years. So even if the averages state that the markets tend to go up, living through years of successive down markets and watching your portfolio slowly diminish might cause you a few sleepless nights . . . even if you knew that markets eventually do go back up again . . . as the assumptions assume.

More Flaws

Before concluding this chapter on assumptions, I think it important to review some of the flaws already stated, as well as new flaws not yet covered . . . flaws caused by assumptions assumed . . . and not yet questioned. Some of the more apparent flaws rich dad saw are:

1. The law has a mandatory withdrawal mechanism. This flaw will cause major problems around the year 2016. In the year 2016, it is estimated that there will be 2,282,887 people turning seventy years of age in America. In 2017, the number of people turning seventy years of age jumps to 2,928,818. The jump is caused because the first of the baby boomers begin turning seventy. That is a jump of nearly 700,000 more people turning seventy than in the year before and the number increases from there on. In one year there is a jump of nearly 30 percent. That may give you an idea of the effect this baby-boom generation will have on DC pension plans and the stock market. As stated earlier, it's tough for a market to keep going up if people are required by law to sell what they own. It's like trying to fill a bathtub while more and more holes are punched in the tub. Pretty soon people do not want to fill the tub.

When people ask why there is a mandatory withdrawal, the answer is simple. The answer is taxes. It appears that when this law was passed, the Internal Revenue Service wanted to know when they were going to get paid. Since the money in a DC plan is contributed tax free and grows tax free, the question was, When will the government get its share, when will the money be taxed? So the government provided the answer: at seventy and a half years of age.

2. The law failed to require the education system to provide the proper financial education. A high financial IQ is mandatory for anyone who is serious about investing. When ERISA was passed, no one told the schools to start teaching financial literacy, and financial literacy is the basis of a person's financial IQ. Most people think investing is risky, when it does not have to be, simply because they have never been trained in the basics of financial matters. As rich dad said, "Anything is risky, even crossing the street, if no one has ever taught you how to do it."

3. No one is questioning the assumptions. The assumptions of the law are based on just that . . . assumptions . . . not facts. What happens if a retiree finds out that at age sixty-five, the assumptions his financial planner used forty years earlier were wrong? Does the retiree have any recourse? Advisors are simply handing out financial advice and people are buying investments without either asking many questions . . . that is until the Enron scandal forced them to.

4. There are too many mutual fund companies. Today, there are more mutual fund companies than publicly listed companies . . . which makes it hard to figure out which funds are good and which funds are bad. That also means the chances are good that the average investor may choose the wrong funds . . . a group of funds that does not provide the gains required for a financially secure retirement.

5. The cost of retirement keeps going up. Having more and more mutual funds chasing only a few real stocks from real companies causes the price of these companies' stock to be overinflated, which means the cost of retirement keeps going up.

6. A DC plan does not protect you after retirement. The stock market may crash after the person retires, wiping out the retiree's nest egg and financial security. Out of a job and out of time, it would be tough to rebuild that nest egg if the funds were lost. That is what happened to many of the Enron employees—they had all their eggs in one basket, Enron, which is why diversify, diversify, diversify is an essential strategy for anyone who has a limited financial education. The problem with diversification is that it is still a risky and poor choice.

7. Many employees are not contributing to their retirement plans. I have seen figures that range from 50 percent or less to 20 percent or less to 10 percent or less of all baby boomers having enough money set aside for retirement. That means an extra financial burden for the generation that follows the baby boomers . . . specifically, your kids.

The May 5, 2002, article in the *Washington Post* "For Many 401(k) Catch-Up Won't Be an Easy Game" reads:

> Data on the size of workers' retirement saving—401(k)s, IRAs, and IRA rollovers—are scarce, but the information available suggests that many people have reason to worry. Forty-four percent of 401(k) balances in 2000 were less than $10,000, according to EBRI, the benefit research institute. Ranking second, at 14 percent, was the $10,000–$20,000 category.

Later in the same article:

> So, if a worker fails to contribute to the account, or if the investments do poorly, there is a risk of running out of money in retirement.
>
> And that appears to be happening, according to another study, released last week by the liberal Economic Policy Institute. This study, by New York University economics professor Edward N. Wolff, found that the "retirement wealth" of all but the wealthiest workers nearing retirement (households headed by someone between 47 and 64 years old) actually declined between 1983 and 1998.

One of the reasons workers are not contributing to their DC pension plans is because their taxes are high, the cost of living is high, the cost of raising and educating children keeps going up, and many workers simply do not realize that time, investing for the long term, is essential for the plan to work. If workers do not begin setting money aside early, the next flaw in the system takes priority.

8. A DC plan may not work for older workers. If a person is forty-five years of age or older when they begin setting money aside for retirement, a DC pension plan may not work. There is simply not enough time for the plan to work. That means if a person begins setting money aside at forty-five or older and has little to invest, or they lose their retirement and must start over again as many of the older Enron workers now must do, the DC strategy may not work.

The May 5 article referred to above includes the following observation:

But consider this: Suppose that a person retires with a $600,000 nest egg and decides he needs $3,000 a month to live on and wants to maintain that level of buying power (meaning he will withdraw increasing amounts to keep up with inflation). If he lives 20 years—to age 85—he has about a 3-in-10 chance of running out of money, according to calculators devised by T. Rowe Price.

Many of the baby-boom generation are only today finding out what they should have found out twenty-five years ago. And the truth is, many of them will have nowhere near $600,000 put away for retirement. It seems that millions of baby boomers are out of time because DC plans are not get-rich-quick plans. If a person is out of time, all the diversification in the world will only make their financial problems worse. Diversification is a defensive investment strategy, and if you are out of time, a defensive strategy won't delay the inevitable.

9. Too many noninvestors are handing out investment advice. Many investment advisors educating the public are not really investors . . . they are salespeople. On top of that, many financial advisors do not really know if their advice will stand the test of time through the ups and downs of financial markets. Many investment advisors do not really know if the person they are advising will be able to survive on the advice and products they are selling. Most investment advisors are required to only sell their company's financial products, which limits their objectivity. On top of that, most advisors only know one category of investments, investments such as paper assets, or real estate, or businesses. Very few have a well-rounded education and are qualified to talk on the synergy of these different asset classes. Or as Warren Buffett says, "Never ask the barber if you need a haircut."

10. Can you afford to stay alive after you retire? As more and more baby boomers begin to retire we will see the real test of the assumptions of a DC plan. While this act focuses on retirement, I wonder if a DC plan will provide for something more important than retirement . . . and that is health care. The question I ask is, "After retirement, will a retiree be able to afford health care for as long as they live?" A person can scale down and live frugally after retirement, but the price of health care is only going up. In the year 2000, the cost of health care and prescription drugs reportedly jumped by 17 percent. In other words, while the rest of the economy was deflating, the cost of health care was inflating. My concern is that in the near future, whether a person lives or dies will be a matter of whether they can afford medical care or not. My concern is that millions of people will not have enough money inside their DC pension plans to afford that medical care.

What about Medicare and other forms of socialized medicine? Well, if the statistics are correct, American socialized medicine may already be bankrupt. If socialized medicine is to be a national right, then taxes will go through the roof, and if taxes go up, businesses will leave the country . . . aggravating an already overtaxed population.

If a person wants to plan for retirement in a DC pension plan, they must start early, put a lot of money away, enough money to not only afford retirement living but also medical survival. In the coming years, many retirees may need to liquidate their portfolios to pay for medical care to extend their lives. My question is, when that financial planner said to the seventy-year-old retiree, "This is called a systematic withdrawal and it works like a charm," was the cost of this retiree's long-term health care factored into that answer? In other words, what were the assumptions behind the financial advisor's answer? Did her assumptions include health care?

In just a few years, not only will the market be hit by millions of baby boomers beginning their systematic withdrawals, the market will also be hit by millions of baby boomers needing money for medical expenses. Using a hypothetical crystal ball, let's say a seventy-five-year-old retiree with a DC plan with $500,000 in assets in his portfolio has limited medical insurance and suddenly needs $150,000 for life-saving cancer surgery. Do you think this retiree will choose to save money and not have the surgery or will he sell $150,000 worth of mutual funds to cover those expenses? My guess is that there will soon be millions of retirees selling large portions of their portfolios, and not following the plan of systematic withdrawal, in order to cover medical expenses. If that happens, what happens to the stock market? Will it continue to go up?

Many financial advisors are handing out financial advice that no one can yet prove will work. But sometime in the near future, we will find out if the assumptions of pension reform were right. Soon we will also find out if the assumptions that the financial planning industry uses can withstand the financial tests that real life after retirement will present . . . assumptions based upon the idea that the stock market, on average, always goes up.

Why a 401(k) Doesn't Make Tax Sense for a High Income Taxpayer

By Diane Kennedy, CPA
Rich Dad's Advisor
Author of _Loopholes of the Rich_

Conventional wisdom says that a high-income taxpayer should contribute the maximum amount to their 401(k) plan. True, it does decrease your current taxable income (the contributions to 401(k) are deductible against earned income), but it can cause a major tax headache later.

First, the assumption is that your income will go down in the future. If you listen to most advisors, they state that your income will always go down when you retire. But, there are some people (mainly my clients) who plan to retire with more income than they have now. For them, a 401(k) plan that defers tax to a later date doesn't make sense. They'll make more money—which means they'll pay more tax! Why pay tax purposely at a higher tax rate?

The second reason why a 401(k) plan doesn't make tax sense for a high-income taxpayer has to do with how we pay income tax. There are three types of income: earned income (you work for your money), passive income (your investments work for you), and portfolio income (your money works for you). Portfolio income is primarily from capital gains, which is typically the type of income you will earn from investments. The maximum capital gains rate for investments held for one year is 20 percent. The rate decreases to 18 percent for investments held for five or more years. However, the federal tax rates for earned income (ordinary income) range up to over 38 percent in 2002.

If you hold your investments outside of a 401(k), the tax rate on gains would be 18 percent–20 percent. If, however, you hold these same investments inside a 401(k), the tax is deferred until you withdraw the income. That withdrawn income is ordinary income, taxed at the highest rate. That means a 401(k) plan doubles your tax rate from the capital gains rate (18–20 percent) to the ordinary tax rate (38 percent).

Even worse, let's assume you die with money still within your pension plan. Upon your death, the pension plan is taxed for income and estate taxes. The total tax on an average estate would be 75 percent. If you assume that your pension plan started out with $100,000 and grows to $400,000, this means that only $100,000 is available for the heirs. The net gain on this 401(k) plan (which quadrupled in size) is actually zero!

There might be benefit to deferring tax to the future, but you must make sure that the solutions you have support the goals you have for the future. Don't settle for conventional advice from conventional advisors.

Are the Assumptions Valid?

Some people have referred to ERISA as a modified Ponzi scheme. Ponzi was a con man who had people give him money on the promise of high interest payments. He would then find a new group of people and promise them the same thing. He would take the money from the second group and give it to the people in the first group. The first group would tell all their friends and then their friends became the nucleus of the third group, which gave the high returns to the second group. The whole Ponzi scheme might have worked if someone had not figured out what Ponzi was doing. So instead of being the name of a hero, the name Ponzi today is infamous. When someone says that someone was caught in a Ponzi scheme that means someone or a group of people were gullible enough to believe in what they knew was too good to be true . . . and the scheme did turn out to be too good to be true.

I suspect that many of us have a part of us that wants to believe in things that are too good to be true. We like believing in magic, fairy godmothers, the Easter Bunny, and good spirits looking over us. That is why when a financial advisor says, "This is called a systematic withdrawal and it works like a charm" people believe it because they want to believe it, even though deep down they know it may not be true. Ponzi knew this about people and that is why there will always be new Ponzi schemes even though Ponzi is long gone. Now I am not saying that ERISA is a Ponzi scheme . . . but I am saying that people do like believing in the idea that things will work like a charm. And things will work like a charm as long as the assumptions come true. If they don't come true, then the word *assume* turns into ass-u-me.

On a Positive Note

In theory, rich dad thought ERISA was built on some excellent ideals and values. The problem was the *theory* part of it. As we all know, there is often a very wide gap between theory and reality.

Upon researching the act, rich dad found that one of its ideals was to give the worker a piece of the action. Up to that point, a worker with a DB pension plan may have had financial security after retirement, but the worker had no real asset base to pass on to his or her heirs. For example, if a worker retired at sixty-five and died at seventy-five, his benefits often ceased and the investment assets remained with the company. By utilizing a DC pension plan, if a worker passed away at age seventy-five and there was still something left in his portfolio, then the remaining assets in the retirement plan would be passed on to the family.

My poor dad had a DB pension plan so he had very little to pass on to his kids. He had a teacher's pension, a small government pension which provided him some degree of financial security each month, but when he died, he really had nothing to pass on. In other words, a DB pension plan is not a plan you pass on to your heirs. On the other hand, if my dad had a DC pension plan, his kids would have inherited the remaining assets in the portfolio, if there were any, less of course death taxes. In theory a DC pension plan has some great benefits that the DB pension plan did not.

So a very positive point of DC pension plans was that it was an attempt to help spread the tremendous wealth of America and the world into the hands of the workers. And in theory, the DC pension plan should work because there is so much wealth that every person could have a small piece of it. After all, there is plenty of wealth to go around.

But of course, that is a great idea that is great only in theory. The reality is, 90 percent of the wealth is held by only 10 percent of the people . . . and there is a reason for that . . . and that reason will be further explained in the next chapter, a chapter about the biggest flaw of all . . . the flaw that will trigger the biggest stock market crash in history, the same flaw that causes the wealth of the world to remain with only 10 percent of the people.

The good news is that if you understand the next flaw, and can overcome it, you have a better chance of becoming part of that 10 percent that does control 90 percent of the wealth.

Chapter 6

Just Because You Invest Does Not Mean You Are an Investor

Of all the flaws of pension reform, rich dad felt the biggest flaw of all was that it forced people who were not investors to invest. To rich dad, the assumption that a change in the law would suddenly turn people into overnight expert investors was an oversight of epic proportions. He said, "How can you take someone who has been programmed from birth to be a job-seeking employee to suddenly becoming a risk-taking investor? A security-seeking person is not the same person as a risk-taking investor." To rich dad, this assumption was the biggest flaw of all and would ultimately lead to the biggest stock market crash in history.

Those of you who have read *Rich Dad's CASHFLOW Quadrant* (book number 2 in the Rich Dad series of books) are very familiar with the following diagram of the quadrant:

For those not familiar with the CASHFLOW Quadrant, or who have not read the book, I will briefly explain what the four letters of the quadrant stand for.

> E stands for employee
> S stands for self-employed or small business owner
> B stands for big business owner
> I stands for investor

These are the four ways you earn money, or the four types of people. Each quadrant represents a different way of thinking about money and financial security.

Rich dad said, "The biggest flaw with ERISA is that the law assumes that people on the left side of the quadrant can easily switch to becoming people on the right side of the quadrant. People in each quadrant are different . . . very, very different. To assume someone in the E quadrant can become an investor in the I quadrant just because a law mandates the change . . . is absurd. You can change laws with the stroke of a pen but you cannot change people with the stroke of a pen."

Simply put, ERISA and subsequent amendments to ERISA mandated the following:

They required millions of employees to become professional investors . . . and as we have seen, did so without developing an educational system to support this small but monumental change.

Our public school system trains people primarily for the E or S quadrants, which is why most people are either Es or Ss. My poor dad, the head of education, constantly said, "Go to school, get good grades, so you can get a safe secure job." In other words, my poor dad was advising me to find safe sanctuary in the E quadrant. My mom, knowing that I wanted to become rich, often said, "I know you want to become rich, so go to medical school and become a doctor." She was advising me to find sanctuary in the S or self-employed quadrant. My response to her was, "There is only one problem with that idea, Mom . . . I'd have to be smart to be a doctor and you know what my grades are." The point being, often the S quadrant could stand for the smart quadrant since that is where doctors, lawyers, accountants, engineers, and so on often reside, although any profession or intelligence level could reside in any of the four quadrants. S can also stand for specialists, people with some unique trade or skill, and it also stands for the millions of small independent business owners.

My rich dad trained his son and me to be people who operated in the B and the I quadrants. For those of you who read my previous books, you may recall rich dad having his son and me do almost every job possible inside his businesses, training us to know how many different types of jobs it took to keep a business running. He also played Monopoly with us by the hour, teaching us to think like investors. One of the primary reasons I have had a normal job for only four years is simply because rich dad trained me to operate on the right side of the quadrant, not the left.

When I was still a boy, rich dad said, "People gravitate to the different quadrants because people are different. A person who seeks the E quadrant wants security. That is why most people in the E quadrant, regardless if they are the president or the janitor of the company, will often say the same thing, which is 'I'm looking for a safe secure job, a steady paycheck, and excellent benefits.' Safety and security are paramount to people in the E quadrant. The world of the I quadrant, the investor quadrant, is not a world perceived as a world of safety and security. It can be but *not* without proper training."

Again, there is a vast difference between the words *security* and *freedom*. Adding to this difference, rich dad pointed out that people in the E and S quadrants often wanted *security,* security from a job for an employee, and security of doing it on your own, not depending upon other people, for people in the S quadrant. People on the B and I side wanted freedom, so they focused on assets that worked for them. Now I can hear the howls of protest from the people in the S quadrant, generally people who want to do their own thing. But before you protest, consider that while most people in the S quadrant are *free to be doing their own thing,* the problem is they still *have to be doing it, regardless of whether they love doing it.* A person who is truly in the B or I quadrants is free to do nothing and still get paid and that is the difference in freedoms. (Again, for those who have not read *Rich Dad's CASHFLOW Quadrant,* you may want to because the book goes into far more detail about the core differences between the different people in the different quadrants. It is a very important book for anyone serious about making changes in their life, rather than simply going from job to job in the E quadrant or working hard all your life in the S quadrant.)

The other day, I was at an investment conference and I was talking to a young man who told me he was an investor. I then asked him what he was invested in. His reply was, "I have a company 401(k) plan that has a well-diversified portfolio of large cap, small cap, a few sector funds, and of course a bond fund."

As I nodded my head, I silently said to myself, "Wall Street has done a good job educating this lifelong customer." Not wanting to burst his bubble, I asked, "How much income do you receive a month from your investments?"

"Income?" he replied. "Why none. I don't have any income. Each month I send a portion of income, through payroll deduction, to these mutual fund companies."

"And when do you expect to receive some income from these investments?" I asked.

"Oh, I'm twenty-seven now. I plan on letting my money grow tax free until I retire, hopefully by age sixty. Then I'll switch my portfolio to a self-directed account and live off my investments. You see, I'm investing for the long term."

"Congratulations," I said, shaking his hand. "Keep on investing."

The point is, this young man may be *investing,* but I would not call him an *investor* . . . at least not from the definition rich dad used when referring to the Cashflow Quadrant. According to rich dad, investors *receive* money from their investments on a regular basis. Until you begin *receiving* money, you may be investing . . . but you are not an investor. To prove to rich dad that I was an investor, I had to prove to him that money was flowing *in* . . . and had stopped flowing *out.* Recently, millions of DC plan investors found out that the money they have been investing flowed out of their pockets and then flowed out of their DC plans . . . that is why there are so many upset investors today. They may have invested but they did not become investors.

When it comes to investing, many people are excellent at having money flow out . . . but only a few are excellent at having money flow in . . . and having money flow in is what makes you a good investor. When it comes to investing, most people have money flowing out and almost nothing flowing back in. After ERISA was passed, millions of people began *investing* but we do not yet know if they will become *investors.* Only time will tell how many make the transition from the E, S, or B quadrant to the I quadrant once their working days are over.

In the movie *Jerry Maguire* there is a classic line that goes "Show me the money." My friends who are hard-core investors consider that line *sacred.* The reason is they know investing money does not mean the investment will return the money. For my circle of friends, an investment is not real until the invested money comes back . . . and once the money comes back, that investment should have more money flowing in. Right now, for millions of people, with DC pension plans, money is flowing out and millions are wondering if it will flow back. Many have called their brokers and asked them to "Show me the money."

The other night, my wife and I were at a party, and the hostess asked my wife what she did for a living. Kim simply said, "I invest in real estate." The hostess's eyes lit up and said, "So do I. My husband and I started with a small house, and sold it when it went up in value. We have done this three times and now look at our home. We kept investing in real estate and now we live in this lovely home."

I know in her mind our friend thinks she is a real investor . . . and technically she is. Yet in our circle of friends, she would *not* be called a real estate investor, she would be called a *homeowner* who got lucky. Although she did have a lovely home, there is a tremendous difference between a real estate investor who owns a home that *costs* them $5,000 a month and a real estate investor who *earns* $5,000 a month in net income. By our investment group's definition, a real estate investor has income coming in every month from rental homes, commercial property, warehouses, office buildings, and so forth. In other words, regardless if we work or not, we can show them the money . . . the money coming in.

The Biggest Flaw of All

So why did rich dad feel that people in the E quadrant being forced into the I quadrant was the biggest flaw of all? The answer again is because they have completely different personalities. A person in the E or S quadrant works for *money* and people in the B and I quadrants work to build or acquire *assets*. This may seem like a small difference on paper, but after a person retires, the differences are substantial. As a professional investor with years of training, learning to show the money on a monthly basis from my investments is not the easiest thing to do . . . and that is what ERISA has asked people to do. Once a person with a DC plan retires, they will be shoved out of the safe sanctuary of their job. For many, they will have to face the real world for the first time in their life . . . the real world rich dad faced at thirteen, I faced at thirty-two, my dad at fifty-three, and the Enron employee on the front page of *USA Today* at fifty-eight.

Meeting the Real World

In the good old days, once an employee retired, there may have been a retirement party, a gold watch, and a DB pension plan to watch over them for the rest of their lives. In other words, they could retire and count on the check being in the mail. That is all they had to do.

Also in the good old days, if the retiree had worked for a generous company or the company had a strong union, they might have received a COLA, a cost-of-living adjustment. As inflation went up, so did their defined benefit payments. Some also had medical plans for as long as the retiree lived. As long as the retiree lived, he or she could go to the doctor and the company would show the doctor the money. In other words DB pension plans became very, very expensive as more people retired and lived longer through improved health care. These large liabilities are some of the real reasons why ERISA was legislated. Employees with DB and medical plans were simply too expensive in a world of increasing global competition.

In today's world, once an employee retires, there may still be a retirement party and a gold watch, but once they retire they may very likely find themselves on their own. Some may keep their money with the company's pension plan, others may elect to roll it over into an IRA, an individual retirement account, and still more will sell their financial assets for cash and put the money in the bank.

The following are the three real reasons why rich dad saw the coming of the biggest stock market crash in history. They are:

1. There will be a market sell-off caused by baby boomers converting to cash. Rich dad said, "Es and Ss work all their lives for money, not for financial assets. Most Es and Ss do not trust the stock market. Once they leave the company, all the fear and insecurity that has always been there—the fear and insecurity that caused them to be an E or S all their lives—will only increase. Once they leave they will cling to what they know and trust and that is cash . . . not stocks or mutual funds."

According to *Business Week* magazine, in 1990 there was $712 billion in 401(k) and similar plans. Only 45 percent of that money was in stocks. By the end of 2000 that amount had swelled to $2.5 trillion, with 72 percent in stocks or similar equities. In other words, as the money from retirement funds came in, a market boom was underway. As the boom increased, so-called investors became more confident and began taking their cash and buying equities with it, simply because they could get a much higher return from equities instead of cash. As the boom progressed, many so-called investors entered the party late and began taking money out of their savings and putting it into the market, primarily into stock mutual funds, swelling that asset class to $4 trillion. About that same time, reports came out that the family savings rate of America had dropped to less than 1 percent. A *mania* was on and people who should never have been in the market were now in the market.

Many people who were investing in their DC pension plans saw their plans increasing in value. Immediately they believed that they were now real investors, and began taking their savings and putting it all into the market. Most of these people came from the E and S quadrants. People who should have remained *savers* suddenly starting *investing*. But they were not investors.

Rich dad believes that the biggest stock market crash in history will be caused when millions of people begin to sell financial assets they do not understand and do not trust. Rich dad said, "People in the E quadrant love security. If they feel their security threatened, *they will not hold on to their financial assets.* If they feel insecure, there will not be any systematic withdrawal as pension reform calls for . . . Instead, there will be a wholesale panic . . . a panic caused by baby boomers converting financial assets back to cash . . . cash for their savings accounts . . . as fast as possible."

At first I did not understand what rich dad was getting at. Now that I am older I am more aware of that subtle difference. Today, I am very aware of that difference whenever I hear people saying, "I am *saving* for my retirement." Or they say, "I am saving for my child's education." Rarely do I ever hear people saying "I am *investing* for my retirement." Or "I am investing for my child's education." As rich dad said, "Savers and investors are not the same people. Savers feel secure with money, not with mutual funds. When push comes to shove they will sell, and when millions of them begin to sell . . . the market will crash. There will be no systematic withdrawal."

Japan has teetered on the brink of a banking and financial disaster for some years now. At the same time, Japan's banks are bursting with money because most Japanese are employees and savers. In fact, Japan has the highest savings rate in the world. Because the banks are so flush with money, the interest rate paid on those savings is nearly 0 percent. Even though the banks pay the Japanese nothing for their savings, the money sits in the banks. Why? The reason is because employees and savers would rather have money earning nothing than take a risk. I predict in a few years U.S. banks will also be flush with money. If banks are filled with money, it's going to be tough for them to pay 10 percent interest to savers on that money. As I write, the U.S. banks are paying 2 percent interest on savings. Two percent is not a very good return on your investment.

So the primary reason for the coming crash is that most people today do not naturally feel secure with mutual funds and stocks. Once they begin to retire, millions of baby boomers will cash in their stocks and mutual funds and return to what they have spent their lives working for . . . cash. As rich dad said, "You can change the law but you cannot change people."

2. The cost of living and medical costs will go up. As stated earlier, with many DB pension plans, there was a cost-of-living adjustment. With a DC pension plan, after retirement, when the cost of living goes up and medical costs go up, the retiree will sell their assets to pay for these life expenses. Again this will blow the systematic withdrawal theory out the window. These slight differences between a DB plan and a DC plan will also add to the coming market crash. People have to have money to live on, not mutual funds. So the mutual funds will be sold for cash.

3. The number of fools will increase. Quoting Warren Buffett: "The fact that people will be full of greed, fear, or folly is predictable. The sequence is not predictable."

Most of us know that any market is run on greed and fear. The reason the market went up in the 1990s was because of *greed*, and the reason it will go down is because of *fear*. In the near future, one more reason people will turn their retirement account into cash is because of *folly*.

I will give you an example of investment *folly*. During the 1990s, I happened to meet many rich employees who thought they became rich because they were investors . . . but in reality, they were lucky employees. One person I met was an employee of Intel. In 1997, just as the market was climbing, he cashed in his options for nearly $35 million. He thought for sure he was an investor rather than just a lucky employee, and was soon out investing in investments only reserved for what the Securities and Exchange Commission classifies as an accredited investor. By definition, an accredited investor is a person with over $1 million net worth or a high paying job. Now, how that qualifies a person to be an accredited investor is beyond me, but those are the rules. *I have a better way of a person proving they are an accredited investor, but the SEC has not called to ask me for my opinion.*

In any event, this ex–Intel investor with his millions of dollars let the money go to his head and he began investing in anything that moved. He bought private placements, he bought partnerships in companies, he bought companies outright and had his sons and daughters run them, and he bought doodads that only truly rich people buy, doodads such as a private jet, a yacht, and two large homes. On top of that he met a woman younger than his daughter and then divorced his wife, who received a sizable sum of money. Rich dad often said, "A fool and his money are one big party." And let me tell you, this guy could throw a party. Today, he is bankrupt. How do I know? I know because he came asking me for a job. He needs a job because his second ex-wife got the rest of the money. He is only one of dozens of such people I met during the roaring 1990s. They were employees who got lucky and thought they were investors—but found out they were fools who threw big parties. Nothing wrong with big parties . . . but just make sure you can afford to throw another one.

This example of investment *folly* is found with sports stars, movie stars, rock stars, lottery winners, people who suddenly inherit a large sum of money, and anyone else who is fooled into believing that investing money and becoming an investor are the same thing. In a few years from now, as some of the luckier baby boomers begin retiring with large sums of money in their DC pension plans, you will begin reading in the paper about fools being swindled out of their retirement money. Many will be swindled because they did not make the distinction between investing money and becoming an investor.

In conclusion, the biggest flaw of all, according to rich dad, was that although people invested, they did not become investors. He said, "This small and seemingly trivial point has the potential to bring down the stock market." So rich dad's prophecy was that sometime in the near future, millions of people will slowly wake up and realize they were forced by law to buy something they really did not want (a DC plan), and could not sell unless they were willing to pay a huge tax penalty for early withdrawal. On top of that many are encouraged to invest in products they do not really value, do not understand, and think they paid too much for. He said, "At that point, savers will begin converting their investments back to what they have worked all their lives for . . . and what they worked for was cash . . . not stocks, bonds, or mutual funds. The market crash will take place because people were encouraged under law to invest but they never learned to become investors. Remember, investors love *assets* and savers love *cash*. And that is why you hear so many people say, "Safe as money in the bank.""

Rich dad once explained to me that his definition of financial *mania* is an irrational conversion of cash to financial assets such as stocks, bonds, real estate, and mutual funds. Over the centuries there have been many manias. One of the more famous or infamous is the tulip bulb mania in Holland from 1634 to 1637. The tulip bulb mania was caused when the Dutch fell madly in love with this new flower imported from China. Soon they began to create

Gouda Tulip Bulb Mania 1634–37
*Based on Historical Estimates

new varieties and it was not long before a mania was on. Certain tulip bulbs were commanding more than a hundred times their weight in gold. Suddenly the mania was over and a panic began, the panic to convert their bulbs back to cash. Today, the tulip bulb mania sounds as ridiculous as the dot.com mania of just a few years ago.

Rich dad's definition of a financial *panic* was an irrational conversion of financial assets back to cash. In other words, people suddenly wake up and realize that what they bought is not worth what they paid for it and they want their money back. It's often called "buyer's remorse." When millions of people who invested in mutual funds and other financial assets experience buyer's remorse and demand their money back a panic will occur and that panic will lead to a crash . . . the biggest crash in the history of the world. As rich dad said, "Just because you invest does not mean you're an investor."

Chapter 7

Everyone Needs to Become an Investor

"Don't they realize how important investing is?" I asked rich dad. We were walking out of a hotel ballroom where rich dad had held a meeting for his key management team and his top employees, about 125 people.

"We shall see," said rich dad. "I've done my best to convince them but I can only push so hard. This 401(k) plan we've implemented is a benefit but many of the workers aren't contributing to the plan. Some only contribute a little. Even some of the management team have stopped contributing. I don't know what they expect to live on once they retire."

The year was 1988. I was passing through Hawaii on my way to the Far East and rich dad asked me if I wanted to attend this meeting. The 1987 stock market crash in October had frightened many of them and they had stopped contributing to their DC retirement plan.

"I called in the representative from the fund management company to explain to the workers once again how their 401(k) plan works. The potential fiduciary liability prevented this investment advisor from giving specific investment advice. She only presented the information but did not advise the person what to buy. So she explained the plan but did not go into much detail. That did not make the employees feel too secure since they have no idea what to invest in. Why does the law prevent the people who run the plan from giving the employees a little bit more specific advice?"

"I did not know that," I said. "All these years I never understood why the advisors just presented the plan but not much advice. Today I learned it was the potential fiduciary liability."

"At least she told them that you were a generous employer because you were willing to match the employee's contribution dollar for dollar. Many employers do not match any funds at all . . . and some only match 50 cents on the dollar. Even though I am willing to be generous, there are still only a few employees contributing on a regular basis," said rich dad.

"Even if they don't get much investment advice, don't the employees realize that every dollar you contribute is like receiving tax free money?" I asked. "All they have to do is put in a dollar that is also tax free."

"They hear the words," said rich dad. "I've been saying the same thing for years but nothing seems to change. I even told them that a person who is contributing to the plan is making more money than those that are not. Even that failed to change things. Then after the stock market crash, some of those that used to contribute stopped contributing. That is why I asked the representative from the fund company to stop by and speak to them. I hope it does some good."

We continued our conversation all the way back to his office, which was just down the street from the hotel where the meeting was held. Again I asked the question, "Don't they realize how important investing is?"

"I believe they do," rich dad replied.

"So why don't they invest?" I asked.

With that question rich dad sat down at his desk and began to write on his yellow legal tablet the following words:

RICH

MIDDLE CLASS

POOR

Looking up at me, he said, "Every one of us invests in one way or another. We simply invest in different things and in different ways." He then wrote the following after each class:

RICH:	Good financial education
	Build business
	Large real estate investments
	Private equity funds
	Hedge funds
	Personal money manager
	Private placements
	Limited partnerships
MIDDLE CLASS:	Good education
	High paying job
	Profession
	Home
	Savings
	Retirement plan
	Mutual funds
	Small real estate investments
POOR:	Large family
	Government support programs

"These are the different investments the different classes invest in," said rich dad. "The poor often have large families, trusting that their kids will take care of them in their old age. They also count on government programs such as Social Security, welfare, and Medicare."

"The poor invest in kids?" I responded incredulously.

Rich dad nodded. "That is a broad generalization but you will find some truth in that statement. They may not say it but they expect their kids to support them when they stop working."

"And the middle class invests in a good education so they can get a high paying job," I said, reading from rich dad's tablet. "To them that is an investment?"

"Sure," smiled rich dad. "Isn't it true in your family? Isn't it important to your mom and dad that you have a college degree, and possibly a profession such as doctor, lawyer, or a job title such as vice president or general manager?"

I agreed. "Education is very important in our family. My mom really wanted me to become a doctor and my dad always thought I should go to law school."

Rich dad chuckled. "And don't they insist you buy a home and have a retirement plan? In fact, didn't you tell me that your dad wanted you to stay in the Marine Corps because it had a great retirement plan with benefits?"

Again I nodded. "But don't the poor want the same things, at least in their work?"

"They may dream of a high paying job. But dreams are dreams and reality is reality. If you notice, most of my lower paid employees move from job to job simply because it's easy to move from job to job, as long as you do not expect high pay. So they may dream of finding a great high paying job but in reality without a good education or some technical skills, a high paying job is out of the question."

"So they spend most of their money just surviving, keeping their kids clothed and fed. That is what they invest in."

Rich dad nodded, tapping his pencil on the investment of the poor. "Now my college-educated managers are different," he said, shifting his pencil to the investments of the middle class. "As employees, they tend to stay longer because they know that if they leave, they have to start all over again, often at the bottom of the ladder. That is why they like job titles and seniority. It also takes longer to find a job if you expect higher pay. So they invest more time in a good education, high pay, job security, promotions, and titles. That is what is important to the middle class. As I said, people invest, but they invest in different ways. People invest time and money only into what they think is important."

"So the rich build businesses and invest in larger pieces of real estate," I said. "Or they invest in private equity funds or hedge funds, while the middle class has mutual funds."

Rich dad went on: "Or the rich invest in syndications, partnerships, or they have personal fund managers who do it for them. They invest in investments reserved only for the rich."

"But isn't a college education important to everyone?" I asked.

"Yes it is," said rich dad. "In fact, if you look at all three classes and their investments, all three classes of investments are important, even to the rich."

"You mean the rich need large families?" I asked.

"Not necessarily large, but family is important to all of us, regardless of which class. And so is government support important for the rich. If the government did not support the poor with welfare programs, there would be beggars in the streets and burglars in the homes of the rich. So the rich invest in government support through their taxes or charitable donations."

Rich dad went on to explain that if I wanted to be rich, I needed to invest in all three classes. In other words, if I wanted to be rich, I had to invest far more than the other two classes of people. He said, "If you want to be rich, I strongly recommend you invest in what the poor invest in, the middle class invest in, and what the rich invest in. Do not . . . I repeat—do not try to skip over any of the first two investments. If you want to be rich, you must invest more . . . not less than the first two groups."

He continued by pointing out to me the importance of family, home, and a retirement plan. He said, "Many people try to get rich without those pillars of support and that is very risky. That is why even I have a 401(k) retirement plan, even though I do not need one. It's there for support. Besides, it's a small tax advantage for me." Pointing to family he said, "Family is very important to me, that is why I invest a lot of time and money in my family. I need them for emotional support just as you need Kim for emotional support. I have met many people who ignore their families. They sacrifice time with family for time at work. Or even worse, people cheat on their families. You and I have met people who cheat on their husband or wife thinking that a little affair doesn't matter, but it does. A strong family is important to me and I trust it is to you."

The discussion of family made sense to me. Before rich dad left the discussion of family, I added, "Because you are rich, you have more time with your family. My dad was often gone for days on business trips. He said he needed to travel if he wanted to get his pay raise and promotion so he can put food on the table and buy a bigger house."

"I know," said rich dad. "Many people ignore their families for a pay raise, promotion, and trying to look rich by buying a big house. As I said, people invest in what they think is important. But in my mind, that is not investing . . . that is financial and family suicide. How many parents today have no time for their kids? Where would you be today if I had not spent so much time with you teaching about business and investing? Your father did not have the time. He was too busy working hard to make big house payments."

As rich dad was talking it was beginning to sink in why he always talked about a plan. In previous books, I wrote about him saying that there were investment plans to be safe, comfortable, and rich. He was a stickler for developing a plan and following it. He had a plan to become rich because he wanted the free time to spend with his kids. My poor dad's plan was to continually go back to school so he could be promoted and receive higher pay. Although he did his best to be at home with the kids, the reality was he was often on the road, while rich dad was at home, letting his employees run his businesses and investments. I now realized how important all three levels of investment were. Suddenly, it struck me that I had many friends who only wanted to get rich, and did not invest in the first two classes of investments. So I asked, "But what about people who invest in the investments of the rich but do not have the first two levels. What happens to them?"

"Some make it," said rich dad. "But very few do. I meet so many people investing in the investments of the rich before investing in the first two steps. I meet people who invest in wild business schemes with lofty tales of making billions of dollars, but most of those people lose their money, falling victim to the con men, crooks, and dreamers of the business world. Most who try to win big without a strong foundation wind up losers."

Nodding, I could only laugh at myself, saying, "I've met many of those people along the way. In fact, I was one of those people when I was just starting out."

Rich dad grinned and said, "I know. You sure had some wild stories about how you were going to strike it rich . . . and the problem is you did strike it rich with your first business. The trouble was you got lucky but you did not have the skills to maintain your luck. That is when you and the three clowns who were your partners went broke. You had the business, the rich level of investment, but you boys forgot about the importance of the first two levels . . . the middle-class and poor levels. That is why when your business struck it rich, instead of you and your partners becoming rich, you became clowns and lost it all."

"So now I have all three levels," I said. "Hopefully, I have the skills and the maturity to develop all three levels."

"I hope so too," said rich dad quietly. "But don't worry. Investing on all three levels is a full-time job and you will have your challenges in the future . . . just as my employees will have their challenges in the future."

"So the lesson of the day is that as individuals we tend to only invest in what we think is important," I added. "Many of your employees know investing is important to them, but investing is not yet important enough. They have other things they invest in that are more important and that is where their time and money goes."

"Exactly," said rich dad. "Look at the differences between your dad and me. Your dad says his house is his biggest investment. To him his home is far more important than his stock portfolio or industrial real estate, which I invest in. That is why his college degrees and job title are more important than going to school to learn to invest. I invest time and money in what I think is important and he invests time and money into what he thinks is important. The problem is, now that he has lost his job and most of his savings, he is finding out how *unimportant* what *he thought was important* really is in the real world. He is finding out that his big house is not really an asset, and he found out that his college degrees and work experience did not help him in the real business world or in the investment markets. The real world is very different than the world of education or the government. What he invested in will not pay off in the real world."

It Takes Little Financial Intelligence to Save Money

In my previous books I wrote about the three different types of education. They are:

1. Academic education
2. Professional education
3. Financial education

My poor dad was well educated in the first two. My rich dad was very well educated in the third level, the level of financial education. When ERISA was passed, rich dad quickly realized that the law failed to make universal financial education essential. In 1988, he also found out that some financial advisors were by law limited in what kind of advice they could offer. The result is that most people will do what they always do. They will not make the transition from the E or S quadrant to the I quadrant when they retire.

Again taking his legal pad, rich dad pointed to his comparison between what the middle class thought was important and the rich. Pointing to the word *save* he said, "How much financial intelligence does it take to save money?"

"I don't know," I replied. "I never really thought about it."

"Well, in my opinion, it takes no financial intelligence at all. I could train a monkey to save money." He chuckled. "And so many people think they're so smart for saving money. All one has to do is walk up to the bank teller, and if you're really incompetent, the teller will fill out the deposit slip for you. What is so hard about that? Saving money may be smart but it doesn't require much financial intelligence."

"You could train a monkey to save money?"

"I'm sure I could," smiled rich dad. "Look, I'm just making a point about how little financial intelligence most people have. If most people have trouble saving money, how much chance do they have when doing more sophisticated investments? Look at your dad. He is a highly educated man but he couldn't make a simple ice cream stand profitable. He was a saver but he was not an investor, much less a businessman. He had no business investing in that venture."

"He felt he got cheated, but the facts were that he could not read a financial statement or the prospectus on the franchise," I said. "I asked him to have you look at the business and the numbers but his pride wouldn't allow that to happen. He said that you did not have a college degree so he would never ask you for any advice."

Rich dad shook his head. Pointing to the investments that the rich invest in he said, "It takes financial education to invest in these investments . . . financial education your dad does not have even though he has a college education," he said, pointing to the investments of the rich.

RICH: Build business
               Large real estate investments
               Private equity funds
               Hedge funds
               Personal money manager
               Private placements
               Limited partnerships

Then pointing to the column of the middle class he said, "It takes very little financial education to invest in any of the investments this group invests in. As I said, I could train a monkey to save money, and after that I would train it to buy mutual funds. In fact every year someone has a contest where a monkey throws darts at a list of stocks to see if the monkey can beat the pros who pick stocks . . . and the monkey often wins."

MIDDLE CLASS:	Good education
	High paying job
	Profession
	Home
	Savings
	Retirement plan
	Mutual funds
	Small real estate investments

"So the reason the middle class does not get rich is because of the lack of financial education?" I asked.

"Well, some do get rich," said rich dad. "But without a sound financial education, it takes a lot of hard work to make a lot of money and it also takes a lot more money to stay rich. Also, the lower your financial IQ, the more at risk you put your money. That is why the middle class focuses on saving money while the rich focus on investing money. That is why the middle class often puts so much money into their home instead of investment real estate. The difference is financial education. If they had a better financial education they would understand why owning a home and saving money was really risky and why investing in investment real estate was more intelligent."

"So after I rebuild my business, then I can begin investing in the investments of the rich," I said, pointing to the top line of what the rich invest in.

"You can do what you want. Today I am only pointing out to you that people only invest in what they think is important. Many of my employees do not think their pension plan is important. They have other things to do with their money . . . things they think are more important," said rich dad. "If you want to invest in the investments of the rich, I'm recommending you continue to invest in your financial education. If you have a high financial IQ, what seems risky to most people will be safe to you. And what seems safe to the poor and the middle class will seem risky to you. It's all a matter of what you think is important and that is what you will ultimately invest in. I leave that decision to you."

A large market crash only frightens people with a limited financial education. A large market crash is the best time to get rich for those with a strong financial education. As rich dad often said, "If you have a strong financial education you are not worried about markets going up or down. You're just happy they are going up and down."

Chapter 8

The Cause of the Problem

ERISA will not be the cause of the coming stock market crash. ERISA, Enron, and the coming giant crash are really only the symptoms of a much deeper problem. This chapter is about the problems behind the problem and how we can begin once and for all to solve them. In this chapter we get to the real reason behind rich dad's prophecy.

Social Security and Medicare are taking on water as well. The Clinton administration's fiscal 2000 budget report stated, "Government trust funds *do not consist of real economic assets* that can be used in the future to fund benefits." In other words, the government is finally admitting that there really is no Social Security trust fund. It is a figment of our imagination. Is Social Security merely a modified Ponzi scheme?

In America today, every employee looks at their pay stub and they see 7.65 percent of their pay, matched by the employer's 7.65 percent, for a total of 15.3 percent, going to Social Security and Medicare. Every employee is hoping that after retirement they will be on the receiving end. They can be if there are enough employees still at the front door turning in their money. The problem is, because people are living longer, there are more and more retired people waiting at the back door. Is this a scheme that works only as long as there are more people at the front door than the back door?

For decades, the federal government has borrowed and spent the Social

Security surplus—the difference between Social Security's tax revenues and outlays. The government replaces the money it borrows with IOUs in the form of U.S. Treasury bonds. In recent years, many critics began to say that the Social Security system was a shell game, that there was nothing in the trust fund. In return, government bureaucrats criticized the critics, denying that there was a problem. In the year 2000, when the Clinton administration came clean and published that statement, the statement fundamentally saying there really is no trust fund, it marked the *first time* that the government finally acknowledged there is a problem. Does the problem sound similar to the problems with Enron?

The Social Security system worked fine when it began in the mid-1930s when there were forty-two workers for every one Social Security recipient. In the year 2000, the number was 3.4 workers per one recipient. By 2016, according to the commission's report, Social Security will collect less money in tax revenues than it pays out. In other words there will be too many people at the back door.

If you remember from an earlier chapter, 2016 is the same year that the first of the baby-boom generation turns seventy, a jump of 700,000 people turning seventy in that year alone, and those statistics do not include the numbers they expect to die before seventy, so that means 700,000 living people . . . and the number of people over seventy years of age will continue to increase with each subsequent year. That is what I call a perfect storm brewing. In 2002, politicians are proposing that younger workers be allowed to invest money either in a personal savings account or the stock market. If this law passes, that will mean even less money entering the system for the older retirees. If this law passes, that means Social Security begins to run at a negative well before 2016.

In 1979, I did not fully understand why rich dad was so concerned about the future. I wondered why a rich man would have such a doom and gloom prophecy. I wondered why he would care. Although I did not fully understand his logic, I trusted him enough to continue building my ark. That is why I did not take the sales manager's job, or any other job, even though the pay and benefits were great. Instead of taking the job, I decided to stand and face the real world early in life rather than face the real world later in life. By 1994, Kim and I were financially free. We had built an ark that kept us afloat. Our ark did well when the stock market went up in the late 1990s and the ark kept us afloat even as the market crashed in March of 2000; in fact we made even more money as the market crashed. Today, because of my own personal experiences on what it takes to build a personal ark, I better understand why rich dad was so concerned about the future . . . a future he knew his son and I would see.

Pushing the Problem Forward

Rich dad saw that the real cause for concern was that the issue of personal financial survival after retirement was being pushed forward. That is why he repeatedly said, "ERISA is my generation passing on its problem to your generation."

One of the more important lessons rich dad taught his son and me was the difference between a businessperson and a government bureaucrat. Rich dad said, "A businessperson is a person who solves financial problems. If they do not solve their financial problems, they are out of business. If a government bureaucrat cannot solve a problem, a bureaucrat can afford to push the problem forward."

Rich dad was not being critical of government; he was just being observant. He said, "Governments solve many problems for the good of society. It is the government that uses our tax dollars to provide military defense, fight fires, provide police protection, build roads, provide schools, and provide welfare for the needy. But there are problems that government cannot solve and when those problems are pushed forward they often become bigger and bigger problems. This problem of financial survival once a person's working years are over is a monster of a problem that is growing bigger. The problem constantly grows bigger because too many people expect the government to solve what is really a personal financial problem."

Rich dad was worried that people were never taught how to build their own ark. Over the years, they have been taught to depend on a company and the government to provide that ark for them. As the problem became too complex to solve, laws were passed to pass the expense of retirement on to the next generation. In other words Social Security and ERISA pass the expense of the care of one generation on to future generations.

Then in 1996, a new DC investment plan entered the market. It is the Roth IRA, named after the senator who championed it. The Roth IRA was a new DC plan designed only for the middle class. If you are rich, you are not allowed to have one.

Soon after the Roth IRA came out, Diane Kennedy, my tax advisor and author of *Loopholes of the Rich,* called me. She was very concerned about this new DC plan, which allows its owner to receive tax free payouts after retirement for funds taxed before entering the plan. The Roth IRA was once again pushing the problem forward, this time from the baby-boom generation to the future generations.

According to Diane, the Roth IRA was primarily created to collect more taxes. She said, "If you notice there was a surplus of money in the budget soon after the Roth IRA was passed. I suspect the Clinton administration passed this law because they needed more taxes and wanted to create the illusion that they were doing a good job. The problem is, when the baby boomers begin to retire, it is their kids who will have to pay those taxes to make up for the future budget shortfalls." In other words, the problem has been passed forward again.

Almost immediately, the Roth IRA was the darling of the middle class. They loved the idea of paying taxes now but being allowed to pull out the gains tax free in the future. Because the market was going up in 1996, many people saw this Roth IRA as a gift from heaven. Money, greed, a rising market, and the new Roth IRA were all these people needed. Money began pouring into these new IRAs and directly into an already overheated stock market. The market took off like a rocket ship.

One of the ways the government made more money was that many people stopped contributing to their 401(k) DC plans and shifted money to their new Roth IRA. That meant the taxman collected more money from the middle class, since only after-tax dollars are allowed to go into a Roth IRA. Explaining a little further for those that might still not be clear on the difference, the traditional 401(k) DC plan, allows the employee and employer to put untaxed dollars into the plan. That means the taxman gets no revenue from those dollars. The taxman then has to wait till the employee retires before the government can begin collecting taxes. By creating the Roth IRA, many people stopped contributing to their company's 401(k) plan, and put the money instead into this new Roth IRA. When this happened, the government got paid today but not tomorrow. The problem is tomorrow. In the future, there will be fewer taxes to be collected. Again, this will be a major problem down the road.

But the Roth IRA did one more thing. It inspired many people without a retirement plan to open one. Not only were there many new people entering the market via their new Roth IRAs, money was also flowing out of savings accounts and some people were even borrowing money to invest. With so much money pouring into the market the market continued its climb. People began to say, "This time it's different. It's the new economy." By 1998 millions of noninvestors who got lucky in the market the year before and who now thought they were investors suddenly began an investing frenzy just because fear and greed had become the same.

People even quit their jobs to become investment advisors. Little old retired ladies formed an investment club, wrote a book, and began handing out investment advice. Unfortunately, it was later disclosed that the little old ladies really hadn't done as well as they thought they had with their investments. Nevertheless, they did inspire others to form investment clubs all across the country, which I think is a very good idea. Investment expos sprung up and they were packed with thousands of people who had been bitten by the bug. By 1999 shoeshine boys and taxi drivers were handing out hot stock tips and the stock market went straight on up to all-new highs. Between 1996 and 2000 many people who had no business investing began pouring money they could not afford to lose into the market . . . a mania was on. Greed and fear had become one . . . twenty-five years after the passage of ERISA. The foxes were grinning as they watched the chickens cluck with excitement. The foxes knew it was time to take a little of their winnings off the table . . . but not all . . . just a little. The foxes know there is still one more run to go.

In March of 2000 the party came to an end . . . but of course, many people did not want to believe it. Yet slowly but surely, the reality of the real world sank in. The opening paragraph of the lead story from the February 25, 2002, *Business Week* says it all:

It's 2 a.m., and Jim Tucci is staring wide-eyed at the ceiling—another sleepless night. Instead of counting sheep, he's anxiously tallying up how much he has lost in the stock market. Half of his $400,000 nest egg, he figures, has evaporated in just two years. Forget the retirement property on the Gulf coast. Forget the long-planned trip to Italy with his wife. Tucci, a 60-year-old sales manager at a voice recording company in Boston, admits he blew a wad on speculative tech stock during the Internet bubble. But a year ago, he dove for safety in blue-chip stocks like IBM, Merrill Lynch, General Motors and Delta Airlines. Now 40% of that is gone. Tucci feels suckered. "I'm paralyzed, I can't sell because I'd take such a big loss. I'm sure as heck not going to buy anything. And even if I were, whom would I listen to for advice? No one seems to give off a whiff of honesty about any of this stuff. These days, I just pray a lot."

The article goes on:

Some 100 million investors—about half of all adult Americans—can relate to that. They're the new Investor Class that has emerged over the past decade. Predominantly middle-class, suburban baby boomers, they bought into the idea that stocks could make them richer. They exulted during the long bull market of the 1990s. But they've lost $5 trillion, or 30% of their stock wealth since the spring of 2000, when the dot-com implosion launched the second-worst bear market since World War II. It wasn't Monopoly money: It was money earmarked for retirement, for college tuition, for medical bills.

The Problem Gets Bigger

The concern with pushing problems forward, rather than solving them, is that the problem only gets worse. When the Enron scandal broke, millions of people got their first glimpse at how big this problem can be . . . and personally devastating . . . especially for older workers, workers who have had their 401(k) wiped out, who know that Social Security and Medicare are going broke, and their kids are not much better off than they are. Instead of retirement being a dream, the retirement has become a nightmare.

Rich dad explained to me how this problem came to be: "When America became a world power back in the early 1900s, millions of farm hands began to move off the farm and into the city for a high paying job in the new factories. Soon our factories were booming, but a new problem was created. The problem of what to do with older workers."

"That's why during the Depression the Social Security Act was passed," I said, remembering that Social Security began in the 1930s. "I'll bet it made a lot of older workers happy."

"It did," rich dad agreed. "And it still does today. But when World War II broke out, the factories picked up and the boom in America continued right on through even after the war ended. Because there was a boom on, many unions began demanding that their workers receive a pension after retiring. In order to keep the union leaders happy, corporate management agreed and DB pension plans began to grow."

"But the problem persists," I said. "The problem of how a person survives once they are no longer able to work."

"That is correct," said rich dad. "That is the problem behind the problem. That is, how does a person survive once they are no longer able to work? This is the problem that led to Social Security, DB pension plans, and ERISA."

"That's the problem that needs to be solved," I said.

Rich dad just nodded his head and said, "The World War I generation solved its problem by passing on its expenses via government legislation to the World War II generation. The World War II generation passed its expenses on to your generation with pension reform."

"So the government passes the problem on rather than solve it," I said. "And that is the basis of your prophecy."

Rich dad looked at me silently and solemnly. He could tell I was beginning to understand why the problem will get worse.

I sat quietly for a while, letting the idea sink in. And as I sat there, I began to recall speeches by famous politicians saying words that made people happy, making promises that would keep them hopeful. Snapping out of my silence I said, "So that is why you say there will be a giant stock market crash. The problem is not the stock market. The problem is the original problem has been passed on rather than solved . . . and someday soon, the problem will become too big. It's all going to come tumbling down like a house of cards."

"That's correct," said rich dad. "We now have too many people who have come to expect the government to solve their problems. And politicians, in their desire to win votes, will promise to solve those problems. But of course, we know that a politician will do and say anything to remain popular, be liked, and get reelected. I don't blame them. If they told people the truth, they would be thrown out of office. So the problem grows, the government gets bigger, and the taxes have to get higher."

The Rise and Fall of the Roman Empire

All through my years growing up with rich dad, he encouraged me to study the history of the rise and fall of great empires. One of the empires he had me study was the Roman Empire. During one of these study sessions rich dad said, "The Roman Empire had great technology for conquering and taxing people so they were able to create a vast empire. Their difficulties began as people moved off the conquered lands and into cities such as Rome. As the city of Rome grew, the leaders became concerned that the urban mobs would revolt because they had no jobs, shelter, or food. So the Romans fed the people and created great distractions such as the Colosseum to entertain the masses. Soon Rome became a great city of people who expected to be entertained and fed."

"So Rome became a welfare state?" I asked.

"More than a welfare state . . ." said rich dad, "it became a large government bureaucracy. Instead of solving problems, they created more problems. It was also a very litigious state. There were more lawsuits per capita than even in America today, because more and more people wanted to blame someone else for their problems, rather than solve their own problems. As a result, the problems only increased. And the more problems they created the more bureaucrats were needed. So as the problem got bigger, so did the government."

"So how did they afford it all and keep control?" I asked.

"Well for one thing they had a strong army. As I said, they knew how to conquer. Conquering people was their technology. In order to pay for this form of mob control, the Romans increased taxes on the working class throughout the empire. Soon the taxes got so high that workers began leaving the land and moving to the cities because life on the land made no sense. All their work was taxed so why not move to where food and entertainment were inexpensive or even free."

"So the problem got worse, not better," I said.

"Well, it was one of the many problems that was getting worse," said rich dad. "As I said, the workers were leaving the land. That meant food production as well as tax collection was beginning to decline as more and more workers moved into the cities."

"So how did they solve that problem?" I asked.

"The same way any military-based conquering nation solves its problems. Rome passed a law making it illegal for a worker to leave the land. In other words the workers were now bound to the land. If the worker left, the law allowed the government to punish the relatives."

"And that did not solve the problem?" I asked.

"No . . . and because the Romans could not solve their problems, the great Roman Empire began its decline," said rich dad. In closing he said, "If we do not solve our problems, the same thing will happen to America."

In 2001, a new president took office in America. Just before he took office, there was a stock market crash, which led to a recession. At the time, we had a surplus in the budget, so to solve the problem, the Bush administration immediately cut taxes and the Federal Reserve Board repeatedly reduced interest rates in hopes of spurring the economy.

The Next Argentina?

Many Americans hate being compared to Japan. Many economic scholars in America say that what is going on in Japan will not go on in America. I tend to agree. If anything, Argentina is a better example of what might happen to America in the future. Argentina, only a few years ago, was a rich industrial powerhouse with a fantastic standard of living. It was a rich land, a favorite place for many Europeans. In many ways it was more European than South American. But in just a few years, this very rich country became a poor, debt-ridden, bankrupt nation with a weak currency. Money has left and so have the rich. Taxes are high and the currency has collapsed. Corruption is everywhere. If the problems are not solved, real anarchy could erupt.

Could that happen to America in twenty to thirty years? Most Americans think not. Unfortunately too many Americans have come to expect that government will solve their problems, and I am afraid rather than solve the problems, an older America will vote for more government and higher taxes. With Social Security the most popular act ever passed, I am afraid that those who depend upon Social Security (soon to be a major voting bloc) will vote once again that the younger workers take care of them. If that happens, taxes will skyrocket. While it took hundreds of years for the Roman Empire to finally collapse, with today's speed of money transfers, the great American Empire could fall pretty fast.

Rich dad noted that one of the reasons the Roman Empire fell was because the Romans never evolved from a basic technology of conquering and taxing. If they had evolved, their empire might have gone on for centuries.

Unfortunately, great empires seem to forget that they need to evolve. Spain was also a great nation that grew by taking and not creating. So it too fell from greatness after attaining great power and great wealth. It fell from power because it did not evolve.

Hopefully this won't happen to America if Americans are willing to face the problem honestly and allow people and business to solve the problem once and for all. In his speech in February 2002, Alan Greenspan, chairman of the Federal Reserve Board, called for the need for financial literacy. He too spoke of the need to evolve. He said it was important that all our children learn financial literacy in our schools if we are to evolve as a civilization and continue to be a world power.

Rich dad would agree wholeheartedly with Alan Greenspan. In fact, in many ways they sound alike. Rich dad often said, "The government tries to solve the problem of poor people by giving them money. Giving poor people money only creates more poor people." He also often said, "If we don't improve our children's financial education, they will not be able to solve the financial problems we have passed forward. If we do not solve these problems, the American Empire will come to an end. It's up to your generation to solve this problem before this happens."

We have a number of years to solve the problem, so I recommend we begin solving it, rather than pushing the problem forward. The problem is too big to be pushed forward anymore. This book is meant to be a call to action. The baby boomers still have time to solve this problem if we will address the problem honestly and truthfully.

Rich dad was very optimistic about America. He said, "Although America is a military power, it does not use its military power to *take*. America uses its military to protect its lines of commerce as well as keep order in the world. America is also a business power and a business power has the ability to *create* rather than *take*." He would say, "It's time to use our business power to create solutions to this very big problem of how a person survives once their working days are over. If we as a nation solve this problem, America can evolve into an even greater world power."

If we do not solve this problem, we contribute to the approaching perfect storm of our financial lives.

Chapter 9

The Perfect Storm

I saw a great movie starring George Clooney, *The Perfect Storm,* which was based on a true story of a series of very severe weather patterns, all coming together at the same time. In other words, it was a story about what would happen if everything went wrong in the weather at once. In many ways, the year 2000 marked the beginning of the coming "perfect financial storm."

The year 2000 has been held as a significant time throughout history. Over four hundred years ago, Nostradamus predicted that in 1998 the third Antichrist would appear. Many believe Osama Bin Laden could fit the description and time. You may also remember the terror around the computer millennium bug that would bring the world to a halt. I have also heard people say that the year 2000 was to be the end of the world . . . and in some ways it has been . . . at least the world we used to know.

I have written about the significance of the change between the DB pension plan and the DC pension plan. The DB pension plan is an Industrial Age pension plan and the DC pension plan is an Information Age pension plan. Many of us are beginning to realize that the rules between the Industrial Age and the Information Age have changed. For example, in the Industrial Age, there was job security and company loyalty. In the Information Age, there is less and less of each. In the Industrial Age, the older you got, the more valuable you became. In the Information Age, the opposite is often true . . . especially in the field of technology. These changes at the end of the Industrial Age and the beginning of the Information Age are adding to the coming of the perfect financial storm.

Sailors all over the world repeat this saying: "Red skies at night, sailor's delight. Red skies in the morning, sailors take warning." Just as Noah had the vision to build an ark, students at the U.S. Merchant Marine Academy, the school from which I received my bachelor's degree, a school that trains ship's officers for the ships of commerce (such as tankers, freighters, passenger liners, tugs, ferries, barges), were taught to always be vigilant for signs of approaching changes in weather . . . changes still out of sight and over the horizon. It is training that has served me well in my business career.

My concern is that many people are not able to see the changes coming simply because they cannot see the differences between the Industrial Age and the Information Age. Just as most people do not know the differences between a DB pension plan and a DC pension plan, most people are not paying attention to changes that are coming . . . but are not yet here.

Before any storm such as a hurricane hits, people on the beach begin to notice a change in the wind, the water, and the mood. Such a period of time is upon us now. Millions of us are aware of this change but most of us are not certain exactly which direction the storm will head, how strong it will be, and exactly where it will come ashore. Nevertheless, if we were on the shore, most of us know we need to do something different. The following are some of the changes I am watching with concern, wonder, and excitement . . . changes that will help fuel the perfect storm.

Change #1: Millions will be left destitute in old age. The World War II generation had secure jobs, secure retirements, and medical care in old age. Beginning with the baby boomers, that all changed. Although we are feeling the shift in the wind today, and we feel the mood change caused by the Enron scandal, I forecast that the full force of this storm will hit around 2025, some fifty years after the act was put into law. By 2025 we will have millions of baby boomers who will be entering their eighties out of money, nearly out of time, and needing the most medical care of their lives. Without government programs such as Social Security and Medicare, which will probably be financially bankrupt, an aged and poor population will be a financial challenge for the generations following the baby boomers.

Change #2: Medical care will get even more expensive. In the year 2000, while the stock market and mutual fund values were crashing down, the cost of medical care was going up by 17 percent. When you add to this the fact that many medical professionals are leaving the industry at a time when more and more baby boomers will need their services, we have another storm cell brewing.

Change #3: Terrorism will increase. On September 11, 2001, Kim and I were just checking into our hotel in Rome, Italy. The bellman put our bags on the floor, grabbed hold of the remote control, turned the television on, and suddenly dropped the remote control on the floor. Kim and I turned to see pictures we have all seen over and over again . . . pictures of airliners flying into the World Trade Center. Since the audio was in Italian, we could not understand what the commentator was saying . . . but the bellman did. He just stood there speechless. Finally switching to an English station, we realized that an event that had been predicted for years was taking place.

The reason I say that this event was predicted is because there is a book I recommend people read, entitled *The Great Reckoning*, by James Dale Davidson and Lord William Rees-Mogg. It is about the coming depression in America. The first edition was published in 1993, written well before the first World Trade Center attack. In this book there are many predictions, many of which have come true, although not at the exact times they were predicted to come true. I have read their earlier books on the future and many of their earlier predictions have come true as well.

In *The Great Reckoning*, Davidson and Rees-Mogg predicted that terrorism will increase because terrorism is cheap. You do not need multitrillion-dollar armed forces to be a terrorist. Columbine High School, the anthrax letters, urban gangs, tribal war lords, drug lords in South America, and of course Bin Laden have proven that concept. Terrorism is on the rise all over the world, and because terrorism feeds on people's fear, the media broadcasts it over and over again. Terrorism is effective even if nothing happens. Just the fear of terrorism can be as effective as the act itself. Every time I hear a political leader warn that the threat of terrorism is high, the terrorists have won. They win because they have a politician doing their work for them. As Davidson and Rees-Mogg state, terrorism is cheap . . . really cheap and it will only spread, and even if we destroy Bin Laden and his network, we will not destroy the cause of terrorism.

A month after the September 11 event, a U.S. television host was interviewing a terrorism specialist from Israel. The American host was intimating that we were now safe because we were bombing Afghanistan. The terrorism specialist in response said, "It's only beginning for America."

The TV host then said, "But you haven't had a hijacking in years. We are following your procedures in stopping hijacking."

"Yes, it is true that we have stopped hijacking but we have not stopped terrorism. Today, we have terrorists bombing shopping centers, nightclubs, and any place else that people gather." The specialist went on to say that the new tactic of terrorists was to steal an army uniform and equipment, walk into a crowded shopping center pretending to be there to protect the shoppers, gain their trust, and then begin shooting them. The terrorism specialist ended by saying, "That tactic has effectively made all of our soldiers and police potential terrorists in the minds of our people. Today, we trust no one. Today, we feel safe nowhere. The same will happen in America." As an airline passenger, I am constantly pulled out of line to be frisked, patted down, and searched. I remember when only crooks were treated that way. Today, every time we fly, we are all treated as suspected terrorists, instead of law-abiding passengers. In other words, the terrorists have won because today we are all treated as terrorists.

In 1920, a truck packed with explosives was parked in front of the New York City Stock Exchange and J. P. Morgan's bank. When it exploded, many were killed and injured. If you go to New York City, you can still see the scars on those buildings. The people responsible for that truck bomb were never apprehended. It was not the first attack on capitalism and it was not the last.

Increased terrorism will mean that many businesses such as shopping centers, restaurants, high school sporting events, churches, and office buildings will be adversely affected just as any business associated with the airlines has been affected. Since terrorism is cheap, any whacko can be an effective terrorist. You do not need to be from a foreign land to be a terrorist. The problem with terrorism is that terrorism's greatest effect is simply the idea of terrorism . . . and ideas in the Information Age spread faster and farther than at any other time in history. In other words, although terrorism has been around forever, in the Information Age, terrorism will be more effective.

Change #4: Japan, currently the world's second largest economy, is on the brink of financial collapse and depression. Many of us remember when just a few years ago Japan's economy was the shining star of the world. Americans by the hundreds of thousands began studying the Japanese way of doing business. Suddenly, almost overnight, everything changed.

Can the same thing happen here in America? Many Americans bristle at the idea. Other Americans are not too sure. Regardless, we can all learn some lessons from Japan's sudden fall as a global economic powerhouse. Some of the lessons are:

1. Japan's counterpart to our baby-boom generation hit retirement age in late 1980–1990. America's baby boomers will become aged in 2010. What effect will an aging American population have on our economy? Will it be similar to Japan's?

2. Japan's aged population has maintained control of the country. The question to America is, In 2010, who will control the U.S.? Will the aging baby boomers still run the country as they did in Japan? If aging baby boomers still run the country, after retirement, there will be laws passed to increase taxes to take care of their needs. If taxes are raised from the younger generation, the economy of America will probably go down faster . . . since businesses move to countries where the tax laws are favorable to businesses . . . not old people.

3. Japan is an old economic culture resistant to change. It has been said that an *indigenous person* is someone whose family has been on the island for over five hundred years. One of Japan's problems is that its people have been on the land and more or less isolated for thousands of years. So its cultural roots cause change to take longer.

Except for the Native Americans, most Americans do not qualify as indigenous people. That means we do not have the thousands of years of cultural traditions to contend with, as the Japanese do. Nevertheless, even though most of us are not indigenous people, we can learn from the lessons of being slow to change and adapt to a changing world. You may notice that the people being left behind financially are often the people who are stuck in old ways of thinking and doing things. So we can learn a lot from indigenous people and their cultures, good and bad.

4. The Japanese are well educated, hardworking, are a tightknit group, religious, and have a very high savings rate. All the virtues we Americans also

desire and want to instill in our children. Yet, even with those virtues, the country is still heading for a depression. Why?

As a fourth-generation Japanese-American, and being familiar with both cultures, I can offer one difference we can all learn from. In the Japanese culture, there is a high need to save face. Shame is disgrace. Shame combined with failure is reason for hara-kiri or suicide. In other words, in the Japanese culture, *death* is more desirable than *disgrace*.

America is different. After the 1986 Tax Reform Act in America, literally trillions of dollars of American real estate became worthless. The 1986 act changed the rules and removed some of the phony tax incentives that had bloated the values of real estate. A stock market, real estate market, and savings and loan (banking) crash followed. Rather than hang on to overvalued and overleveraged real estate, the federal government stepped in and bankrupted a bankrupt industry (the Savings and Loan industry).

A federal agency known as the Resolution Trust Corporation, the RTC, was formed and it bundled trillions of dollars of real estate and sold it for pennies on the dollar. In other words, the U.S. government realized that the country was in trouble because several mistakes had been made and it tried to clean house as quickly as possible. Japan has not yet done that. They are about to . . . but their banks have hung on to real estate they loaned too much money for, refusing to admit they made a mistake, continuing to save face, and hoping that the price of real estate in their portfolios will increase in value . . . for years.

In other words, they hung on instead of cleaning house. In their attempt to save face, the Japanese banks, its politicians, and people have become a worldwide disgrace. The need to save face has destroyed an economy, an economy of well-educated, hardworking, high-savings-rate people . . . everything everyone in the world should all strive to be. If America does not learn from this lesson, it too could follow in Japan's footsteps.

I have written about the difference between savers and investors as well as the difference between people in the E quadrant and people in the I quadrant. One of the biggest differences between Es and Is is that a professional investor knows to cut their losses quickly. Professional investors are not afraid to admit they made a mistake quickly. Professional investors are not into saving face . . . they are into saving money. When they make a bad investment, they cut and run, even if they lose some money. I have seen so many noninvestors buy an investment, and hold on to it all the way down to the bottom. That is what happened to many Enron employees. What is a good trait as an employee—loyalty and tenacity—is a bad trait in the investor quadrant. A true investor has very little loyalty to any investment. If the investment turns and begins to go bad, they cut their losses and go looking for a good investment. I have seen many average investors do exactly what the Japanese have been doing . . . they refuse to admit they made a mistake and hang on till all the money is gone.

Over the years, I have heard the following words from many loser investors . . . investors who refuse to admit they made a mistake. I have used these words myself. As the stock price is going down, I hear them say, "This is only a minor correction. I know it will come back up. After all, the market on average always goes up." And after their stock hits rock bottom they say, "You don't lose as long as you don't sell. I'll hold on till the stock price comes back up and then I'll sell." In other words, "As soon as the stock begins to win I'm going to sell it—and as long as it is a loser I will hang on to it." After the stock is dead and has been down for months, I hear them say, "I'm investing for the long term." When I hear people of any nationality saying those words, I am reminded of my Japanese heritage . . . a heritage that puts a high importance on being smart, being right, and saving face. Funny, that sounds sort of like my American heritage also.

If you want to be a professional investor, you need to learn from the American example of cutting losses quickly rather than following the Japanese example of *death* is preferable to *disgrace*. Losing money is not a disgrace. Losing money and becoming a loser is primarily an issue of arrogance and ignorance . . . and arrogance and ignorance are abundantly available to people everywhere.

Always remember what my rich dad taught me about the difference between winners and losers. He said, "Losers cut their winners and hang on to their losers. Winners cut their losers and hang on to their winners." To rich dad, that was one of his golden rules of life. Now that I am older, I know how valuable that rule has been for me, especially when I violated it. I have also seen so many people violate that golden rule by hanging on to losing jobs, losing businesses, losing marriages, losing friends, losing investments, and losing ideas . . . just to avoid admitting they may not be right or they made a mistake. In America, we don't usually call it saving face. In America, we call it "looking good and going nowhere."

Change #5: China will become the world's largest economy. While Japan is on the brink of falling from the number two spot in the world economy, China is set to become number one. America is contracting financially, while at the same time China is booming. It is estimated that sometime around the year 2020, China is expected to pass the U.S. as the economic powerhouse of the world. As reported in the May 6, 2002, *Business Week*, China has 21 percent of the world's population. It has an almost unlimited supply of human capital, and now as it opens its borders through joining the World Trade Organization, its economic impact is just beginning to be seen.

All of these factors are leading up to a perfect financial storm. Just when the U.S. baby boomers enter old age, China's boom will be in full force. China's rise to power, along with the expansion of the World Wide Web and all the new technology it will spawn, will definitely cause the future to be different than today. One thing is for certain, the gap between the haves and have-nots in America and the world will definitely widen. Those who move with these global changes will become richer than ever before. Those who do not change will be left even further behind financially and professionally.

Back in 1271, a young man named Marco Polo traveled to China to find a large nation booming with industry and trade. Europe at that time was just at the brink of entering into the world of business. Sure enough, when Marco Polo returned from China, Europe passed China as the world economic power. In 1492, Christopher Columbus sailed west looking for a shorter route to Asia . . . and the world changed forever after that. Spain soon became the world financial power in the 1500s by plundering the gold from South America. The financial power then shifted to Europe, from France, Holland, and then to England. From the 1600s to the 1900s, America was considered a Third World nation . . . a very risky place to invest . . . much like China is viewed today. In 1920, right after the end of World War I, the financial power shifted to the U.S. But now, after all these years, China's era of dominance is about to return. With a massive labor force, low labor prices, and great technology, who knows what will happen?

I found it interesting in 2001, just as we began retaliation bombing in

Afghanistan, that President Bush was not in the White House or the country. Where was he? Was he cheering our troops on in Afghanistan? No. He was in China with business leaders such as Bill Gates of Microsoft and Carly Fiorina of Hewlett-Packard talking about trade, not war. If I were in my thirties and thinking about climbing the corporate ladder I would be worried. Why? Because the saying goes, "Whatever can be made in America will now be made in China." So much for a nice secure job in middle management or on the assembly line.

Every time I travel to China, I can still hear Ross Perot saying: "That loud sucking sound from South of the Border will be jobs . . ." He was referring to jobs being lost to Mexico after NAFTA, the North American Free Trade Agreement. In a few years the sucking sound will get louder but it will not be coming from Mexico. Rather, it will be coming from China and other countries . . . as technology spreads to countries with lower labor costs, bright younger minds, and a hunger to get rich and enjoy the good life we have enjoyed.

In 1805 William Playfair wrote: "The general conclusion is that wealth and power have never been long permanent in any place . . . and that they travel over the face of the earth, something like a caravan of merchants. On their arrival everything is found green and fresh; while they remain, all is bustle and abundance; and when gone, all is left trampled down, barren, and bare."

We have all heard stories that, by the third generation, the fortune of a family is gone. The family fortune is gone because the third generation has not appreciated the hard work of the previous generations to gain and preserve the wealth . . . so instead of reinvesting and rebuilding true wealth, the third generation is spoiled and expects life to be rich and easy. Why should they study hard or work hard? After all, Mom, Dad, Grandma, and Grandpa worked hard and now have money. They'll give the kids anything they want. The kids expect life to be easy. They expect simply to go to school, get a high paying job, nice house, nice car, put money in the stock market, the stock price goes up, and they become rich. Is that what we have come to expect? If a generation is approximately twenty-five years in length, then America is on its third and fourth generations after 1920. Has the baby-boom generation, the third generation after 1920, squandered our wealth—or has wealth and power simply decided that it is time to move on?

Change #6. The world population will continue to age. Many of us have heard the theory of an asteroid that collided with earth millions of years ago and wiped out the great dinosaurs. If Japan's economic reforms do not work and work quickly, Japan could be the financial asteroid that collides with the world's economic system and wipes out many financial dinosaurs. Friends who are economists in Japan say that the chances are 50/50 that Japan could go bankrupt by 2006 if not sooner. If it happens, the financial world will be in turmoil.

Here's what might happen. As we have seen, the Japanese by nature are frugal, savers, and hardworking. If their economy goes down, the Japanese people will cut down on consumption, work harder, and attempt to export their way out of their financial problems. That will mean that they will cut prices drastically on everything they make . . . which will mean the world will also have to cut prices in order to compete. That means lower wages for most people worldwide.

Even if Japan does not go bankrupt its economy faces the same problem that America, France, and Germany face, the problem of a large aging population followed by a smaller younger generation. How these three economic giants deal with this challenge will also have great impact upon our economic future.

Looking at the population of workers and retirees as assets and liabilities, the picture looks like this:

Japan, France, Germany, and America Today

Assets	Liabilities
Lots of Workers	Retirees

Japan, France, Germany, and America Tomorrow

Assets	*Liabilities*
Few Workers	*Many of Retirees*

In the Industrial Age, there were more workers than retirees. As we enter the Information Age, retirees are living longer and the rules of how we as a society care for our elders will need to be addressed.

China faces a similar but different problem. China's challenge is the law of one child per family. This is their problem in the near future:

China Prior To Birth Restrictions

A couple could count on their numerous children and grandchildren to support them in their old age.

China with Birth Restrictions

In a few years, that one grandchild may have to support two parents and four grandparents. If you extend this government-enforced policy one more generation, you will have a single great-grandchild responsible for two parents, four grandparents, and eight great-grandparents. Talk about a strain on the budget.

A similar challenge is going on in Singapore. The birth rates there are so low that the government is offering cash incentives for couples to have more children. On top of that, the government of Singapore has passed a law requiring a child to be financially responsible for their parents. In other words, a child can go to jail if they do not support their parents.

As you can see, the challenge of how people support themselves financially and medically once their working days are over is a worldwide problem.

Change #7. Wall Street is obsolete. After dominating the world economic scene, the idea of a physical trading floor, like the floor of the New York Stock Exchange, is an obsolete idea. Today, we have stock markets in cyberspace. With the rest of the world coming online and waking up to the idea of buying and selling stocks, millions of online traders, with their portable computers and real-time quotes coming from the markets, will be the stock market floors of the future . . . stock markets in cyberspace.

In many ways that makes stockbrokers actually an icon of the Industrial Age and it makes mutual funds big slow dirigibles, airships that fast independent investors watch and whose every move they can anticipate. That means investors using traditional brokers and large mutual funds to do their investing for them are also dinosaurs of the Industrial Age. In the Information Age, faster, more nimble, better-trained, less-regulated individual investors will win the richest, and the fastest, global, 24/7 game in the world . . . in fact, they already are.

The February 25, 2002, cover of *Business Week* ran the headline "The Betrayed Investor." Under the headline on the cover, the magazine wrote, "In the 1990s, a new class of investors became a powerful economic and political force. Now many feel misled by Wall Street, corporations, accountants, and the government." The article inside the magazine writes that investors slapped a record 341 class action lawsuits on brokers, lawsuits that cost brokerage houses as much as $14 billion, "charging them [the brokers] with everything from issuing misleading prospectuses to taking kickbacks for IPO allocations. Individual complaints for bad advice soared as well." Instead of titling the cover "The Betrayed Investor," a more accurate statement would be "The Obsolete Investor." That whole system of buying and selling stocks and other securities through a traditional broker and brokerage house is a dinosaur, a Tyrannosaurus rex of the Industrial Age. Now if you have a laptop with a connection to the World Wide Web, you can beat the Street and the slower investors from anywhere in the world. The stock markets of today are in cyberspace and so are the *real* investors.

Change #8. Big corporations are losing the public trust and failing. The May 6, 2002, issue of *Business Week*'s cover story was "The Crisis in Corporate Governance: Excessive Pay. Weak Leadership. Corrupt Analysts. Complacent Boards. Questionable Accounting—How to Fix the System." In the article were the following observations:

> The latest wave of skepticism may have started with Enron Corp.'s ugly demise, but with each revelation of corporate excess or wrongdoing, the goodwill built up by business during the boom of the last decade has eroded a little more, giving way to widespread suspicion and mistrust. An unrelenting barrage of headlines that tell of Securities & Exchange Commission investigations, indictments, guilty pleas, government settlements, financial re-statements, and fines has only lent greater credence to the belief that the system in inherently unfair. . . .

In many ways, Enron and its dealings with Arthur Andersen are an anomaly, a *perfect storm* [italics added] where greed, lax oversight, and outright fraud combined to unravel two of the nation's largest companies. But a certain moral laxity has come to pervade even the bluest of the blue chips. . . .

At risk is the very integrity of capitalism.

(As a side note, the *Business Week* quotations in Change #8 were added in the final draft of this book, well after we had titled this chapter "The Perfect Storm." We find it interesting that the *Business Week* writers chose the same term in their article. Maybe we should pay attention!)

Life Outside the Chicken Coop

In 1974, when I had to make the decision to follow in my poor dad's footsteps or my rich dad's footsteps, rich dad gave me this bit of advice that helped me in my decision-making process. He said, "When your dad advises you to go back to school to get your master's degree so you can find a better, more secure job, he is talking about security within the chicken coop. Most people think that your dad's advice is good advice, since most people seek security inside the chicken coop. Most people want a secure job, a steady paycheck, great benefits, and a secure retirement. That is life inside the chicken coop. My advice is for life outside the chicken coop. So you need to choose between the two. When I was thirteen years old, I was forced to face life outside of the coop . . . and I have stayed outside all my life. That is the choice you face today. You need to choose between a life inside the coop or a life outside the coop . . . and believe me, they are not the same." In 1974 I chose to prepare for life outside the coop.

In 1979, I had to rechoose again. As you know I had nothing . . . no money, no job, no roof over my head. When I was interviewing for that high paying sales manager's job, the lure of the coop was very tempting. One of the things that gave me the courage to stand up and turn down the job was rich dad's simple story of the chicken coop.

Although it took me another fifteen years to feel comfortable surviving outside the coop, I would say the process was worth it. Today when I hear of people losing their jobs, their retirement savings, their homes, their hopes for the future, I cannot help but reflect back on rich dad's simple story of the coop. I know that the world outside the coop looks frightening for many people. Jobs seem scarce, money seems scarce, and opportunities dwindling. But I assure you, life outside the coop is strong, optimistic, vibrant, and filled with more opportunity than ever before. My friends and I open the paper and read tales of doom and gloom, yet in our world, there is more money available, more opportunity, and more excitement than ever before. In my opinion, it is simply a matter of seeing the world from inside the chicken coop, or from outside of it. It is also a matter of who you listen to. Do you take advice from people who are also in the coop or do you listen to people outside the coop, people who are saying, "It's great out here."

Obviously, in 1974, I chose to learn about life outside the chicken coop. After my decision rich dad said to me, "Life outside the chicken coop is filled with liars, cheats, whores, cowards, crooks, idiots, losers, and con men. It is also filled with saints, warriors, noble people, winners, and geniuses." He then said, "If you choose to live your life outside the chicken coop, you must learn to do business with all of them . . . simply because you will not know who they really are until after you have done business with them." In other words, every deal I have gone into outside the chicken coop, everyone puts forth the face of saints, warriors, noble people, and geniuses. Sometime into the deal, regardless if things go bad or things go good, you find out if the people you were dealing with are liars, cheats, whores, cowards, crooks, idiots, and con men . . . or they really were the saints, warriors, noble people, and geniuses they appeared to be when you first met them.

Rich dad explained to me that many people leaving school and searching for a secure job with a big company or the government are searching for a place where they are protected from the real world. When they invest, they often search for similar investments that protect them from the real world . . . which is why mutual funds became the investment vehicle of choice over the last few years. As my friend Rolf Parta, a person with his MBA, CPA, and a former bank product manager, says, "People like mutual funds because they believe mutual funds are sanitized. Many new investors feel safe with mutual funds because they think their fund manager has the power to wipe off the germs from the real world and deliver them a safe, secure investment."

After the Enron scandal and the demise of so many blue chip companies, many investors are waking up to the reality that life *inside* the chicken coop is beginning to look a lot like life *outside* the coop. The problem is, most are not prepared for that outside life and that is why we are cruising for a very large stock market crash.

Business Week's article "The Betrayed Investor" is about an investor who is still in the market and still hoping that the government can tighten things up to protect them. Instead of learning to become professional investors, I predict that most of these betrayed but smarter investors will stay in the market and just before retirement they will sell their mutual funds and cling to what they know and trust the most: cash. When that happens, the biggest stock market crash in the history of the world will be on, and those outside the chicken coop will find life more exciting than ever before. Unfortunately, those still inside the chicken coop will find life frightening, very, very, frightening.

Many have designated the year 2000 as the year that the world shifted from the Industrial Age to the Information Age. It is this shift that is the cause of much of the volatility in the markets and also in our lives. As the winds of the perfect storm pick up, there are those *inside* the chicken coop who are dusting off their résumés looking for a new "secure" coop, or are sitting tight at their job, yet they are afraid of opening their retirement account statements. Many others may find themselves outside the chicken coop unvoluntarily through layoffs or unemployment, frightened and without the financial education to survive. While the sounds of the howling winds scare many people, as the winds pick up, there are others *outside* the coop who are having hurricane parties. In the next section of this book, I will go into how to prepare for the years to come regardless if you plan to live inside the chicken coop or outside it.

Section Two

Building the Ark

Rich dad said, "Everyone has the ability to build a financial ark to survive and flourish in the future. But you must invest time in your financial education to build an ark with a solid foundation."

This section of the book is for people who want to build their own arks rather than expect someone else, or their government, to provide one for them.

Chapter 10

How Do You Build an Ark?

Many people already know they need to build their own ark. The need to build an ark and build it quickly is not news to them. But the question remains, "How do you build an ark?" And the answer is, "It depends upon who you ask." For example, if you ask a:

1. Politician. Many politicians today are saying that the way to save Social Security is to allow younger workers to invest 2 percent to 4 percent of their Social Security–taxed money into personal investment accounts and then reduce the benefits promised to them by the Social Security Administration.

I don't know about you, but that solution sounds vaguely familiar. To me, it has a ring similar to defined contribution plans. Once again we are forcing people to become investors without the necessary financial education to help them. Not only does it sound familiar, if this law passes, it will mean that Social Security will begin to run negative before 2016 because less money will be coming in to pay for the older retirees. The politicians who are proposing this today, in 2002, know they will be out of office long before this happens. Again, the problem is pushed forward.

2. Union leader. Union leaders would recommend you find a job with a company that has a strong well-organized union, with a well-funded pension plan and benefits.

My poor dad, as head of the Hawaii State Teachers Association was a strong advocate of this idea. If you like this idea, get a job with the government.

3. Schoolteacher. A schoolteacher would probably recommend staying in school to get as high an advanced degree as possible. In fact, get several of them. Then go find a safe, secure job with benefits.

Our institutions of higher learning are filled with students who are in school because the job market is tight. Only a few years ago, during the dot.com mania, students were leaving school early in search of jobs with start-up companies offering stock options. Many of them are back in school or are looking for jobs.

4. Professional person. There are many people who recommend going to school so you can learn a profession such as doctor, lawyer, plumber, accountant, electrician, or chef. People who believe in this course of action often say, "Get a skill or trade you can always fall back on."

In other words, in this era of job insecurity, be sure you can work on your own. This group includes the millions of small business owners, often called mom-and-pop businesses.

5. Financial planner. We know what these people say. This group always recommends that you start early, invest for the long term, stick with the plan, and diversify, diversify, diversify.

While this is great advice for the average investor, it is what the financial planners don't tell the average investor that concerns me. Also, if you are a baby boomer over forty-five years of age, this advice may not work.

6. Religious person. They recommend attending church regularly and praying twice a day. They know God will save them and provide for them.

I am not knocking the power of prayer, but I believe this is an entitlement mentality. I believe that God wants people to take control of their own lives and provide for themselves and their families.

7. Stockbroker. Many recommend picking individual stocks over mutual funds . . . but they are happy to sell you mutual funds also.

8. Real estate agent. Most real estate agents support the idea that your home is your biggest investment and your most important asset . . . even though in most cases a home is a liability.

9. Poor person. Many of this group believe that the rich and the government should help care for the less fortunate.

10. Hardworking person. They believe in working until the day they cannot work any longer, saying, "I never plan on retiring."

11. Animal lover. Since this group loves animals they would recommend buying a monkey. They would recommend training the monkey to first save money, then diversify with mutual funds, and after that, teach it to throw darts at a mutual funds dartboard.

12. Gambler. Wait till you feel lucky and then go to Las Vegas. But even if you do not feel lucky, always stop to buy a lottery ticket on your way home.

13. Gold digger. Find a rich person and do whatever it takes to marry them.

14. Optimist. What, me worry? In their mind-set the stock market always goes up.

15. Pessimist. Build a fallout shelter, hoard food, water, gold, guns, and cash.

16. Dreamer. The dreamer would suggest belief in magic and creative visualization. They have crystals, aromatherapy candles, and wind chimes to keep away the evil spirits.

17. Banker. Bankers always recommend that you save, save, save. After you save some money, they call to inform you that they also sell mutual funds, stocks, insurance, annuities, and other financial planning products.

Today, even CPAs, tax preparers, and attorneys are also getting into the act. Many professionals such as accountants also have a financial planning service in the next room from where they do your taxes. All that separates them is a thin corporate wall and business license. It's hard to tell who's doing what in the financial world and they all have some advice on how to build your ark.

18. Rich dad. Take control of your own financial ark and buy or build assets that generate cash flow. Include real estate, businesses, and paper assets. As soon as your income from your assets (your money working for you) exceeds your expenses you are financially free.

All eighteen categories exist . . . some have more merit than others. So the real question is, which of the eighteen sounds best to you? Rather than getting into which of the eighteen possible answers works best, I think it important to say that there are many ways to build an ark. As Warren Buffett said:

"Happily there is more than one way to get to financial heaven."

The point is, find a way that works best for you. We are all different. We have different strengths and different weaknesses. How I built my ark was very different from the way rich dad built his ark, although we often used similar asset classes to do the job . . . the job of building an ark. Rich dad used businesses and real estate and I too used businesses and real estate. The difference is we built very different businesses and invested in very different types of real estate. So a very important point in building an ark is to find the way that works best for you.

Years ago, rich dad said to me, "If you want to find true financial security, or even become financially rich, you must play your own game. Don't play someone else's game." After ERISA passed into law, rich dad felt that millions of people would be forced to play Wall Street's game. Rich dad said, "The problem with playing Wall Street's game is that Wall Street is in control and you aren't. Find your own game, become good at it, and then take control of your life."

On to Building Your Ark

The first thing I recommend is deciding how big an ark you want to build. Obviously, the poor person's ark would be a small and leaky boat. If all you desire is a poor person's ark, you really do not have to do that much. Social Security remains the most popular government program in the history of the U.S. Personally I would not want to depend upon my family to care for me, nor do I want to be dependent upon the government or charities for support.

The middle-class ark was a good ark for the World War II generation. All the middle class had to do prior to 1950 was go to school, get a job, work hard, buy a house, save money, and retire. This plan may still work if you get a job with the government, or a well-unionized business. But ever since the shift from the DB to the DC pension plan, this new middle-class ark may not be strong enough to survive the rough seas ahead. If this DC pension plan is all you want for your ark, then rigorously follow traditional financial planning advice, which is to have a plan, start early, work for years, and diversify. A middle-class ark can work but there may be rough sailing the next few years.

If you want to have a rich ark, obviously you will need to dramatically commit to increasing your financial education. There is one thing a person who wants to become wealthy must understand . . . and that is in building a rich ark, many of their traditional middle-class ideas and values will have to be expanded. For example, many people in the middle class think saving money, having a DC pension plan, and owning a home are the most intelligent financial decisions. While these are important to a person's overall financial well-being, the truth is that saving, DC pension plans, and a home are not cornerstones of a rich person's ark. The rich know that buying or building assets that generate passive income is the real foundation needed for a rich ark.

Why Savers Are Losers

One caution I put forth is to be careful about the word *save.* The act of saving worked well for the World War II generation . . . a generation that lived in an era of inflation. In fact, for the generation that lived before 1900, there was very little inflation and also no taxes. So saving worked even better for the parents of the World War II generation. But ever since 1950, savers have been losers simply because savings are taxed at a high rate and inflation wipes out most of the gains. In early 2002, the interest rate paid on saving is about 2 percent. Many savers have been severely crippled because of this drop in interest. For example, only a few years ago, if a person had a million dollars in cash in the bank, and the bank paid them 5 percent interest, the saver then received $50,000 in interest income, before taxes. But when the rate hit 2 percent, that same million dollars paid them $20,000 in interest income before taxes. That means in just a few years savers took a 40 percent cut in pay . . . before taxes. The point is, advising people to save used to be good advice . . . and it still is good advice for the poor and the middle class. But for anyone wanting to build a rich ark, simply saving money in the old-fashioned way is bad advice.

7.75 Percent Interest Versus 1.85 Percent Interest

Even though the interest rates today are approximately 2 percent and taxable, by shopping around and knowing what questions to ask, it is possible to find higher rates of interest, often tax free. For example, on February 22, 2002, by having my stockbroker watch the market, Kim and I were able to find a tax free government bond paying 7.75 percent. Being that they are tax free, that is the equivalent of earning 12 percent taxable interest, while everyone else who has money in passbook savings is earning approximately 2 percent, 1.85 percent to be exact, interest that is taxable.

Obviously to receive a 7.75 percent tax free rate there is a little more risk . . . but very little. Earlier I wrote about how a person with a strong financial education could make more money with less money and less risk. This is an example of that. For Kim and me, this is a very low-risk investment simply because we understand the investment and its risks. For a person without much financial education, a traditional bank passbook savings account paying a 1.85 percent taxable interest rate would make more sense. Again the point is that your investment in your financial education can pay a greater percentage return, even on something as simple as a savings account.

If you feel you have a sound financial education and are interested in such types of investments, call your stockbroker and inquire about real estate development companies selling shares secured by low-income-housing new construction real estate, and using government tax free bonds to pay a higher tax free interest. A simpler name might be municipal mortgage REITS, real estate investment trusts. Basically, it is a real estate mutual fund that offers a tax free rate of return from interest and the potential of capital gains. But it also carries with it the potential of loss of investment.

A strong word of caution. If you *do not* like real estate, or understand low income housing, or understand municipal bonds, or how the stock market works, or you have limited amounts of money, I would not place money into these investments. Kim and I invest in these types because we have extensive experience in all of the relevant investment categories. In other words, this is more than a savings account that pays interest. As Warren Buffett says, "Investing must be rational; if you can't understand it, don't do it."

The point of discussing a 7.75 percent tax free interest return and a 1.85 percent bank passbook, taxable interest return is not to toot my horn or brag . . . but to make a point.

Without a financial education, it takes a lot more money to get rich and a lot more money to stay rich. The *higher* your financial IQ the less money it takes to get rich. The lower your financial IQ the more money it takes.

"My friend Dolf de Roos, author of the Rich Dad's Advisors book *Real Estate Riches,* says, "If you think education is expensive, you should try ignorance.""

In other words, don't invest in something you do not understand, even if it is paying 7.75 percent tax free interest with the potential of a capital gains play. Rich dad would say, "Before you invest in something, invest the time to understand it." Kim has personally invested nearly fifteen years in this market and I have a few more years in the business. That is where financial intelligence comes from. It comes from investing time in the real world. Financial intelligence does not come from handing your money over to a fund manager and hoping and praying he or she does a good job. You do not increase your financial intelligence investing in that way. As stated earlier, many people *invest* but they fail to become *investors.* Investing in your financial education may not pay off early in the process but it does seem to pay off later. So I repeat that I am *not* recommending you call your stock broker and invest in municipal mortgage REITs, because as with all investments, there are good REITs and bad REITs. What I am strongly recommending is that you invest in your financial education . . . especially if you want to build a rich ark. In fact, I would say your financial education is mandatory for building a rich ark and keeping it afloat once it's built.

Why the Middle Class Is Risky Even Though They Play It Safe

Rich dad said to me, "The middle class plays it risky financially . . . and that is why they are such risky investors." He went on to say, "The reason the middle class is taking a huge financial risk with a DC plan is because they invest a lot of money into the plan but they invest very little time learning to invest.

If you want to become rich, start out investing a lot of time before you begin investing a lot of money." So before you switch your savings account over, invest some time finding out about the investment.

Obviously, 7.75 percent return is not a high rate of return. But as I said, I used it as an example of the difference between a financially educated investor and a middle-class investor. I used the example only to point out the cost of the lack of financial education. In reality, as a professional investor, I like a minimum of 40 percent cash-on-cash return from my investments . . . which is why I do not invest any time saving money.

On many of our investments, Kim and I receive a return of infinity, which means we have no money making a lot of money. Our last real estate investment rental property yields a 45 percent return, cash-on-cash, most of it tax free. This 45 percent is actually received in two parts. We receive a cash-on-cash return of 15 percent, which means that our net rental income exceeds the amount of cash we invested each year by 15 percent. Then when you add the impact of depreciation we have an additional tax savings, and therefore, additional cash return (cash we get to keep instead of paying the government) of 30 percent for this property. For us this 45 percent return is an average return on investment. Yet when I mention that rate of return to some of my friends, they think I am exaggerating or lying to them. Again, it is the difference in one's financial education.

So a 7.75 percent tax free interest return is interesting, but not particularly exciting. We use that rate simply to park excess money for periods of six months or more, while we work on putting the next investment together. When we need the money, we simply liquidate our position, often for a capital gain, and invest the cash. We sometimes use a vehicle called a C share annuity to park our money . . . and today a C share is paying 3.5 percent while a passbook is paying 1.85 percent. The advantage of the C share annuity is that it is as liquid as a Municipal mortgage REIT, it has lower risk, and for that lower risk, there is a lower rate of return. Since Kim and I do not need the money and we have time to play the share price or the REIT in the market, we prefer the REIT and its higher return. So far we have made money from the tax free dividends and the capital gains from selling the shares of the REIT. As I said, a financial education does pay in the long run.

Saving money in a bank may sound intelligent to many people, but for me it is a waste of both time and money. The reason I began with the subject of savings is because so many of the middle class think that saving money is intelligent . . . and it is for that class of people. But it is a financial drag for a rich person to save money because saving in the traditional ways makes no financial sense for a rich person. So before going into building a rich ark I want to bring up a few important points.

Point #1: If you plan on building a rich person's ark, saving money will eventually not make sense. Why? The answer is because the interest from savings is taxed at ordinary income levels . . . the highest tax rate there is. For example if you have a million dollars in savings, earning $20,000 from 2 percent taxable interest rate, and you earn more than $65,000 as a single person or $110,000 as a couple a year, that $20,000 will be taxed at approximately 30 percent, leaving you an effective return from your million dollars of about $14,000, which equates to an effective return of 1.4 percent before inflation. If you earn even more money, and are in the 40 percent tax bracket, that 2 percent interest rate return drops to a 1.2 percent effective interest rate. Let me assure you that inflation is running at more than 1.2 percent, so a rich saver is a loser. The point is if you are poor and at a lower tax bracket, the interest on your money is taxed at a lower rate. But if you are rich, your higher tax bracket causes that same interest rate to be taxed higher. So the more you save, if you are rich, the more you lose.

Point #2: If you plan on building a rich person's ark and you have a traditional DC plan, for example a 401(k), again, when you begin to withdraw money from your DC retirement plan, that income will be taxed at the highest levels. Again, the tax rates today are 30 percent for a single person earning over $65,000 a year. So for every $1,000 you receive in income from your 401(k) after retiring, that $1,000 will be reduced to $700 due to taxes. Again, a 401(k) or most other traditional retirement plans do not make tax sense if you plan on retiring rich.

One of the reasons Kim and I use real estate is because with proper planning, we can reduce our taxes to 0 percent from our real estate income. That is why Dolf de Roos, my real estate advisor, states that the rich either made their money in real estate or hold their money in real estate. In other words, if you build a rich ark, income from real estate investments makes far more sense than income from a DC pension plan.

Point #3: Most people who aspire to higher income levels are not aware that they will lose the benefits of their itemized deductions as their income grows, including their home mortgage interest. A big house—the dream of the middle class—is not a write-off if you are rich. In America, if you earn less than approximately $137,300 in 2002, you are allowed by the tax code to write off some of your mortgage interest as a deduction from your taxes. But if you are rich, you lose that interest deduction. In fact, the higher your income the less you may deduct, to the point of not being able to deduct any of it.

High Income—Lost Deductions

by Diane Kennedy, CPA
Rich Dad's Advisor
Author of *Loopholes of the Rich*

If your income is over $137,300 in 2002, you might find a big surprise on your tax return . . . lost deductions! And, of course, lost deductions means you pay more tax.

Itemized deductions such as mortgage interest, state, local, and property taxes, and charitable donations phase out as income passes the designated threshold amount. For 2002, that designated threshold amount for a married couple (filing jointly) is $137,300. For every dollar that your income is more than that threshold, you lose 3% of most itemized deductions. (Medical expenses, investment interest, and casualty, theft, or wagering losses are not subject to this limitation.)

This comes as a big (and bad) tax surprise to many taxpayers who get a raise and, following standard advice from their banker or accountant, buy a bigger house for the added deductions. They actually end up losing some of the mortgage interest deduction.

And, even more sad, those high income taxpayers who believe in charitable giving will find that they lose a significant part of their charity deduction as well. The government is cutting social programs from their budget. This forces the charities to rely on individual contributors. But the charities are losing contributors as the high income taxpayer loses the tax benefit. This deduction phases out too!

This itemized deduction phase-out is in addition to the loss of medical expenses and miscellaneous deductions that are built into the system. These deductions are limited based on a percentage of your income. For example, your medical expenses are only deductible when they are more than 7.5 percent of your adjusted gross income. As your income increases, the 7.5 percent calculated exclusion increases and so you lose part of your medical expenses deduction!

But wait! That's not all! You also lose your exemptions as your income increases. For 2002, as your income increases over $206,000, you lose progressively more of the exemption deduction for yourself, your spouse, and your dependents.

The rich also lose passive loss offsets from real estate losses against other income (lost at $150,000 adjustable gross income) and the ability to use strategies such as the ROTH IRA, which allows your money to grow tax free.

Sometimes it just costs more to be rich.

The Main Point

The main point is that if you plan on building a big rich ark for retirement, you may have to let go of many of the traditional middle-class values . . . investments the middle class think are important. In other words there are some investments that work for the middle class, investments such as savings, DC pension plans, and interest deductions from your personal residence. But if you want to be rich, and plan on building a rich ark, those middle-class money values will have to go.

So the first step is to decide on what size ark you want to build. If you want to build a poor person's ark, or a middle-class ark, then stop here—the rest of this book is not for you. There are other books that will go into further detail on how to build those sizes of financial arks.

This chapter started with the eighteen different opinions on how to build an ark . . . today almost everyone is handing out advice on ark building. That is because you and I are not the only ones that know the perfect storm is coming. You and I are not the only ones who know the problem has been pushed forward for too long. So after you decide on building an ark, then you decide if you want a poor ark, a middle-class ark, or a rich ark to ride out the storm in. As rich dad said to me years ago, "If you know the storm is coming, the size of the ark really does not matter. The first step is to simply make up your mind to build one. After you have made that decision, then you decide on the kind of ark you want to build, then begin building it, build it as quickly as possible, and don't stop until it's built."

Build Your Ark

1. Do you need to build a financial ark for yourself and your family?

       Yes _____   No _____

2. How much time do you have to build your ark?

       Years before you turn 65 _____
       Years before 2016 _____
       (Take the lower number of years)

3. Do you believe you need to change your investing habits to build your ark?

       Yes _____   No _____

4. From what quadrant in the CASHFLOW Quadrant do you derive your income?

5. Review the investment vehicles of the poor, middle class, and rich outlined in Chapter 7. Which investments do you want to start with?

6. If you want to become rich, are you willing to start out investing time before you begin investing a lot of money?

Chapter 11

Taking Control of the Ark

"If you are going to build a *rich* ark," rich dad said, "you need to be in control of its construction, what is loaded in the cargo holds, and who is steering it." After the market crash of March 2000, millions of people came to feel less secure about their financial future. Why? Because they were *not* in control of their ark or its cargo, and many did not know who their skipper was.

Rich dad stated that *security* and *freedom* were not the same words, in fact they were almost opposite from each other. Rich dad said, "The more security you *gain,* the more freedom you *lose.*" He also said, "A person who seeks security often gives up control over parts of their lives. The more *control* you give up, the less *freedom* you have." Many people feel insecure about their financial future and retirement because they have given up most of the control over their financial future.

In *Rich Dad Poor Dad,* I stated that rich dad said *the most important word* in business was *cash flow.* In *Retire Young Retire Rich* (book number five in the Rich Dad series), I wrote that *the second most important word* was *leverage,* the ability to do more and more with less and less. Although rich dad never directly said it, if there was *a third most important word* in his vocabulary, I believe it would be the word *control.* Here are a few observations about the word *control* as it relates to cash flow:

1. One of the most important *life skills* to develop is to learn to gain *control* of your cash flow.

2. When I saw the picture of the fifty-eight-year-old Enron employee on the front page of *USA Today*'s "Money" section who had lost a significant amount of his retirement due to the fall of Enron, I saw a picture of a person who found out late in life that he had very little *control* over which way his cash was flowing.

3. Most financial problems are caused by personal lack of *control* over cash flow.

4. Kim and I were able to retire early in life because we took *control* over which direction our cash flowed.

One of the reasons so many millions feel less secure about their financial future is because they lack control of many aspects of their lives. Simply looking at a 401(k) defined contribution plan—the ark of choice of the American middle class—most people have very little control over it. Rich dad was in control of his arks. He worked on design, cargoes, and knew his skippers well. The reason he had many skippers was because he had many arks. Obviously, if you decide to build a rich ark, one of the most important things to consider is whether you are willing to take back control of the entire ark or fleet of arks. If not, then stay with a defined contribution plan, invest for the long term, diversify, pray a lot, and hope your skipper knows what to do.

By taking greater control over your entire ark you may also slowly take back more and more control of your life and then your freedom. Warren Buffett says, "I'm the luckiest guy in the world in terms of what I do for a living. No one can tell me to do things I don't believe in or things I think are stupid." In other words, he is in *control* of his arks . . . and he has a fleet of them.

Before going on to what it takes to take control over your ark, I think it important that you hear the word from Warren Buffett himself on his style of ark control. Buffett controls but is not into overcontrol. He buys companies with excellent management and treats them like owners of their businesses . . . in fact many are allocated ownership positions. To this point he says:

"We wish to see the unit's managers become wealthy through ownership, not simply free-riding on the ownership of others. I think, in fact, that ownership can in time bring our best managers substantial wealth, perhaps in amounts well beyond what they now think possible."

The remark *not simply free-riding on the ownership of others* was made about a famous investment house, whose name shall remain anonymous. He felt this large investment firm did not care about the shareholders or their investments. The second half of this remark is about how he treats his managers . . . he lets them share in the profits of his arks.

He also hires the best people he can find to be skippers of his arks. He does that because he wants them to run the ark, not him. He says: "If they need my help to manage the enterprise we're probably both in trouble."

Rich dad had the same style of ownership and management. That is why both men could manage many arks. It is a style of management that comes from the B and I quadrants rather than the hands-on approach that many E and S quadrant people envision. It is the same style I am learning. I state this because many people say to me, "I don't have time to do my own investing. I'm just too busy." Many people from the E and S quadrants think they have to do everything rather than learn to find people smarter than them to build, load, and sail their arks. So the word *control* does not necessarily mean you have to do it all by yourself. People from different quadrants control their arks in different ways. If you control in the style of the B and I side, you can control many arks. If you control in the style of the E and S, you may only be able to control one ark, and for that one ark you will be ark designer, ark builder, cargo loader, crew, and skipper. As I have said in other books and tapes, people from the E and S side tend to have two theme songs running in their heads. One song is "Nobody Does It Better" and the other theme song is "I Did It My Way." In my opinion, those are theme songs of people who tend to *overcontrol.*

Taking Control of Your Ark

Repeating a question asked earlier in this chapter: "Are you willing to take control of your ark?" That is the question. If the answer is no, then the rest of this book may be too problematic . . . seeming to involve much too much time, effort, study, and money. For many people, it is much easier to work hard at their jobs and just hand their money over to someone they hope is better at managing arks than they are.

But if the answer is yes, then read on. Remember, being in control of an ark does not mean you have to do much. All you have to do is be willing to be in control. Warren Buffett is in control and lets other captains run the ships. You can do the same thing . . . if you want.

Learning About the Ark Business

From 1965 to 1969, I attended the U.S. Merchant Marine Academy in New York. For four years, that federal school trained young men, and now young women, to become ship's officers. Our training began with four weeks of rigorous physical and military indoctrination, which military academies are noted for. We got up early in the morning and ran till late at night. After our heads were shaved, we learned everything from military discipline, to how to wear a uniform, how to properly shoot a gun, exercise, and even proper etiquette at a dining table.

After the month of indoctrination, school began. We had to fulfill the academic requirements of a traditional college or university, which meant we had courses such as English, calculus, spherical trigonometry, thermodynamics, physics, literature, electronics, and the humanities. In addition to those traditional academic courses of study, we had to learn about life at sea . . . so we also had to learn Morse code, knot tying, wire rope splicing, semaphore, sailing, rowing, rescue at sea, astronomy, celestial navigation, weather, small boat handling, large ship steering, running an engine room, docking and undocking, handling a tugboat, business law, maritime law, cargo handling, naval architecture, oceanography, and other seagoing subjects.

On top of that, we spent a year at sea, taking a correspondence course while actually on merchant ships sailing the cargo lanes of the world, learning in the real world about what we had been learning in the classroom. My classmates and I literally went to every famous seaport throughout the world. To me, that was the best part of the program. Because of this year at sea, we had to finish a traditional four-year college curriculum in three years. It was a great well-rounded education. By the time my class graduated in 1969, we had lost over 50 percent of the class, but the rest of us were ready to take control of a ship, as junior officers, ready to apprentice under the captain and other senior ship's officers. On graduation day, one of my instructors said, "Our training program is rigorous because we are training you to be more than captains of ships, we are training you to be captains of this industry." And many of my classmates did go on to become leaders in the shipping industry.

Rich dad put his son and me through a similar program, beginning at the age of nine. That is why he had us working in every aspect of his business. We cleaned rooms, waited on tables, cleaned the grounds, picked up trash, hung wallpaper, worked on construction of buildings, worked in accounts receivable and payable, accounting, sales, management, banking, human relations, and investing.

I meet many college kids coming out of their MBA programs today who have great formal education but very little practical real-world education. For many of them, the only job they had was working in a fast food restaurant flipping burgers, as waiters, or clerks in retail stores. Upon graduation, many of these young people are put into positions of management lacking in real-world people skills.

Because they are smart, some are promoted quickly before gaining those real-world people skills. Instead of knowing what it feels like to be the janitor, the clerk, the warehouse foreman, the receptionist, in the company, all they know is their fraternity or sorority friends who move up the corporate ladder with them. Too many of these very bright students become captains but lose touch with the workers, the real engine of business. When people lose touch with their workers, then disasters like Enron happen. Did those so-called well-educated leaders recommend that their employees buy shares of the company while they were selling? It may not be technically illegal, but to me, it is definitely unethical. The problem is, this practice of recommending a *buy* while in fact you are *selling* is very common practice not only at Enron, but it is a common practice in business, especially the business of the stock market.

One thing both of my dads demanded of me was that I never lose touch with people at all levels of society. My rich dad said, "Never lose your humanity. Always remember that each member of your business is a human being with a family, and your job as the leader of the business is to do your best to protect their welfare and their well-being." Rich dad reminded Mike and me of this very often. That is why he had us work in every corner of the business, not only to learn that part of the business, but also to get to know the people responsible for that part of the business.

A few years before he died, my poor dad said, "I have no doubt that some-day you will be a rich man. Please never forget the home you come from and the values we hold. Always remember the people who have touched your life along the way. You may never see them again but always remember them and be grateful for the gifts they have given you. And when you get to where you are going, have the humility to remember that rich or poor, friend or enemy, we are all human beings. Money does not make you superior to anyone. Please remember that you are a human being too." In my humble opinion, there are too many skippers of ships who have forgotten that they are re-sponsible for human beings as well as the ship, and the ship's cargo.

Rich Dad's Lesson

At the start of this book, I related a story of how my rich dad began our meet-ings with my showing him my current financial statements. That is how we started almost every meeting. As a child, he had me do very simple ones. As an adult, my financials became more adultlike. As I grew richer, my financials became more complex. Once I became financially free, my financials became even much more sophisticated. As I grow older and hopefully wealthier, my financials will also grow in sophistication . . . and so must I. Getting into the habit of always having up-to-date personal financials is a learning process, a habit my rich dad stressed I develop.

Needless to say, my poor dad never had one, much less a current up-to-date one. He knew how to fill out credit applications, for such things as a home loan or to buy a car. But he never made it a habit of having a book-keeper do his monthly personal financial statements.

All through this book, I refer to financial greats such as Warren Buffett, America's richest investor, Alan Greenspan, chairman of the powerful Fed-eral Reserve Board, and Paul O'Neill, the secretary of the treasury, who all say basically the same thing my rich dad said to me. All of these financially smart men stress the importance of financial literacy and that financial liter-acy begins with a financial statement. None of these men said start with real estate, savings, a business, tax liens, stocks, day trading, options trading, or mutual funds, which is where most people start building their arks . . . and that is why so many arks cannot stand rough seas.

To repeat a question I asked before in this chapter: "Are you willing to take control of your ark?" If the answer is still yes, then the next question is, "Are you willing to have current, up-to-date, audited, personal financial statements?" If the answer is no, then a DC pension plan such as personal savings, government retirement plans, a 401(k), and a home become very, very, very important.

If you are going to take control of your ark and maybe build a rich ark, you must make it a habit of having at least monthly income statements and balance sheet statements . . . the two documents that make up the basic financial statement. If you are to become richer and richer, regardless of the storms ahead, you must constantly work on improving your financial literacy and the best place to start your real-life education is with your own personal, up-to-date, real-life financial statement—even if it has nothing in it. I stress this point because I meet many people who read financial statements and annual reports of other companies, but they do not have financial statements on themselves. The most important financial statement of all, if you are going to be in control of your ark, is your own personal financial statement.

At the start of most meetings with rich dad, he had me show him my personal as well as business's financial statements. Without those statements, he could not have helped me. He could only guess as to what my problems were and where they were. In 1977, my financials looked pretty good, because the business was just starting out and we had some investor money in the treasury. Rich dad helped me by making specific suggestions on what to do on my personal financial statement as well as the business's financial statements. But by 1978, the financial statements from my business were getting murky, a little cloudy. By 1979, you heard what rich dad said, "Your company has financial cancer." He also thought the cancer would prove terminal . . . and it did. The company soon disappeared. Nevertheless, with his help, and my constant reporting to him, my personal financial wounds healed and my fortune began to grow again . . . although I did lose it all again, one more time. Again, by constantly checking in, handing over my financials, my rich dad was able to help me heal and grow. Today, that process of making mistakes, learning, correcting, and reporting to rich dad with my financials has been the process that helped me evolve into a better ship's officer. Today instead of fearing the storms brewing ahead, I look forward to them, knowing that it is by confronting life's challenges that we all become stronger, even though sometimes I feel fear just as anyone else would.

Before closing this chapter, I would like to point out that health and wealth are very similar. When we go to a doctor, the first thing a doctor does is take a blood sample or X-rays. That is the way the doctor can pinpoint exactly what is wrong and what needs to be corrected. The other day, I went to my doctor and from reviewing my blood test, he gave me some disturbing news. As much as I did not like the news, I was glad I received it early because receiving the bad news early allowed me to make corrections early . . . before the problem becomes worse.

A financial statement with clean clear numbers serves the same purpose as a blood test or X-ray. Regular updated financials give you a chance to find out the bad news early and take corrective action early. Unfortunately, because our school system has failed to educate people financially, millions of people will find out that they have financial cancer only after it is too late. That is what happened to that fifty-eight-year-old Enron employee in *USA Today*. He found out that his ship was rotting, so was its cargo, and the skippers had abandoned ship without telling the crew. The problem was, this worker found this out a little late in life . . . but it's not *too* late. If that employee is willing to take control of his own ark, that fifty-eight-year-old employee may sail into a whole new world of financial wealth and financial well-being. All he has to do is look in the Yellow Pages for professional bookkeepers, interview many, hire one, begin receiving at least monthly financial statements, and review them with a financial expert like a banker or accountant once a month, and start making corrections. By facing his real-world finances, with real-world financial documents, he enters a whole new real world of financial possibilities.

In the following chapters I will go into the controls a person needs in order to begin to gain greater control over the ark of his or her financial future. These controls are the basis of becoming a better captain of your own ark.

Build Your Ark

1. Are you willing to take control of your ark?

2. Develop your own financial statement. Use the format from the game sheet of CASHFLOW 101 to assist you. A sample is found in the next chapter.

3. Find a bookkeeper or accountant—ask for references from successful people you know—or use the Yellow Pages. Interview many, select one.

4. Make an appointment with an accountant or bookkeeper to review your financial statements to make sure you have completed them properly.

5. Now you are ready to analyze where you are today and what changes you need to make in your investing habits.

Chapter 12

Control #1:
Control over Yourself

The most important control of all is to take control over yourself and how you manage your money. If you can do that, you can build a rich ark and captain it wisely.

In 1996, I was in Peru looking for a gold mine to buy. Due to economic turmoil and terrorist attacks, many gold mines had been abandoned or left in the hands of poor management. Up at fifteen thousand feet, high in the Andes Mountains, a banker showed me a mine he thought I could buy. Due to the altitude, the best I could do was take three steps, stop, and gain control of my dizziness and my breathing.

Finally, down in the small, dark shaft of the mine, the banker, who owned the mine through foreclosure, pointed to a vein of quartz running through the rock. "Here," he said. "Look at how rich the vein is."

Stumbling over to the spot where he stood, I gazed at the spot his flashlight was hitting. "Wow," I said. "Look at all the gold." I could not believe the sparkling glitter of gold reflected in the light.

"*Sí, señor,* I told you this was a good mine," smiled the banker.

Inching closer, I put my hand up to the milky green and white quartz vein and began touching the sparkling gold. I said, "I can't believe how beautiful it is."

"*Señor,*" said the banker. "What you are looking at is not gold. That is iron pyrites, or fool's gold. The gold I am looking at is in the quartz below the fool's gold. The real gold is in the dark part of the quartz vein. The gold is the part of the vein that does not shine."

Modern-Day Alchemist

When I was a little boy, rich dad often spoke of alchemy. Not knowing what alchemy was I asked rich dad for an explanation. He said, "Years ago, many people were trying to turn different materials such as iron or coal into gold."

"Did anyone ever do it?" I asked.

"No," said rich dad. "No one has ever turned something into gold. Gold is just gold. But people have learned to create something even better than gold."

"What is better than gold?" I asked.

"Assets," said rich dad. "Today's modern alchemists turn money, resources, or ideas into wealth via assets."

"You mean assets they buy or build," I said.

Rich dad said, "That is correct. Today's modern alchemists can create assets out of thin air. They turn their ideas into assets and those assets make them rich. A patent or trademark are examples of turning ideas into such assets. Or they turn trash into an asset. Or they turn real estate into assets. That is modern-day alchemy."

As I rode down the twisting and bumpy road with the banker, staring out at the spectacular vistas high on the Peruvian Andes, I knew the banker knew he had a fool, not an alchemist, as a potential investor. If I could not tell the difference between veins of fool's gold and the vein of real gold, what chance did I have of turning that abandoned mine into an asset? Needless to say, I did not do a deal in Peru. I am just grateful today there are many ways to be an alchemist other than mining for gold.

How Does a Banker Know the Difference Between a Fool and an Alchemist?

I began this book with my rich dad going over my personal and business financial statements in 1979. One of his comments is still appropriate today. As rich dad was going over my financials, rich dad said, "The world is filled with fools and alchemists. Fools turn cash to trash and alchemists turn trash to cash. You and your partners are fools, not alchemists. You boys have taken a business and turned the cash into trash."

"But our banker said he would lend us more money," I replied. "We can't be doing that bad."

Rich dad chuckled and smiled, then said, "First of all, bankers lend money to both fools and alchemists. Bankers do not really care as long as you have the money to pay them back. And secondly, if you are a fool, you will pay higher rates of interest. The bigger the fool, the higher the interest rate. So your bankers love you boys. Your business makes a lot of money and you boys are turning that cash into trash. These financials show that at one end of the business you are alchemists and at the other end you boys are fools. Why wouldn't a banker lend money to you?

"The problem is you boys are about to go broke. Instead of reinvesting the money from your business back into your business, I can see here in the liability column of your financial statement that you boys have invested in one Porsche, two Mercedeses, and one Jaguar. Look at the interest rates you are paying on those cars. No wonder your banker loves you and no wonder you're going broke. You boys must look good driving around in your flashy cars. I'm sure the women love you. But when I look at your financials, your financials tell me that you have financial cancer. Your financials tell me that you are fools, not alchemists. You seem to have forgotten everything I have taught you."

All That Glitters Is Not Gold

Rich dad then said something I recalled years later, as I rode down from the mine way on top of the Peruvian Andes. Sitting in the bumpy four-wheel-drive vehicle, I could hear rich dad saying, "All that glitters is not gold. Fools are fooled by the glitter. That is why it is called fool's gold. Alchemists can find gold in the darkness."

Retirement Plans That Glitter

One of my routines is to get up and turn on the financial news on two financial networks. I check the mood of the market in the morning and then the mood of the market at the end of the day. One thing I have found interesting as a sideline is to watch which mutual fund, stock, public company, or financial advisory service is doing the most advertising. In other words, which one is glittering?

Many people, low-income wage earners to high-income wage earners, are in financial trouble because too much of their money goes to buy things that glitter. We have all heard of poor kids spending $150 for a new pair of name-brand athletic shoes. On my inspection tours of apartment houses I am interested in buying, I always find name-brand large-screen TV sets and video games in many of the apartments. I have friends who live in name-brand suburbs, drive European cars, and send their kids to private schools. In other words, when you look at their expense and liability columns, they are awash with glitter.

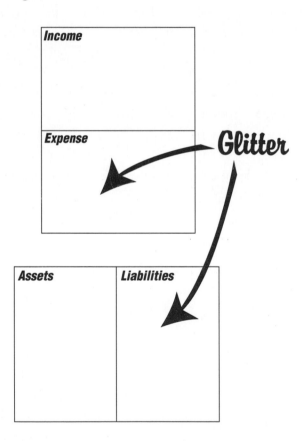

There is nothing wrong with name-brand glitter. I too love brand names such as Porsche, Ferrari, Armani, and Rolex. What good is life without a little glitter?

The problem is, too many people have asset columns overwhelmingly invested in glitter.

Income

Expense

Assets	Liabilities
Glitter	

When I hear someone say, "I buy only blue chip stocks," I know this person buys stocks of companies that glitter. Or if I hear "My broker is so-and-so" and this person is mentioning this name-brand brokerage firm as a form of *name dropping,* I know this person has bought the glitter. I become a little suspicious of mutual fund companies or stock brokerage firms that advertise a lot. Those ads are expensive, costing millions of dollars. Someone has to pay for those ads and that someone is obviously the investor. As mentioned earlier Warren Buffett's mutual fund, Berkshire Hathaway, doesn't advertise for investors, and discourages people from investing in the fund. The point is, I do not *see* Berkshire Hathaway advertisements but I do *hear* ordinary people talking about Berkshire Hathaway a lot. Maybe I hear about Berkshire Hathaway because Berkshire Hathaway is run by an investor, rather than a large corporation.

Many professional investors look only in the darkness. They do not follow Microsoft. Instead they are looking for the next Microsoft. They are looking for the small start-up company that will grow into an international giant. They are not looking for a name-brand CEO with the silver hair, the Ivy League degree, and the movie star smile. Many are looking for an entrepreneur, laboring away in a basement or garage, working on the next product that will solve the next big problem facing humanity.

When playing Monopoly my rich dad would remind me that many people also look for the glitter in real estate and want Boardwalk and Park Place, but the true wealth is from owning the other properties and loading them up with houses and hotels. It's not the glitter that counts, it's the cash flow. In fact, in a recent Harvard Business Review article by Phil Orbanes, titled "Everything I Know About Business I Learned from Monopoly" (March 2002), he references *The Monopoly Companion: The Player's Guide* when he quotes "Casual players don't know this, but the 28 properties around the Monopoly board are not equally valuable in terms of ROI. Boardwalk and Park Place, which many regard as the most precious, actually are not. It turns out that the oranges and reds have the hightest ROI and are the best properties to own."

When I look for real estate investments, I generally do not go to the new home subdivisions where there are flags, helium balloons, large eye-catching signs, flashy model homes, and a sales trailer on site offering easy financing plans. I know these marketing ploys are to attract potential homeowners who are seeking emotional satisfaction. When I look for real estate, I am often looking at unattractive buildings, many with major problems, and generally in older neighborhoods. Often that is where the highest yielding investments are . . . but not always. I have bought brand-new real estate in hot new areas that has turned out to be a financial home run. I do know that sometimes things that do glitter *are* gold. Again it is financial education, being able to read financial statements, the deal, the trends, the needs of the buyer and seller, that can turn glittery fool's gold into glittery real gold. That is financial alchemy.

The point is, millions of people, rich and poor, are in financial trouble because they are fools for the glitter. In just a few years, millions of aging people throughout the world will find out they are in financial trouble because their DC pension plans are invested in glitter but not gold.

The following is the income statement and balance statement from my patented and trademarked board game CASHFLOW 101:

INCOME from ASSETS

| Profession | | Player | |

Goal: To get out of the Rat Race and onto the Fast Track by building up your Passive Income to be greater than your Total Expenses

Income Statement

Income			Auditor	
Description		Cash Flow		Person on your right
Salary:				
Interest:			Passive Income= _____	
Dividends:			(Cash Flows from Interest +	
			Dividends + Real Estate + Businesses)	
Real Estate:				
Businesses:				
			Total Income:_____	

Expenses

Expenses		
Taxes:		
Home Mortgage:		
School Loan Payment:		Number of Children: _____
Car Payment:		(Begin game with 0 Children)
Credit Card Payment:		Per Child Expense: _____
Retail Payment:		
Other Expenses:		
Child Expenses:		Total Expenses: _____
Bank Loan Payment:		

Monthly
Cash Flow: _____
(Pay Check)

Balance Sheet

Assets			Liabilities	
Savings:			Home Mortgage:	
Stocks/Mutual's/CDs	No. of Shares:	Cost/Share:	School Loans:	
			Car Loans:	
			Credit Cards:	
Real Estate:	Down Pay:	Cost:	Retail Debt:	
			RE Mortgage:	
Business:	Down Pay:	Cost:	Liability: (Business)	
			Bank Loan:	

When a banker or captain of an ark looks at the lines on the income state-ment that the arrows are pointing to, and there is income there, they know that this ark has a cargo of assets on board.

If there are no lines and numbers under the salary line entry, a banker or captain of an ark knows this person has no cargo on board and is sailing empty, or, if there is cargo on board, this person has loaded his or her ark with fool's gold.

To find out if the ship is empty or loaded with fool's gold, the banker or ship's captain simply looks down at the balance sheet as shown on page 169.

If the balance sheet, which is the cargo hold of an ark, shows the asset column as empty, they know the ship is empty. It could be the financial state-ment of a poor person or a young person just starting out.

If the balance sheet shows a cargo manifest of a retirement plan, stocks, bonds, mutual funds, or real estate but no cash flow arrows to the income statement, the banker or the ship's captain becomes suspicious, suspecting that the cargo hold might have been filled with fool's gold. And if the assets are name-brand assets, then you know this person loaded the cargo hold with fool's gold that merely glitters.

As a student at the U.S. Merchant Marine Academy, I was taught to watch the cargo holds closely. We were taught to be careful about what type of cargo was being loaded, how it was being loaded, where it was stored, if it was securely stored, and how and where it was to be unloaded. The subject of cargo and cargo operations was a very big subject at the academy. It was a subject we studied in depth for four years.

One of the cargo operations instructors was a retired sea captain with years of experience. His classes were very interesting because he would tell us great stories as he explained the technical side of a rather boring subject. One of the stories he told was about a load of cargo that broke loose on the port side (left side) of the number two cargo hold (the large cargo hold, that is, second from the bow of the ship) during a storm. He said, "Suddenly there was a large cracking sound and the ship began to list [tilt] to starboard [the right side]. Immediately the ship began to sail off course and the helms-man [the seaman steering the ship] had to swing the wheel hard to port [turn the steering wheel to the left]. Immediately the large waves began to come over the ship from the port side instead of hitting the ship on the bow. As the helmsman fought to get the bow of the ship headed back into the

Profession _____   **Player** _____

Goal: *To get out of the Rat Race and onto the Fast Track by building up your Passive Income to be greater than your Total Expenses*

Income Statement

Income		
	Description	Cash Flow
Salary:	_____	_____
Interest:	_____	_____
Dividends:	_____	_____
	_____	_____
Real Estate:	_____	_____
	_____	_____
	_____	_____
	_____	_____
Businesses:	_____	_____
	_____	_____

Auditor	
	Person on your right

Passive Income= _____
(Cash Flows from Interest +
Dividends + Real Estate + Businesses)

**Total
Income:** _____

Expenses

Taxes:	_____
Home Mortgage:	_____
School Loan Payment:	_____
Car Payment:	_____
Credit Card Payment:	_____
Retail Payment:	_____
Other Expenses:	_____
Child Expenses:	_____
Bank Loan Payment:	_____

Number of
Children: _____
(Begin game with 0 Children)
Per Child
Expense: _____

**Total
Expenses:** _____

**Monthly
Cash Flow:** _____
(Pay Check)

Balance Sheet

Assets		
Savings:		
Stocks/Mutual's/CDs	No. of Shares:	Cost/Share:
Real Estate:	Down Pay:	Cost:
Business:	Down Pay:	Cost:

Liabilities	
Home Mortgage:	
School Loans:	
Car Loans:	
Credit Cards:	
Retail Debt:	
RE Mortgage:	
Liability: (Business)	
Bank Loan:	

Profession _____

Player _____

Goal: _To get out of the Rat Race and onto the Fast Track by building up your Passive Income to be greater than your Total Expenses_

Income Statement

Income

Description	Cash Flow
Salary:	
Interest:	
Dividends:	
Income from assets	**$0**
Real Estate:	
Businesses:	

Auditor

_____

Person on your right

Passive Income= _____
(Cash Flows from Interest +
Dividends + Real Estate + Businesses)

Total Income: _____

Expenses

Taxes:	
Home Mortgage:	
School Loan Payment:	
Car Payment:	
Credit Card Payment:	
Retail Payment:	
Other Expenses:	
Child Expenses:	
Bank Loan Payment:	

Number of
Children: _____
(Begin game with 0 Children)

Per Child
Expense: _____

Total Expenses: _____

Monthly Cash Flow: _____
(Pay Check)

Balance Sheet

Assets

Savings:		
Stocks/Mutual's/CDs	No. of Shares:	Cost/Share:
Real Estate:	Down Pay:	Cost:
	Retirement Plan	
Fool's	**Stocks**	
Gold:	**Bonds**	
	GLITTER	
Business:	Down Pay:	Cost:

Liabilities

Home Mortgage:	
School Loans:	
Car Loans:	
Credit Cards:	
Retail Debt:	
RE Mortgage:	
Liability: (Business)	
Bank Loan:	

waves, there was another loud cracking sound. It was the cargo in number four hold [the biggest hold, just in front of the bridge of the ship] breaking loose. Instead of the ship correcting, the weight of the cargo in hold number four breaking loose and shifting to starboard made the list to starboard even worse. The monster waves were now hitting the ship broadside."

As the old sea captain was speaking, the rest of the class was right there on board the ship with him. Since we were now seniors, we had all been to sea for a year. We knew what it was like to be out on the ocean on a large ship loaded with cargo. Many of us, myself included, had been through hurricanes, accidents, deaths, and other hazards and disasters associated with the industry. As the old captain spoke, I could feel the ship listing to starboard with the helmsman fighting to regain control over the forces of the cargo, the ship, the weather, and the ocean. We all knew that having your cargo break loose from its lashing at sea during a storm is a nightmare that few people live through.

The retired captain told us that the helmsman did eventually lose control of the ship. The ship's cargo continued to break loose and suddenly the ship rolled rapidly to starboard and capsized when a large wave hit it. Luckily, the crew was picked up two days later by another passing freighter. The teacher's final words were, "Before you leave the harbor, make sure your cargo is tied down securely. All it takes is one hold to be tied down improperly and the cargo that was supposed to make you rich could kill you." The rest of the class, all of us students, paid especially close attention to a normally boring subject, the subject of how to check cargo ties and make sure they are secure.

When the next monster stock market crash comes, many people will find out that their cargo holds are not securely tied down. Many of their assets will suddenly turn into liabilities, as many did in March of 2000. Many will not be able to handle the financial storm because although millions of people have invested, they failed to become investors. When the financial crash comes, the real investors will be at the helm, working hard to keep the cash flowing from the asset column into the income column. Many of the people who invested but failed to become investors will find their little arks capsized and find themselves adrift at sea, hoping the government or some charitable organization rescues them.

Take Control of Your Financial Statement

The reason the financial statement is such an important financial tool is because it gives the banker or the captain of the ship a quick snapshot as to whether your cargo is gold or fool's gold. In book number four of the Rich Dad series, *Rich Kid Smart Kid*, the introduction to the book is entitled, "Why Your Banker Does Not Ask for Your Report Card." The reason the banker does not ask you for your report card, or what your grade-point average was, or what school you went to is because your academic success or professional success has little to do with your financial success As the crew of the good ship SS *Enron* found out, employees with Ph.D.s, MBAs, CPAs, and JDs after their names were swimming right alongside employees who had not finished high school. Unfortunately, in just a few years, millions of highly educated people will also be swimming, swimming for their lives and hoping to be rescued.

The number one control if you are to be captain of your own ark is to take control of yourself, your financial statement, your cargo, how it is stored, and who is securing it. Your balance sheet is the cargo hold of your ark. In large financial storms, which do occur on a regular basis, people will find out that Porsches, Ferraris, Rolexes, their home, mutual funds, stocks, real estate, suddenly shift in value . . . a shift from the port side (assets) to the starboard side (liabilities) in a flash. When that happens, and it will, people will find out how *worth less* their *net worth* really is. So, the message is, if you love the glitter, you should not be captain of the ship. If you are to become captain, you must control the fool in you that tends to be attracted to the glitter rather than the gold. To be captain of your ship, take control of yourself, which means taking control of your income statement and your balance sheet. Always remember that your balance sheet is the cargo hold of your ark regardless if you load it or not.

Is Your Retirement Plan Filled with Assets or Liabilities?

"If you want to be rich, you must know the difference between an asset and a liability," rich dad repeatedly said to his son and me. The reason he spent so much time on our financial education is because without a solid financial education a person cannot tell the difference between an asset and a liability. One of the fundamentals of building a rich ark is to know the difference between an asset and a liability.

A Book on Accounting

In January of 2002, I was asked to give a talk to a small group of very prominent business people in Phoenix, Arizona. After my talk, a senior vice president of a large regional bank asked, "I understand your book *Rich Dad Poor
Dad* has sold more than 11 million copies, in over thirty-five languages,
worldwide. Is that true?"

Nodding, I said, "Yes, and the numbers sold keep increasing. *Rich Dad
Poor Dad* has been on best-seller lists for years, lists such as those of the
New York Times and the *Wall Street Journal.* Have you read the book?"

"No I haven't," he replied pleasantly. "Tell me what the book is about."

"It's a book on accounting," I said with a smile.

"What?" stammered the banker. "How can a book on accounting be a
worldwide best-seller? That makes no sense. I have an accounting degree
and accounting could never be the subject of a best-seller."

I spent the next few minutes telling him the story of my poor dad and my
rich dad. I explained how my poor dad was an advocate of *word literacy* and
my rich dad was an advocate of *financial literacy.* After explaining the story
behind the book, I then asked the banker, "How many of your customers are
financially illiterate?"

The banker shook his head, smiled and said, "Some of my clients are
very financially literate. Many of the richest clients are well versed financially.
But most of my clients have no idea what a financial statement is, much less
anything about accounting. Many of them make a lot of money but they have
no idea what to do with their money. It's good for me since most of them
keep their money in savings. So yes, you are correct. Most of the people I
meet are not financially literate."

Those of you who have read *Rich Dad Poor Dad* know how important
the basics of accounting . . . the income statement and balance sheet . . .
were to my rich dad. Rich dad often said, "Without both the income statement and a balance sheet, you really cannot tell the difference between an
asset and a liability." In *Rich Dad Poor Dad,* the part of the book that caused
such a roar of protest was the idea that your home was not an asset. In most
cases, a person's home is a liability. Some people put the book down after
that point and refuse to read further. My rich dad never said not to buy a
home . . . in fact he encouraged home ownership. His main point was that

we need to know the difference between an asset and a liability. Rich dad's point was that many people struggled financially simply because they purchased liabilities they thought were assets.

"So how can a book on accounting be so popular?" asked the banker.

Smiling, I said, "Well, it's more than a book on accounting. It's also a book on personal accountability."

"Personal accountability?" replied the banker. "Why personal accountability?"

"First of all, understanding accounting gives me control over my finances and my future. I can run my own businesses and I don't need someone else to do my investing for me," I said. "Secondly, personal accountability means I do not let people lie to me."

"Lie to you?" said the banker. "What do you mean by lie?"

"Well look at this Enron case."

"Oh," smiled the banker. "I understand."

How Do You Tell Gold from Fool's Gold?

Warren Buffett, America's richest investor, believes that understanding accounting is a form of self-defense. On this subject he said:

> "When managers want to get across the facts of a business to you, it can be done within the rules of accounting. Unfortunately, when they want to play games, at least in some industries, it can also be done within the rules of accounting. If you can't recognize the differences, you shouldn't be in the equity-picking business."

When the Enron affair broke, one of the questions asked was, "What is proforma accounting?" which was one of the methods of accounting Enron was using when the roof caved in. Rich dad would say, "Proforma accounting is an accounting report that should begin with the words, "Once upon a time . . ." Or, "In a perfect world . . ." Or, "If everything goes as planned . . ."

In 1999, at the height of the stock market boom, I was invited to a school to talk about the importance of teaching young people financial literacy. A teacher raised his hand and proudly said, "We do teach financial literacy in our school. We're teaching kids how to pick stocks."

"Do you first teach them to read the annual reports and financial statements?" I asked.

"No. I just have them read the reports from the market analysts. If the analyst gives the stock a *buy* recommendation, we buy, and when they recommend a *sell*, we sell."

Not wanting to be obnoxious, I simply smiled and nodded my head saying, "How are they doing?"

He beamed and said, "The average portfolio is up over 20 percent."

I smiled and thanked him for teaching. I did not say anything after the word *teaching.* I did not want to say what I feared he was teaching those kids to be.

Just before the Enron scandal broke, sixteen out of seventeen market analysts were giving Enron a buy recommendation.

When Warren Buffett says, "If you can't recognize the differences, you shouldn't be in the equity-picking business," he means if you are not financially literate, you shouldn't be picking stocks. Rich dad would say, "Picking stocks without first knowing how to read a company's financial statements is *gambling* . . . not stock picking." In rich dad's mind, ERISA forced millions of people to become *gamblers* . . . not investors . . . gambling with their future financial security. Instead of filling their retirement arks up with gold, they spent a lifetime being fooled and filled their arks with fool's gold. So the problem of a worldwide lack of financial literacy is a problem far beyond just the ENRON and the Arthur Andersen scandal.

Rich Dad Poor Dad is a book about accounting, but it is also a book about accountability. As accounting questions continue to surface with companies such as with Enron, WorldCom, and Xerox, it is obvious that the basics of financial accountability, not just accounting, are being overlooked.

Enron used "off balance sheet" accounting to account for liabilities. In other words, its financial statement did not correctly show all liabilities. This would be similar to a person who doesn't want to list all of his credit card debt on his own financial statement. It's not only bad accounting, it's a lack of accountability.

With the financial collapse of WorldCom, we have to consider Rich Dad's definition of assets versus that of the conventional "banker's" definition. Rich dad told us that an asset puts money in your pocket. When an expense is "capitalized" (moved to an asset) and then amortized or depreciated over time (gradually expensed), it increases assets and decreases expenses. But, remember that Rich Dad told us that an asset has to put money in your pocket. Changing an expense into an asset doesn't put more money in your pocket.

Should savvy analysts have discovered the shortcomings of the World-Com accounting? It stands to be the largest accounting fraud in history at close to $4 billion, and new allegations of additional irregularities are arising every day. It seems a careful study of the Statement of Cash Flows could have revealed this alarming exercise of re-classifying expenses to assets. The net impact was to increase revenue (by decreasing expenses) and increase assets—all while the cash was flowing out of the company!

Many analysts and accountants place too much reliance on the accrual form of accounting, which is reflected in the Income Statement and Balance Sheet, where WorldCom as overstating its revenues and assets. Warren Buffett in his 2001 Annual Report for Berkshire Hathaway, stated: "When companies or investment professionals use terms such as 'EBITDA' and 'pro forma,' they want you to unthinkingly accept concepts that are dangerously flawed. (In golf, my score is frequently below par on a pro forma basis: I have firm plans to 'restructure' my putting stroke and therefore only count the swings I take before reaching the green)." Later in the same report, he continued with: "Those who believe that EBITDA is in any way equivalent to true earnings are welcome to pick up the tab."

In fact, the creation of the Statement of Cash Flows is usually one of the last statements put together for the financial statements. It seems the accountants start with two known amounts, beginning cash and ending cash, and the rest is a jigsaw puzzle until the difference is explained. Could more time analyzing the Statement of Cash Flows have prevented many of the accounting irregularities in corporate America today?

Is a company a good investment? The answer is shown by reviewing all parts of all of the financial statements—the Balance Sheet, the Income Statement, and especially the Statement of Cash Flows. Look for which way the cash flows for an investment. Does it flow in or does it flow out? Look for the clues that can give evidence of the Board's accountability. Cash flow is a good place to start, but no one line item can ever give the answer as to a company's viability.

Bear in mind what Alan Greenspan has said:

1. "Many studies have pointed to a critical need to improve financial literacy, the lack of which leaves millions of Americans vulnerable to unscrupulous business practices."

2. "An informed borrower is simply less vulnerable to fraud and abuse."

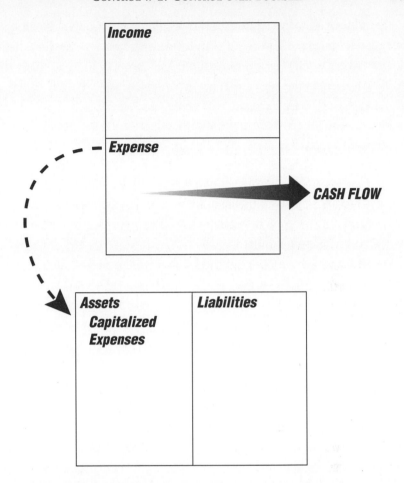

3. "Schools should teach basic financial concepts better in elementary and secondary schools."

4. "Improved financial literacy would help prevent younger people from making poor financial decisions that can take years to overcome."

As I watched Greenspan on TV delivering this speech, what I was most impressed with was his emphasis on the need for the American civilization to evolve . . . and given the financial complexities we all face today, financial literacy is important for that evolution.

At the same Senate Banking Committee meeting, Treasury Secretary Paul O'Neill said, "People need to be able to read, write, and speak basic concepts in order to make informed investment decisions." He continued, "Financial literacy is more important now with the decline in the number of companies offering defined benefit pension plans and the growth in pension plans in which workers make their own investing decisions." In the year 2002, these prominent men sound very much like my rich dad did a couple of decades ago. At least they share the same concerns.

Understanding Assets Versus Liabilities

In *Rich Dad Poor Dad*, I wrote about my rich dad teaching me to become financially literate starting at the age of nine. I believe one of the reasons for the success of the book is because it really never gets above a nine-year-old child's level of understanding.

For those who have not read the book, I will go over some of the core points it covered. For those of you who have read the book, I will add a few more important bits of information as I cover what rich dad taught me years ago.

Years ago, rich dad drew this simple diagram for me:

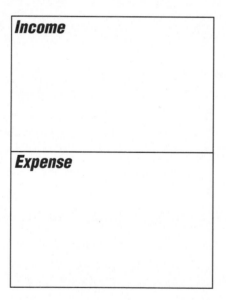

Rich dad taught me that an income and expense statement was also known as a profit and loss statement, or P&L.

He drew the following diagram:

Assets	Liabilities

He taught me that this accounting form is called a balance sheet, simply because it was supposed to balance. In other words, your assets had to balance your liabilities. At that point he said, "This is where the confusion in accounting begins for most people."

My poor dad sincerely believed our house was an asset. My rich dad would say, "If your dad were financially literate, he would know that his house was not an asset, it was a liability."

Rich dad explained to me that the reason so many people called their home an asset is simply because a home is listed under the asset column. That meant that even accountants and bankers call your home an asset because that is the column your home is listed under. For example, let's say your home costs $100,000; you put $20,000 as a down payment, and take out an $80,000 mortgage. The balance sheet would then look like this:

Assets	Liabilities
$ 100,000	$ 80,000
	Net Worth
	$ 20,000

The difference between assets and liabilities is net worth, in this case your $20,000 deposit. The balance sheet balances and the accountants are happy and the new homeowner is happy.

For most people, this is all they want to know about accounting . . . and all they believe they need to know about the subject of accounting. For many people there is a lot of emotional comfort, pride, and a feeling that they are doing the right thing because they purchased a home and because in their mind they think it is an asset. The word *asset* sounds better than *liability*.

In teaching his son and me to be business owners and investors, rich dad often said, "If you want to be wealthy, you need to know more than the average person knows about accounting." Starting at the age of nine, he began pushing our financial education far beyond the financial education of most adults . . . and he did it in very simple language.

Rich dad said, "It is impossible to tell the difference between an asset and a liability, just by looking at a *balance sheet.* To know that difference, you must also have an *income statement.* Without both an income statement and balance sheet, it is impossible to tell the difference between an asset and a liability."

To make his point, rich dad drew the following diagram for his son and me.

The book *Rich Dad Poor Dad* is really a book about the relationship between the income statement and balance sheet as much as it is the story of two dads and two sons. Without understanding the relationships it is easy to be fooled.

A Most Important Lesson

Rich dad then said, "The most important words in business are the words *cash flow.*" He went on to explain that rich people are *rich* because they can control cash flow and poor people are *poor* because they cannot. "One of the most important *life skills* to develop is to learn to gain control of your cash flow. Most financial problems are caused by personal lack of control over cash flow." This is one of the most important lessons I learned as a nine-year-old boy.

To repeat Alan Greenspan's words: "Improved financial literacy would help prevent younger people from making poor financial decisions that can take years to overcome."

Income
Expense

Assets	Liabilities

Rich dad's lesson, "One of the most important *life skills* to develop is to learn to gain control of your cash flow," parallels Alan Greenspan's statement. When I saw the picture of that fifty-eight-year-old Enron employee on the front page of *USA Today*'s "Money" section, I saw a picture of a person who found out late in life that he had very little control over which way his cash was flowing. Alan Greenspan's reference to "making poor financial decisions that can take years to overcome" is especially prophetic here.

In March of 2000, millions of employees in America found out that they have no control over the cash flowing out of their retirement plans . . . out of what they were led to believe were assets. To rich dad and to me, that is one of the greatest flaws of these new DC pension plans. The worker puts money in, hoping that the money grows. But instead, what workers are finding out is that they do not have much control over their cash flow once their cash buys a stock, bond, or mutual fund. Again, to repeat:

"One of the most important *life skills* to develop is to learn to gain control of your cash flow. Most financial problems are caused by personal lack of control over cash flow." This is one of the most important lessons I learned as a nine-year-old boy. As I grew up, I had to gain more and more control over my cash flow . . . not less.

Kim and I were able to retire early in life because we took control over which direction our cash flowed. When the stock market went up, we made money because we had control over our cash flow. When the market crashed, we made even more money because we had control over our cash flow. We do not sit around watching our money flowing down the drain doing nothing as most people did after the March 2000 crash.

When I said to that banker that my book *Rich Dad Poor Dad* was a book on *accounting* and *accountability*, I believe it is the word *accountability* that was more important. The question from this Enron scandal is, How can workers be accountable for their own lives if they never learned to account for their money and they have no control over which way their retirement money flows? Millions, and I do mean millions, of people all over the world are in grave financial danger simply because they never learned accounting, how to be accountable, have little control over the cash flow in their retirement accounts . . . and hence have little to no control over their later lives.

Cash Flow Determines if Something Is an Asset or a Liability

Continuing on with rich dad's simple yet most important lesson, he said, "Which direction the cash is flowing determines if something is an asset or a liability."

He said, "Assets cash flow money into the income column," as the diagram illustrates on the next page.

He then said, "Liabilities cash flow money into and out of the expense column," as the diagram on page 178 illustrates.

The lesson again is that it is the relationship of cash flow between an income statement and a balance sheet that tells if something is an asset or a liability. More simply stated, rich dad often said, "If you stop working, as-

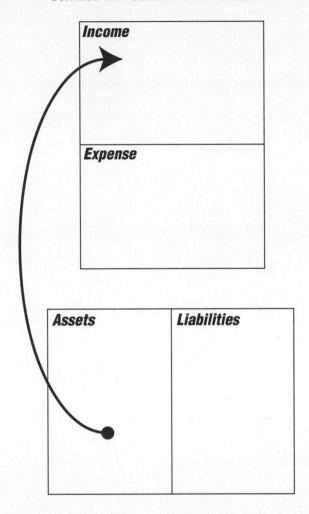

sets will put money into your pocket and liabilities will take money out of your pocket." More graphically he said, "If you stop working, assets feed you and liabilities eat you." After March of 2000, millions of people, not just Enron workers, found out that their arks, their retirement plans, were eating them alive, simply because they had no control over which way the cash was flowing.

A liability is anything that takes money from your pocket. That means a personal residence, the dream of the middle class, is more often a liability, rather than an asset. If a person rented out that home and the rental income was greater than all the expenses, then that same home would shift from the liability column to the asset column.

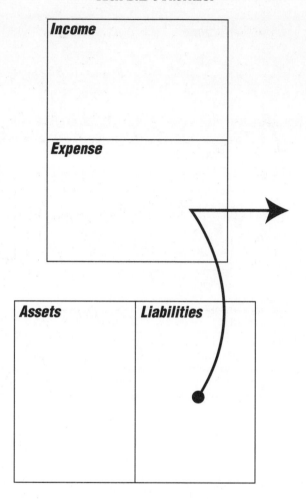

Personal Residence Turned into Rental Property

As a young boy, I learned that *a house could be either an asset or a liability.* That simple little lesson changed the direction of my life because I was less apt to be fooled . . . fooled into blindly believing my house is an asset. If not for that simple little lesson early in life, I am certain I would have wound up like my parents, buying a house, car, furniture, television sets, jewelry, believing in my mind and in my heart that I was buying assets. My mom and dad truly believed in their hearts they were buying assets . . . instead they were fooled by popular cultural myths, the financial myths of the middle class and poor.

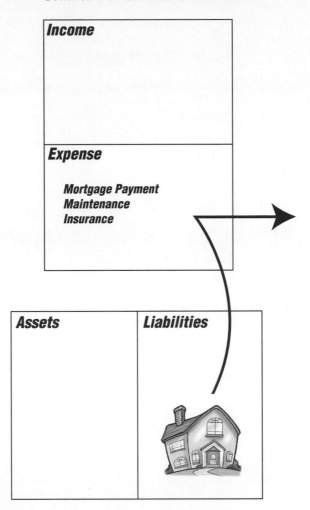

Now I can hear some of you saying, "What if I do not have a mortgage on my house? What if it is free and clear?" Or "What about all the appreciation my house has gained?" Or "What about my car? Isn't that an asset?"

Those questions are answered in *Rich Dad Poor Dad* and in other books and tapes. But in short, the answer is the same—it is cash flow that determines if something is an asset or a liability. In other words, a house without debt can still be a liability . . . because it is not debt that determines if something is an asset or liability . . . it is the direction of cash flowing between the income statement and balance sheet.

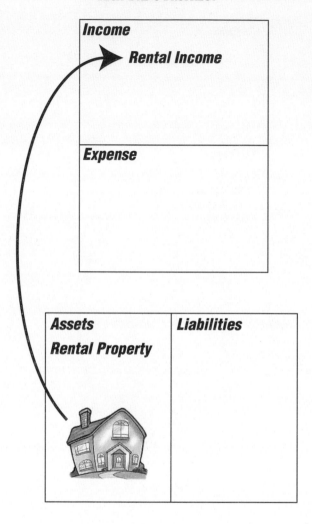

The point of this book is not to discuss the idea of your home being an asset or liability. The point of this book is to point out that millions of people have their retirement in jeopardy because they have not been buying assets . . . they have been buying liabilities for their retirement arks. Millions and millions of workers are opening their retirement account statements and wondering where the money went. In other words, which way did the cash flow? In millions of cases, the cash flowed out, meaning they had invested in liabilities they thought were assets.

Facts Versus Opinion

Many people think that accounting is dealing with facts . . . and in some ways that is true. Yet . . . for the most part, accounting is based upon opinions . . . not facts. I promised those who have read my other books or listened to my audio products that I would go deeper into what rich dad taught me. This is where we go deeper. The point that accounting is made up of opinions rather than facts . . . is a very, very important point to grasp.

Rich dad tells this story on how to find a good accountant. He said, "When interviewing the first accountant you ask him, 'How much is 1 + 1?' If the first candidate answers '2,' don't hire him because he is not smart enough. If the second accountant answers '3' to the same question, again don't hire him because he's stupid. If the third candidate answers the question with 'What do you want 1 + 1 to be,' hire him because you have found your accountant."

Is Your Retirement Account an Asset or a Liability?

Taking this point that accounting is primarily opinion rather than fact, I use this example. When I ask people "Is your retirement plan an asset?" most people would say yes. After all, they may have several hundred thousands of dollars or even millions of dollars in it. After pension reform, rich dad saw his employees' 401(k)s as *liabilities* . . . not assets, even though there was money, stocks, bonds, or mutual funds in the accounts. The question is, who was right?

In February 2002, General Motors happily announced to the world that they would be posting a profit. Given the tough economic environment of 2001, that news was worth celebrating. Yet critics began to talk about GM's underfunded liability, their pension plan. As I watched a discussion on television, one commentator was calling the billions of dollars in General Motors' pension plan an asset. The second commentator was calling the same billions of dollars a major liability. Again, they were talking about the same billions of dollars, yet one expert called it an asset and the other called it a liability. The point here is that accounting is more often a matter of opinion rather than fact.

Starting at a very young age, a major part of rich dad's financial education was to teach us to be *critical* thinkers. Now I use the word *critical* because I can hear some of the readers at this point being *cynical*, not critical. I can hear some of you saying, "Well, a billion dollars is an asset no matter which way you look at it." In other words, that person is *cynical* rather than being simply critical, and here is a very big difference between critical and cynical.

Repeating Warren Buffett's statement: "When managers want to get across the facts of the business to you, it can be done within the rules of accounting. Unfortunately, when they want to play games, at least in some industries, it can also be done within the rules of accounting. If you can't recognize the differences, you shouldn't be in the equity-picking business."

Warren Buffett is advising a person to be a *critical* thinker, not a *cynical* thinker. He is saying, if your mind cannot discern the finer differences, you can easily be fooled.

Millions of people believe their DC pension plans are assets. Another person can see those same pension plans as liabilities. The point rich dad would make is that to be a more sophisticated investor, you need to see it both ways. If you cannot see it both ways, as Buffett says, "you shouldn't be in the equity-picking business."

Assets Are Liabilities

Another vitally important lesson rich dad taught his son and me was that *all assets could become liabilities.* He said, "All assets have the potential to turn into liabilities in the blink of an eye. That is why you must be careful when you buy an asset and be even more careful after you buy it."

Millions of people may have technically bought assets before March of 2000 but those same so-called assets quickly turned into liabilities after March of 2000. It is this shift, the sudden shift from the perception that they had assets in their retirement accounts to the reality that they have purchased liabilities, that causes so many millions of people today to feel uncertain about their retirement.

Today millions of people want to know what a real asset is and what a real liability is. The real answer is that all *assets are also liabilities.* That is why, if you want to build a rich ark, you must do as Alan Greenspan, Warren Buffett, Treasury Secretary Paul O'Neill, and rich dad recommend, which is to become financially literate. Financial literacy is essential to building a rich ark because if you are not financially literate, you may spend years filling your ark with fool's gold, rather than real gold.

It's Time Now to Prepare for the Storm

This book is being written in spring 2002. Given the needs of the massive baby-boom generation, the generation generally defined by those born in America between 1946 and 1964, a mass of approximately 75 million people, 83 million when immigrants are measured, there should be another stock market boom . . . a big one, when they are ready to start retiring.

Many of these baby boomers will be forced once again to enter the stock market through their DC pension plans. This last-chance gasp for some degree of financial security will cause the big boom before the big bust. This means that we all have till approximately 2012 to load our arks with good assets rather than bad assets . . . assets that will break loose in the storm and turn into liabilities. Two thousand twelve is only ten years from now! Of course, the big crash could happen tonight or tomorrow night. If nothing happens, the big bust may take till 2016 . . . but the big bust will come. It will come simply because there are too many millions of baby boomers and their parents who are not in control of their arks, or don't have the financial education to be in control of their arks during rough seas.

This book is not so much about *predicting* the exact date as much as it is about *preparing* . . . and the good news is that we all have time to prepare. I point out action steps to assist in your preparation for the coming perfect storm, a storm that will probably cause a giant boom and a giant bust. Remember rich dad's words, "If you want to become rich, start out investing a lot of time before you begin investing a lot of money."

Build Your Ark

1. Review your financial statement. Analyze each item listed as an asset. For each, answer the following question:

Does it put money in your pocket? Yes_____   No _____

2. If the asset does not put money in your pocket, label it as fool's gold.

3. How much of your income is from assets? In other words, is your money (assets) working for you?

4. Do you have assets that are not working for you today that you could turn into cash-flow-producing assets?

Additional Resources

If you are interested in learning how to take more control of your own ark and its cargo the following educational products are designed to assist your in that learning process:

1. *The Retirement Myth:* A book written by author Craig S. Karpel and published by HarperCollins, first published in 1995.

This book shares the same concerns my rich dad had about DC pension plans. If you would like more detail on how severe the problem is and what you can do to protect yourself, read this book. The book explains why the near future holds great risk to job security, pension plans, Social Security, the stock market, housing prices, and more.

2. *Your 1st Step to Financial Freedom:* An audio cassette program with workbook by Diane Kennedy, CPA, and Robert Kiyosaki, available from richdad.com.

As this chapter states, the first control is to take control of you. This audio cassette and workbook program was created for people who have spent a lot of money on the glitter of fool's gold and want to straighten things out. Not only does it help you put your personal finances in proper order according to sound accounting principles, this program then goes into how you might begin lowering your number one expense, the expense of taxes.

Once you learn to put your finances in order and reduce your taxes, you will be on the road to setting more money aside so you can invest with more money and more wisdom. This simple audio program is the perfect first step for anyone wanting to take control of his or her financial ark.

3. *CASHFLOW 101:* I created this board game in 1996 to teach the basics

of both accounting and investing simultaneously. It is a patented board game available from richdad.com and other authorized distributors.

As the name of the game states, it is designed to teach people who want to be investors how to take control over the cash flow from their assets. It is not the easiest game, but once learned, people report their lives changing as the lights go on in their heads. Players learn how to turn their paychecks into assets and keep the cash flowing from those assets back into their pockets. Simply put, it is a powerful life-changing game.

4. *CASHFLOW for Kids:* This educational game is the simplified version of the adult version of CASHFLOW 101. The child's game is designed for children between the ages of six and twelve. Many parents find the kids' game a great place to start before going on to the adult version.

This game was developed to teach young people how to avoid the glitter of all the fool's gold in the world and learn to take control of their own financial arks. CASHFLOW for Kids gives your children the opportunity to be the CFO of their lives. As Alan Greenspan, the chairman of the Federal Reserve Board, said, "Improved financial literacy would help prevent younger people from making poor financial decisions that can take years to overcome."

Exciting News

We have developed an electronic curriculum called *Rich Kid Smart Kid* that will be offered to schools throughout the world for free. We at richdad.com feel it is important that we give to the children of the world the vital financial education required for the Information Age.

As stated earlier in this book, "Government pushes financial problems forward." We at richdad.com believe it is up to people and business to solve this problem. As Alan Greenspan emphasized, financial education for children is important if we are to evolve as a civilization.

So we at richdad.com and all of our supporters are happy to be part of the solution rather than part of the problem. For those of you who have purchased our products, participated on our Web site, and attended our seminars, we at richdad.com say thank you because your support assists us in giving back to the children of the world. Again thank you to all of you who support our efforts, our business, and the mission statement of our organization *to elevate the financial well-being of all humanity.*

Case Study

The Rich Dad Organization is a learning company. Our goal is for our employees and all members of our team to become financially independent. Once a month, we close the office in the afternoon and play CASHFLOW so we can continue learning together.

Cecilia came to the Rich Dad Organization as a two-week temporary employee. It is now four years later and she still works with us as an independent contractor. To quote her, "Now I choose to work here, for the priceless financial education I receive and the support I receive from the Rich Dad Team."

Cecilia and her husband, George, have taken control of their future. In addition to their incomes from their professions, they have recently purchased a Laundromat and are hoping to own three in the next year. Their goal is to have passive income from these businesses to allow them to have the freedom to work only when they choose to.

Chapter 13

Control #2: Control over Your Emotions

Warren Buffett often says, "If you cannot control your emotions you cannot control your money."

In the late 1990s a friend's wife said to me, "As a close friend, you're aware that we've recently made a lot of money. We've never had so much money. But now I'm terrified that we are going to lose it all." By the end of 2001 they had indeed nearly lost it all. What they were afraid would happen, did, in fact, happen. Their fear of losing became a self-fulfilling prophecy.

Rich dad said, "Money is an emotional subject. If you cannot control your emotions, your emotions will control your money." He also said, "When it comes to money, many people are financial hypochondriacs."

In the fifth grade, I began to read books on the great seagoing explorers such as Columbus, Magellan, Cortéz, Cook, and others. It was because of their stories that I believe I wound up at the U.S. Merchant Marine Academy, at Kings Point, New York. Although I went into the Marine Corps after graduation from Kings Point, my love of the sea has never left me.

Recently, I read one of the best books I have ever read about life on ships, *In the Heart of the Sea: The Tragedy of the Whaleship Essex,* written by Nathaniel Philbrick. The book is based upon a true story about the whaling ship *Essex.* In the early 1800s, the *Essex* sailed from Nantucket, twenty-five miles off the coast of Cape Cod, Massachusetts, around South America and out into the middle of the Pacific Ocean near the equator. It was supposed to be a voyage that would last two to three years. Unfortunately, the voyage came to a sudden end when a giant sperm whale rammed the ship and sank it.

If this story sounds familiar, it is because Herman Melville's *Moby-Dick* was taken from the true story of the *Essex*. Having read both books, the story of *Moby-Dick* pales in comparison to the real tale of what happened to the crew of the *Essex* after it sank. In fact, the story of *Moby-Dick ends* after the ship is rammed; the story of the *Essex begins* after the ship is rammed.

As the *Essex* slowly began to sink, the crew of approximately twenty men climbed onto the three smaller whaleboats. Once provisions were transferred from the *Essex* to the whaleboats, the captain and the crew had to decide what they would do next. One option they discussed was simply raising their sails and letting the wind blow them to Tahiti, an easy trip they estimated would take about a week.

Suddenly one of the crewmen said, "But the Tahitians are cannibals!" That was all it took. With that frightening thought, the mood of the crew in the three whaleboats changed and they decided it was best they sail and row back to Chile, even though it was much farther away and it meant traveling against the wind. They chose Chile because they were familiar with Chile and felt they would be safer there than with the "cannibals of Tahiti." So off they sailed, straight into the wind.

More than ninety days later, one of the small whaleboats was sighted by another whaling ship from New England. As the captain of the whaling ship pulled alongside, he saw a man who looked like a skeleton in the bow of the boat and another man, just as skeletal, in the stern. In the middle of the boat was a pile of bones, the bleached bones of their fellow crewmembers. The men of the *Essex* had become what they were afraid of. Their fears had become a self-fulfilling prophecy.

The story of the *Essex* is much more than a gruesome story of cannibalism, it is also about a weak captain and a group of people who let their emotions do their thinking. It is about a group of men letting the thought of security determine their future. Instead of sailing to Tahiti, they chose to sail back to what they felt familiar with, even though professionally they knew that sailing back to Chile was almost impossible.

It is also a story of assumptions. Remember assumptions from earlier in this book? Well, no one ever questioned the sailor who made the comment that the Tahitians were cannibals. All of the men were from New England. None had ever been to Tahiti. No one simply asked, "Have you ever been to Tahiti?"

Soon after the *Essex* tragedy, both Hawaii and Tahiti became paradise for whalers from all over the world. As a young boy, after reading about the great times whalers had in Tahiti, I used to dream of one day sailing a ship to Tahiti, a dream that came true in 1967. In fact, it was my dream of sailing to Tahiti that most inspired me to go to school in New York. In 1967 I sailed from Hawaii to Tahiti as a student on board an oil tanker. Instead of finding cannibals, I found a paradise far better than that of all my youthful dreams. I still dream of Tahiti and the beautiful people I met there.

Investing Is Paradise

For my wife, Kim, and me, investing is paradise. Investing means freedom, wealth, and security. While there is risk in investing, as there is risk in sailing to Tahiti . . . the risk and the alternative are worth it. Sadly, many people take investment advice from so-called investment professionals who themselves have never been to paradise. Instead, many people assume that the people advising them know what they are talking about.

The underlying point is that when it comes to money, too many people allow their emotions to do their thinking for them. Our emotions are powerful forces . . . and emotional thoughts have the power to become self-fulfilling prophecies if not controlled. If you are to become captain of your own ark, one of the most important controls is the control over your emotions. Once I heard my friend's wife say, "I'm terrified that we are going to lose it all," I then knew her emotions had taken over her life. Even though they had more than enough money to live in paradise, they never made it. Instead their fear determined their fate, and indeed they nearly lost it all.

Three Levels of Controlling Thought

In explaining this phenomenon to his son and me, rich dad said there were *three levels of controlling thought*. They are, lower, middle, and higher thought. He said, "When someone is speaking from their lower levels of thought, they often say things such as 'investing is risky' or 'what if I lose'—they are speaking from their lower level emotions." Rich dad explained further by saying, "When it comes to money, most people never get out of the lower levels of thought." As usual, I did not fully understand what he meant, but as I grow older, I notice that many people are stuck in lower levels of thought, especially around the subject of money. I have dear friends who live in fear of investing, taking risks, and losing money. They cannot seem to shake these thoughts, and in some cases these thoughts become self-fulfilling prophecies. Some of these friends have millions of dollars in the bank, living as cheaply as possible, living in fear of losing that money. In many ways they have lost—simply because they live like they do not have any money. They live like they *have* lost it.

Teaching us how to get out of lower levels of thought, rich dad said, "If you decide that you do not want these lower level emotions to run your thinking, you need both the middle level as well as the higher levels to pull you out." He was saying that it was our middle mind—the rational mind—that needed to learn the technical financial skills required. For example, when I was afraid of investing in real estate, rich dad suggested I take a course on real estate investing. By following that advice, my rational mind overcame my emotional mind and off I went to a weekend course on real estate investing. After the course, my fears were still there but at least I felt better prepared to undertake the learning process that lay ahead. In 1973, that real estate course cost me $385 but over the years I have made millions of dollars from taking that seminar.

Now, this is where the higher mind comes in. In spite of the fact that I have looked at thousands of potential real estate investments, have done nearly a hundred real estate transactions, and I consider myself successful at real estate investing, my lower mind's doubts and fears still kick in. My wife, Kim, and I are about to close on over $10 million worth of real estate this month alone. The nervousness and doubt from my lower mind are still with me. This is where the higher mind comes to the rescue. Because I have gone through the process of finding, buying, selling, and managing property so many times, when the fears of my lower mind act up, it is my higher mind that takes control. It comforts the doubts and fears of the lower mind and tells my middle brain to begin searching for the new information, advice, or education that my lower mind needs to feel more secure. Most noninvestors do not have the technical skills in the middle mind, or the years of experience of the higher mind, to pull them out of the powerful grip of the emotions of the lower mind . . . so ultimately their lower mind runs the show.

This is one reason why financial education is so important. Because once you learn about finances, you can rely upon your middle mind to break the grip of fear and doubt of your lower emotional mind. When I look back upon my life, it was my rich dad playing Monopoly with me, and supplementing the game with real-world advice and experience, that helped me overcome those doubts and fears that we all have.

After he finished college, Warren Buffett invested $100 in a Dale Carnegie course. Reflecting on his investment he said, "I did not take the course to prevent my knees from shaking when public speaking . . . but to do public speaking while my knees were knocking."

Kim and I invest even though we have fears and doubts. It is the challenges offered by our own personal fears and doubts that make investing so exciting. In other words, we do not let our lower mind run our lives. We use our doubts and fears to make our lives better.

The reason that $385 real estate course in 1973 was so important was because the course and my rich dad's prior financial education provided the bridge to my higher mind. Even though I know that any piece of real estate can turn from an asset into a liability quickly, it is my higher mind that keeps me stable and thinking clearly through the challenges of being a professional investor.

Being skipper of your own ark does not mean you are free of doubts and fears. Being human means that we all have those doubts and fears. In fact, you would not be a good skipper if you did not have those worries. But if you are going to be a good skipper, you will need the help of your middle mind and your higher mind in guiding your ark, especially if you want to get through the rough seas that lie ahead and still get to paradise.

Mutiny on the Bounty

As a young boy, I saw the movie *Mutiny on the Bounty* with Marlon Brando. I can still remember the scene where the *Bounty* pulls into a harbor in Tahiti and several outrigger canoes approach the ship, filled with beautiful Tahitian maidens, smiling, waving, and shouting "Hi sailors." I know it wasn't possible back then, but if the crew of the *Essex* had seen that movie, instead of deciding to sail to Chile, they would probably have said, "Who cares about the cannibals? Let's go to Tahiti." That's the power of a little education.

A Different World

It takes very little financial education to save money. As rich dad said, "I could train a monkey to save money." Similarly, it takes very little financial education to diversify. The reason most people save, and if they invest, they diversify, is because they lack the proper financial education of their middle mind. If they had that financial education they might be more willing to venture out into the real world outside the chicken coop and find a world filled with opportunity and abundance. They will also find a world of crooks and liars . . . but after Enron, we know crooks and liars are also found inside the coop. The point is, without that financial education to their middle mind, staying inside the safety of the coop, saving money and diversifying their mutual funds, is the smart thing to do and often the only thing they can do.

Good Debt Bad Debt

Many people inside the coop think it's smart is to be debt free. Early in my life, rich dad pointed out that there was good debt and bad debt. He said, "Good debt is debt that makes you rich and bad debt is debt that makes you poor." The reason so many people inside the chicken coop think debt is bad and being debt free is smart is because in their world, the only kind of debt they know is bad debt. So again, in their world, being debt free is smart.

If you are going to be the captain of your own ark, you will need to know the difference between good debt and bad debt. As students at the Merchant Marine Academy, we studied ship design extensively. One of the things we were taught was that small boats did not need ballast and big ships did. Ballast is, of course, the weight put in the bottom of the ship, so that the ship will remain upright. For example, when large sailing ships went from Europe to the New World of America, most of the ships went over empty. If they did not put ballast in the holds of those ships, they would have capsized. A favorite form of ballast in the good old days of sailing ships was river rock. That is why today, wherever sailing ships tied up in America, you can still find piles of river rock, which came over from Europe in the bottom of sailing ships.

Obviously, once the ship arrived in America, the river rock ballast was taken out and the cargo bound for Europe took its place.

The point is if you build a tiny ark, let's say an ark the size of an eight-foot rowboat, you do not need any ballast. In a small boat, the less ballast the better. But if you are to build a big ark, ballast is always a factor. In the world of the B and I quadrants, the science of using debt as leverage, i.e., good debt, is an important science. If you build a small ark, being debt free or ballast free is smart and you do not need to learn the science of managing good debt. In a small ark, any kind of debt is bad debt.

Early in my life, rich dad taught us how to borrow money rather than get out of debt. His reasoning for teaching us to be borrowers was so that we would someday be able to manage big arks. One of the most important lessons he taught us was that if you are going to acquire bad debt, a financial education or financial statements were not required. He said, "If all you want is bad debt, the banker will not require you to have a financial statement. All you need to buy a home, car, or receive a credit card is a simple credit application. But if you want good debt, debt that makes you rich, the banker will require you to have a financial statement. Before letting you have good debt the banker first wants to see your financial report card—your financial statement—to find out if you are smart enough to handle good debt."

I now more fully understand and appreciate rich dad's lessons on the differences between good debt and bad debt. I know that bad debt comes at higher interest rates. If a person does not have a financial statement, the banker assumes the person is not financially educated and naturally charges a higher rate of interest for the risk of loaning money to someone without much financial training. Yet, if I come in to borrow money for a business or investment real estate, he will require a financial statement. In this case, the banker wants to see your financial report card before he risks lending you money at a lower interest rate.

Good Interest and Bad Interest

The same is true for people who save money. If you lack a solid financial education, the banker will pay you the lowest interest rate possible. If you are financially savvy, there are many programs that will pay far higher interest rates. An example of this is the 2 percent taxable interest versus the 7.75 percent tax free interest I wrote about in an earlier chapter. In other words, the fear of the lower mind is also very expensive to people who save. So if you want to be the captain of a big ark, you need to know the difference between good debt and bad debt as well as good interest and bad interest.

Mandatory Education

Diane Kennedy, CPA, my tax strategist, and a Rich Dad's advisor, makes the following point. Referring to the CASHFLOW Quadrant she says, "If you live in the world of the E and S quadrants, you do not need financial statements."

Continuing, she says, "If you live in the world of the B and I quadrants, financial statements and a good financial education are mandatory." And she does emphasize the word *mandatory*. She also adds, "Many times, a financial statement is required by law in the B and I quadrants. In most instances, the law does not require them for people in the E and S quadrants."

The point is that ERISA and its subsequent amendments resulted in millions of people moving from the E and S quadrants into the I quadrant . . . but without the proper financial education. Because they lack this financial education to their middle mind, millions of people have become financial prisoners, held hostage by the doubts and fears of their lower mind.

Analysis Paralysis

Some people are not good investors because they are too well educated and become trapped in a world of analysis paralysis. They live in what rich dad called *The World of What If* . . . what if this goes wrong, what if that goes wrong. In the world of investing, the term *can't pull the trigger* often refers to someone who knows all the answers, but just cannot bring themselves to put money on the table. They come right up to the brink of investing but their lower mind overpowers their middle mind and they do not go through with the investment and enter the real world. These people are best staying with the pat formula—invest for the long term, dollar cost average, and diversify, diversify, diversify. Their fear and doubt are in control.

Warren Buffett says, "If you have to go through too much investigation, something is wrong."

Education Reduces the Fear

It was the financial education I received from rich dad starting at the age of nine that helped me control the fear of investing. I still have fear but through education and experience I was able to start building my ark. One of the biggest surprises in my life was to finally become financially free. I had always thought that once I had enough money I could retire, sit on my ark, and take life easy. In 1994 at the age of forty-seven I finally completed the ark. Then I found out how boring life was just sitting on my ark and that is why in 1996 I created the board game CASHFLOW 101.

In 1997 *Rich Dad Poor Dad,* the first in the Rich Dad series, was published with the assistance of my business partner, Sharon Lechter, who took my notes and transformed them into a book. Today we are busier than ever, sometimes longing for those days of boredom sitting on the ark, but nonetheless, I am grateful for the opportunity to be productive and contributing to society again. I created CASHFLOW to share the lessons I have learned from my rich dad and from real-life investments I have made. Some have been very successful and others have been failures. But most importantly, it teaches the vocabulary of money. Best yet, by simply playing it, your fears about money and investing will start to disappear.

Case Study

John was a middle manager who realized he could be downsized at any time. His boss was in control of his financial security. Rather than wait in fear, he kept his daytime job and began to learn a second profession.

Always in love with health more than medicine, in his spare time he went back to school to become a naturopathic doctor. A few years later he began his practice and soon made enough money to quit his job. Today he still knows he will work all his life, the difference is he is doing what he loves and no one can fire him. He saw the future, took control of his emotions, and took control of his financial future.

Chapter 14

How I Built My Ark

CASHFLOW 101 not only teaches the basics of financial literacy, but the educational game also points out the four different levels of investing found in the real world. In building our ark, Kim and I followed the real-life investment plan found in the game itself.

The Four Investment Levels

LEVEL #1: SMALL DEALS

On the CASHFLOW game board small deal investment cards and big deal investment cards are found. When most investors start out, they start out with small deals. Of course there is always the egotist, just as in real life, who wants to start with a big deal, even though they do not have any money.

In real life, in the early 1970s, I purchased my first piece of investment real estate. It was an $18,000 condominium on the island of Maui. Even though I did not have much money, I was able to buy three of those $18,000 condominiums, raising investor money for the down payment. I then sold them for $48,000 each in less than a year, netting me $90,000, which was split between myself and my investors. I made more that year from my investments than I did at my job at Xerox and, from then on, I was hooked on learning to become a better investor.

In real life, Kim purchased her first investment property in 1989. It was a two-bedroom, one-bath rental home that sold for $45,000. It took a $5,000 down payment and she made approximately $25 a month positive cash flow.

Although Kim was very nervous, she gained a tremendous amount of experience, experience that serves her well today.

Today, we continue to do a few small deals. I wrote earlier about investing in municipal mortgage REITs, which pay a 7.75 percent tax free return on our money. While most people are only receiving 2 percent taxable interest from their banks, we receive nearly a 12 percent effective return on our money. In order to play this investment, you must watch stock market trends and the short-term interest rates dictated by the Federal Reserve Bank. That means every time someone like Alan Greenspan talks, you had best listen.

LEVEL #2: BIG DEALS
Once a CASHFLOW player has made some money from investing in small deals, they are now ready to take on bigger deals.

Kim and I did this in real life. After we had purchased nearly twelve small properties, we were ready to sell them through a tax-deferred 1031 exchange, which means we did not have to pay the capital gains tax that stock investors often have to pay. After we sold our twelve small deals we were ready to move on to bigger deals. With the proceeds from those small deals we purchased two larger apartment houses and we were able to retire in 1994. In other words, it took Kim and me less than five years to move from small deals to big deals and retire.

After we retired we began looking for other big deals, capitalizing on our experience. Following are examples of other types of big deals:

PREPs. Kim and I like to invest in private real estate partnerships, or what we call PREPs. No one else calls them that. It is simply a code name we gave to this form of real estate investing. A PREP is more often called a *real estate syndication* and is simply a private partnership that is formed to buy a large real estate investment.

The following is an example of a PREP. In an earlier book I wrote about wanting to buy a new Porsche for $50,000. Instead of wasting my money on the Porsche, which is a liability, Kim and I pooled our money with nine other investors, raising $500,000 equity, and purchased a mini–storage warehouse with the mortgage financing coming from a bank.

That warehouse paid each partner approximately $1,000 to $1,400 a month in cash flow. I do not know what the other partners did with their monthly cash flow check but Kim and I used our checks to make the monthly payments for the Porsche. After three years, the mini—storage warehouse was refinanced. We then got our initial $50,000 back, which we reinvested in another PREP. And we continue to receive our monthly cash flow, which has grown to approximately $2,000 a month, since the rents went up. If the property were sold today, we stand to make an additional $100,000 to $200,000 from capital gains . . . and I still have the Porsche. This is an example of an asset buying our liability and helping us with our early retirement. Since we no longer have any money in the investment, and we still receive our $2,000 a month, what is our new ROI (return on investment)? Infinite.

Kim and I invest in one or two of these types of PREPs a year. Our average returns are 15 percent to 25 percent cash-on-cash returns, *plus* the offsetting depreciation deductions, which are not really losses but phantom cash flow. This can easily put our returns in the 50 percent or more range. Try doing that with most mutual funds.

We like these investments because the risk is shared, we use our banker's money, the investment is secured to real estate, we receive monthly cash flow, there is a strong potential for capital gains if the property goes up in value, the income is tax-advantaged, and the capital gains are tax-advantaged at the time of sale. Most stocks and mutual funds do not offer such tax advantages, steady cash flow, or security.

The latest PREP Kim and I invested in was a 240-unit apartment building that pays a 15 percent tax-advantaged return, which is comparable to a 30 percent taxable return, with capital gains potential. We are in this partnership with three other investors.

But best of all, in a little over three years we will have all of our initial investment back, we will still own the property, still receive the monthly cash flow, *and* then be able to go out and use the same initial investment money to do it all again on another property!

Triple net lease real estate. A similar big deal, but a slightly different investment, is called a *triple net lease.* Kim and I like these investments for many reasons. The reasons are:

1. Triple net lease investments are often in excellent commercial locations, such as a street corner of a busy intersection.

2. The tenant is often a public company such as a major drugstore, fast food franchise, or national retail chain. That means the cash flow is often steady and secure.

3. The tenant is responsible for everything. Triple net means that in addition to their lease payment, the tenant pays for the maintenance of the building, the insurance, the taxes, and structural repairs. For those who hate the idea of managing and maintaining real estate, these triple net investments are the best. The problem is, these investments require a rich investor.

While the steady cash flow is excellent, the risk is low and the tax advantages are great. But the main reason Kim and I invest in such properties is to own the land at the corner of the intersection. Once the lease is up, in fifteen to twenty years, that piece of corner land at the busy intersection should have increased tremendously in value. One of the reasons McDonald's is such a rich company is not because it sells a lot of burgers but because it owns the land at some of the best intersections in the world.

A friend of mine recently took an early retirement and cashed in his 401(k) with $3 million in it, prior to the crash of 2000. He took $1 million and purchased a publicly traded famous hamburger franchise (not McDonald's) triple net lease property. He did not take out a loan. He simply paid the $1 million dollar price and retired. His $1 million dollar investment pays an 8.5 percent annual return, which means he receives approximately $85,000 a year tax-advantaged cash flow, which increases every five years. In other words, his 8.5 percent tax-advantaged return is similar to receiving a 17 percent return from the stock market each and every year.

The difference is, because he can count on this money regardless of whether the stock market goes up or down, he sleeps well. Each month the money is wired to his bank account, and at the end of twenty years, he will own a great piece of real estate he can pass on to his children and grandchildren. While 8.5 percent is not a great return to me, for him it is a smart and secure return. I do not know what he did with the remaining $2 million but I think most went to pay taxes and to pay for his new boat.

If you are tired of the ups and downs of the stock market, and wondering how the rich feel secure, just drive to a busy intersection and look at the commercial buildings on each corner. The chances are the buildings (including the drugstore, the supermarket, and the fast food franchise) are owned by a single investor. They do not own the business, just the building and often the land under the business, without the headache of running the business or maintaining the property. Instead, each month while millions watch the ups and downs of the stock market, that triple net investor is having a check wired to his or her bank account each month. To me, that makes much more investment sense.

The beauty of this type of investment is that you receive the monthly cash flow, your tenants pay for the debt on the property, and in the end you own the underlying real estate so you also benefit from the appreciation during the term of the lease.

There are two issues with triple net lease purchases. One is that they usually require a substantial down payment. The second problem is that most financial planners who sell mutual funds and insurance do not recommend them because they do not make a commission on such investments. I have heard financial planners say that these real estate investments are risky and instead they recommend a diversified mutual fund portfolio . . . which to me is extremely risky. To invest in these investments, you will need to find an experienced commercial real estate broker with at least five years of experience, and do not be afraid to ask to speak to satisfied clients, if he or she has any. As with any investment, there are good and bad triple net lease purchases.

A real-life investment we just turned down. The following is an example of an investment I recently looked at but turned down because it did not return enough money.

The real estate was a newly built supermarket in the Midwest. The tenant is a public company with excellent credit. The company does $15 billion in sales, it has three thousand grocery stores and two thousand convenience stores.

Purchase price	$6,600,000
Down payment	1,600,000
Mortgage	5,000,000

Positive cash flows:

Years 1–2	$198,000 (11%)
Years 3–8	$240,000 (14%)
Years 9–10	$282,000 (16%)

Although this was a very safe and secure investment, Kim and I turned it down because it was not a great investment. We turned it down because we can find investments with higher returns sitting on better pieces of real estate. The location of this property was not as solid as we like to see in a triple net lease. If you have a prime location, even if your tenant defaults, you should have an easier time releasing the property.

The Starting Point

A point to remember here is that both Kim and I started with small deals. But as our wealth grew, so did our experience and hence the size of the investments, the security, and the higher returns. In other words, it is education and experience that ultimately makes a person richer and richer. Kim and I tend to add two such investments to our ark each year so our passive income increases each year. That is the power of education and experience. Many mutual fund investors would love to receive $200,000 passive income each year for twenty years, rather than sweat the ups and downs of the stock market. If you can do just five of these big deals in your lifetime, you could easily earn over $1 million a year for as long as you live.

LEVEL #3: THE FAST TRACK:

As many of you know, the CASHFLOW board game has two tracks. One is the rat race and the second track is the fast track. In real life, investments on the fast track are by law reserved only for the rich. The following are some real-life examples of investments Kim and I have added to our ark since our retirement in 1994.

PRIVATE PLACEMENTS

Being entrepreneurs, we also like investing in small start-up companies that have the potential of going public. Along the way we have invested in two oil companies, one silver company, a gold company, and a consumer products company. One oil company ran into trouble when it failed to strike oil and ran out of money. The other oil company discovered gas and is now being acquired by a publicly listed company. The silver company was acquired by a company listed on the Toronto Stock Exchange in 2001 and is beginning to attract investor attention. It is in production and has cash flow from the ore it sells. The gold company has secured rights to an advanced exploration project with a resource of 3 million ounces of gold and is set to go public in 2003 through an IPO. The consumer products company is also set to go public in 2002 through a reverse merger.

Most of these small start-up companies have taken four to five years to develop, to get them ready to bring to the market. I wrote about this process of starting companies and getting them ready for the public markets in book number three, *Rich Dad's Guide to Investing*. I remember after the book came out in 1999 a few people commented that I was wasting my time starting gold, silver, and oil companies. The reason was because the high-tech boom and dot.com boom was on. Today, due to changes in market conditions, gold, silver, and oil are coming back into favor. Again, an entrepreneur must have vision and be able to build a company for a market five years out.

Going Public: The advantage to building a company and taking it public is that because the founders receive the largest blocks of shares at very favorable prices, prices as low as $.02 a share to $.25 a share. One may be able to buy a substantial percentage of the company at that price. After the stock goes public—and let's say the share price hits $3 a share—the founders can begin to sell a few shares to recoup their initial investment and go on to reap the benefits of a growing public company. Of course, these are the riskiest of all investments in the stock market and only the very rich or the very savvy should invest in such companies. This end of the stock market is where most of the crooks and con men hang out. That is why if you should venture into this market, your business and investment training must be the best. If your business and investment skills are limited, you may fall prey to these crooks and con men or, even worse, become one of them.

LEVEL #4: CASHFLOW 202

After a person has their millions securely stored in their ark, they are ready to move on to CASHFLOW 202, the game that introduces the fundamentals of technical investing. Although many people who are not rich play the options market, I chose to follow my rich dad's advice and waited until I had a steady source of cash flow before playing this high-speed game involving paper assets.

I personally feel picking stock and mutual funds is the riskiest of all investment strategies. I would rather have steady cash flow from a business and real estate, or use options to protect my positions in volatile markets. But that is just my opinion.

One of the benefits from playing both CASHFLOW 101 and 202 multiple times is that you too can begin to see the four different levels of investments and find out how you too can learn to invest for greater returns, steady income, and with far less risk. Of course, to invest in the four levels will require that you commit to studying for a number of years to gain your education and experience. If you are not willing to invest in your education, then investing in mutual funds or picking stocks is much safer than the four other levels of investments.

Warning!

When you look at my CASHFLOW board game, you notice that there are two tracks. The small circular track is fondly called the *rat race*, which is where 90 percent of all investors are. The larger outer track is called the *fast track*. Kim and I invest in primarily investments from the *fast track*. They are not investments for the average investor. If you talk to most financial advisors they will say that the investments that Kim and I invest in are far too risky and should *not* be invested in. I agree. They are too risky for the average investor. Yet they are not risky if you educate yourself and gain experience on the B and I side of the quadrant. If you do gain the education and experience on the B and I side of the quadrant, you may find that these investments are the safest, highest yielding, most exciting investments in the world . . . but you must do your part.

Over the years, Kim and I have lost money in businesses and in these other types of investments. We have had businesses not succeed and we have invested in private investment partnerships that failed. In the last five years, we have lost approximately $125,000 in such ventures. We have also made tens of millions of dollars during that same period of time. So our education and experience continue.

The point in sharing descriptions of our investments is not to brag but to encourage and inspire some of you to begin your journey to greatly improve your financial education and find your way to financial freedom. While we agree that these investments are too risky for most people, with the proper education and experience we have found these pathways to actually be the safest and most secure. We have also found that it is not the investment that is necessarily risky but in most cases it is the investor that is risky.

Start a Part-Time Business

If you do not have the money to invest in these investments, then I often recommend you keep your daytime job and start a part-time business. Read the book *Protecting Your #1 Asset: Creating Fortunes from Your Ideas* by Michael Lechter. The greatest fortunes have been created through building businesses. If you do not have the money to start a business or lack the experience, then join a network marketing company with a great educational plan to teach you and give you the opportunity to gain the money to invest with. When people say to me, "I don't have the money," I often reply with, "Then start a part-time business." Some do, but most would rather still say, "I don't have the money."

Build Your Ark

1. Analyze your level of thought when it comes to money:

   a) Do you have fear of losing money?
   b) Do you have fear of not having enough money?
   c) Do you find yourself saying "I can't afford it" instead of "How can I afford it?"
   d) Do you want to develop a higher level of thought when it comes to money?

2. Analyze your personal financial statement for each liability and expense listed: Is it good debt or bad debt?
3. Will you commit to start with a small deal?

4. Start jotting down your negative thoughts about:

   a. a part-time business
   b. real estate
   c. stocks
   d. options

   Now analyze those negative thoughts: Are they based on fact or fear?

Chapter 15

Control #3: Control over Your Excuses

Rich dad said, "Excuses are the words coming from the loser in you."

Time to Grow Up

A few years ago, I was speaking to a group of about a hundred people about investing. They were between the ages of twenty-five and thirty-five; bright, well dressed, most had college degrees and good jobs. For a group that seemed to have everything going for them, they whined about whatever I had to say. For example, when I said, "I usually look at a hundred properties before actually acquiring one," immediately a young woman raised her hand and said, "A hundred properties? Who has time for that? Besides, I think I'm too old to begin investing in real estate."

Letting that comment go, I continued with my discussion on financing a property. I explained that I sometimes used a larger down payment just to keep my debt-to-equity ratios in line. Immediately a hand went up and this time a young man said, "But what if you don't have any money for a down payment? I still have student loans to pay off."

Before I could say anything, another young man stood up and said, "Real estate won't work for me. I have credit problems."

With that I stopped the class. "Look," I said. "I know this was advertised to be a talk on investing in real estate. But before I go on, I want to offer you a lesson far more important than making money with real estate. I'm going to share with you a very important lesson from rich dad."

With that I turned and wrote on my flip chart the question, *What do you want to be when you grow up?* Turning to the group I then asked, "How many of you have ever been asked this question?"

All of the hands in the room went up with that question.

"Who would like to say what they wanted to be when they grew up?"

"I wanted to be a medical doctor," said one of the women. "And I became one."

"Good," I replied. "Anyone else?"

"My dad wanted me to go into business with him but after college I opened my own business," said a young man.

"Okay," I replied. "Now when rich dad asked his son, Mike, and me that question he was not talking about what professions we wanted to become when we grew up. He was asking us if we wanted to grow up to become more honest or less honest. More reliable, or less reliable. Have more integrity or less integrity. That was what he wanted to find out when he asked that question."

There was a long silent pause. Finally someone asked, "You mean honesty and integrity really are important in investing?"

"Well I can't speak for everyone, but to me they are," I replied. "But I am not just talking about investing. I am asking if honesty, reliability, and integrity are important to you."

"Well of course they are," replied a young woman in the front row.

"Then let me pass on a lesson from rich dad," I responded. "A lesson far more important than investing, but a lesson that will make you a better investor nonetheless."

Turning to my flip chart I wrote in quotes, "Excuses are lies you tell yourself."

Putting my marker down, I turned back to the group and paused awhile. I wanted to let the words on the flip chart sink in. Finally I began again, saying, "Today I heard people saying, 'I don't have time,' 'I don't have money,' 'My credit is bad.' Are those lies or truths?"

"Well I don't have the money," shouted the young man who had used that excuse. "That's a fact. That's not a lie."

"And who has time to look at a hundred stupid properties?" said the young woman who had said she had no time. "Do you know how busy I am? I have a business to run and kids to feed. When I say I don't have time, I don't have time. I'm busy. I'm not lying."

"My student loans are a mile high," said the young man who mentioned his debt problem. "That too is a fact, not a lie."

"All right, rich dad's lesson on growing up is about to begin," I said, smiling. "Rich dad told me years ago that if I wanted to grow up to be an honest person, I had to become more and more honest. . . . not stay the same. In other words, I had to be tougher on myself by being more honest with myself. For example, when I personally use the excuse 'I have no time' a more honest and truthful statement would be that 'I am not willing to make the time.'"

"So instead of making an excuse you become more honest with yourself?" asked one of the participants.

"Exactly," I said. "Years ago rich dad taught his son and me that all excuses are lies."

Upon hearing that, the young man sat back in his seat and said quietly, "I get what you're saying. So growing up means not using the facts of our lives as excuses for our lives. If we do that we become more honest."

"You're getting it," I replied. "In sports a person might say that the referee calls the game tighter. That means the referee is demanding a higher standard of play from the players. What rich dad was saying is that as you grow up, call your own game tighter. Be more honest with yourself. Raise the standards on yourself. If you don't, your life stays the same."

"But what about me? I am busy. I really don't have any time—especially to go looking at a hundred properties."

I noticed she had dropped the excuse about being too old. Since she didn't bring it up, I wasn't going to either. "Then just be honest about it," I said. "Just say, 'I'm not going to make the time.'"

"So all you are saying is stop whining, complaining, and acting like babies."

"That's a great way of saying it," I said. "Grow up and stop acting like babies. Every time you make an excuse, you're acting like a baby."

"Well, not everyone is rich like you with all the free time and money in the world," said someone from a back row.

The room groaned with that remark.

Smiling, I said, "I would not have the free time and money if I had let excuses be truths instead of lies. I too started without any money. I too had mountains of debt, nearly a million dollars. And I too am busy."

"And you would still have those problems if you had used those problems as excuses," said the woman with no time. "I get what you are saying. Excuses hold us back . . . no one else."

"That's correct," I said. "Rich dad often said excuses are the words coming from the loser in you."

"So by being more honest with your excuses, that honesty allowed the winner in you to take over," said the woman with no time. "If you are truthful with your excuses, then the loser shuts up and the winner can be heard."

"Exactly," I said. "And the more the winner in you speaks, the more you grow up. But first, you need to be willing to call your game tighter and raise your own standards."

"So how can I find more time?" asked the woman with no time.

"Great question," I said with a big smile. "The winner in you is now talking."

"It is? I am?" said the woman with no time in confusion.

"Sure. Instead of complaining to me that you have no time and letting the loser in you speak to you, the winner in you is asking me how I found the time. If the loser speaks you learn nothing, but if the winner speaks you might learn something."

"So that is how you find the money even when you have no money," said the man with no money.

"You got it," I said. "Look, we all have the same amount of time. We all have twenty-four hours in a day. A winner just finds ways of making better use of that time and a loser lets not having enough time be the excuse for not getting things done. Rarely have I ever invested in a piece of property when I had enough money. And I often have credit problems because I always want to borrow as much as possible when I find a great real estate investment."

"So how do you find the time to look at a hundred properties?" asked the woman with no time.

"Another good question," I replied with a smile. "I estimated that I look at approximately three hundred to five hundred properties a year. I may not buy anything that year . . . yet I still look. Sometimes looking at a property may be simply looking only at the sales flyer the real estate agent puts out on the property. The analysis might take less than five minutes of my time. Sometimes I will spend three months chasing one deal and then have it fall apart. So time is relative. The point is, I am always looking. For example, regardless if I am in New York, Sydney, Paris, Singapore, or Athens, I always stop and look at properties. Regardless of how busy I am, I always look. I'm always looking for a good deal to put into my assets column. I'm looking at the same time I'm running my businesses, investing in stocks and stock options, and leading a normal life."

"So you don't always buy," said the man without money.

"No. In fact rarely do I buy. But it costs you nothing to look. Just as it costs you no money to walk into a department store and look around, it costs you no money to look at property, businesses, or stocks."

"Oh, I go shopping all the time when I'm on business trips. Especially between appointments," said the woman without any time. "You and I just shop in different places."

"So how do you find the money when you find a deal . . . especially when you do not have any money?" asked the man without money.

"Well that is where right-brained creativity comes in. Not having money after finding a great investment is how I gained most of my financial education. You'd be surprised how intelligent you become when you must use your creative mind to solve financial problems. Solving financial problems or challenges increases your financial intelligence. I have money today simply because I did not let not having money be an excuse. Even though I had no time, I still looked at property, even if it was only for a few minutes. Every time I looked at a property, even if only from a sales information sheet, I would analyze the deal, working on how I could turn this piece of real estate into an asset that put money in my pocket. That is what made me rich . . . money did not make me rich . . . investing time when I had no time and investing money when I had very little money is what made me rich."

"So excuses don't make you rich. Excuses keep you poor," said the young woman in the front row.

"Well said," I replied with a great big smile. The class had gotten a lesson far more important than how to invest in real estate. I could tell that most of them got the lesson about the importance of growing up to be more honest . . . by being more truthful with themselves.

Developing Your Sixth Sense

In a previous chapter, I wrote about the lower, middle, and higher mind. Excuses generally come from the lower mind. With a little financial education of the middle mind, and a little *dedication*, the higher mind can develop. After looking at and analyzing thousands of properties, the process is much easier because I have all three minds working rather than just one or two.

Finding a good deal is almost a psychic experience. Many times, I have intuitively known without much research that a certain property was a great deal. Something just goes off inside me and I become like a bloodhound on the trail. But this sixth sense would not have been developed if I had allowed my excuses to run my life.

The same is true with developing a sixth sense about people. Operating outside the chicken coop, I have met characters with all sorts of deals. I have done business with some less than honest characters, not because I knew they were less than honest but because I simply lacked enough real-world experience. I was not able to tell the con artists from the more honest people.

Today, my sixth sense from my higher mind plays a very important role in detecting the phonies, liars, con men, flakes, and others who operate outside the boundaries of the chicken coop. I am still not always right, but I learn from my mistakes and get better each time. I believe that without rich dad's lesson on growing up to be more honest, I might have easily become one of those phony con men, operating outside the coop.

One of the reasons my real dad lost all his savings in his ice cream franchise was not because of the franchise, but because of the people he went into business with. His partners were not crooks. But his partners were all schoolteachers just like my dad, teachers without much real-world business experience. None had much financial training to the middle brain and none had much real-world business experience. When the business started going bad, instead of admitting they knew nothing, the group began making excuses and then they began blaming each other for the problems. Once that happened, the business fell apart and my dad lost everything. They went into the ice cream shop business as adults and wound up acting like a bunch of kids. So bad things can happen to good people, especially if they are not willing to face their own truths and call their own game tighter.

After the ice cream franchise, and swearing on a stack of Bibles that he would not do business with schoolteachers again, my dad entered into two more outside-the-coop business ventures, this time with people he thought were businesspeople. Again the same things happened. The businesses did not perform as expected, sales dropped, money was lost, and again adults began behaving like children.

Now, the same things have happened to me and I have behaved in the same way, sometimes even worse. Many times, things did not go as expected on several real estate deals, or on my first two major business ventures; and more recently in the stock and options market. Each time things went bad, I too found myself acting like a kid. If not for my rich dad's advice on not making excuses or blaming someone else . . . as well as being more truthful and growing up, I think I would still be a kid.

Unfortunately, my father did not have a person like my rich dad to talk to each time a business venture went bad. Instead of being more truthful to himself, he sank deeper into his lower mind, becoming angrier with his ex-partners, harder on himself, and less confident about his future. After the third business failure, he gave up. In my opinion, he retreated to his lower mind and stayed there. To me, that is the price of not having the proper education for the middle mind and allowing the wisdom of the higher mind to develop.

Fortunately for me, rich dad taught me about my lower, middle, and higher minds. He reminded me to return to my higher mind and begin to assess what things my middle mind could learn from these experiences. Instead of blaming others or being hard on myself, he asked me to search for deeper truths and more meaningful insights into me so I could find out more about me.

Please allow me a little repetition. Rich dad started my investing career at the age of nine, simply by playing Monopoly. I purchased my first property in my mid-twenties. My first failure in real estate came at age twenty-six. I started my first real business at twenty-seven, the nylon and Velcro wallet business. That business and the business that followed went bust. My third business and most of my subsequent businesses have done very well. I started my options trading education, after I was financially stable in 1994, at the age of forty-seven. I have made a lot of money but I have also lost almost as much money. The point is, each time I failed I did retreat into my lower mind . . . the place where *fight or flight* occurs. I too acted like a kid and sometimes a baby. But after I got through with my thumb-sucking treat, it was my rich dad's lesson on not making excuses, not blaming, being more honest with myself, and then seeking more information and education that pulled me out of my funk and allowed the wisdom of my higher mind to develop. Without that guidance, I do not know where I would be today. Without that guidance, I doubt if I would have grown up, a process I am still actively involved in.

The point is, too many people give up too early. If they are disappointed, lose a few dollars, or have their feelings hurt, most people retreat back to the world of the lower mind. I believe this is one of the primary reasons why so few people attain great wealth, even in the richest country in the world. I also believe it is the reason why so many people choose security over freedom.

Lessons Learned

I learned two very important lessons from this process. The first thing is that once I developed some real-life experience, it was easier for me to remain calm even if things were not going my way. For example, in real estate or business, if things were going bad, I could remain calm because the emotion from my higher mind would kick in, and that emotion is love . . . the love of the game. Today, regardless of what is happening in business or real estate, winning or losing, I remain happy because I have learned to love the game and love comes from the higher mind.

The second thing I learned was that when I find myself thrashing around in my lower mind, ready to fight or run, I remember the rule that *silence is golden*. Instead of lashing out and saying something I will regret later, I do my best (I don't always succeed in this one) to remain silent and ask my higher mind to think of a higher thought. If my higher mind does kick in, I am then able to find a better way of saying the same thing, without all the blame, anger, or self-justification.

At the academy, in flight school, and in the real world of business and investing, one of the most important of lessons for me to learn was to remain calm, think from my higher mind, and focus on the mission, regardless of what was happening with the ship.

If you want to be the captain of your ark, then the *buck* and the *excuses all* stop with you.

Build Your Ark

1. Are you lying to yourself?
2. What do you want to be when you grow up (even if you think you are already grown up)?
3. Do you make excuses about not having enough time or money?
4. Excuses are lies you tell yourself. Make a sign with this saying and post it where you will see it daily: "Make an effort, not an excuse."
5. Review your negative thoughts in the exercise from Chapter 14 and decide if any of your negative thoughts are really excuses.
6. Challenge yourself to find a minimum of five hours a week to devote to building your ark.
7. Make the five-hour exercise a personal commitment or a family activity.
   Walk, bike, or drive neighborhoods looking at real estate.
   Visit a real estate broker to inquire about investment properties.
   Spend dinner one night a week discussing new business ideas.
   Attend franchise shows in your area.
   Attend local seminars on real estate, building businesses, or investing in the stock market.
8. Decide which asset class you want to start with: business, real estate, or investing in stocks and/or options.

Case Study

A couple of years ago, Chuck and Denise took a trip to visit Denise's sister in California. She had started a part-time furniture business out of her home that was fairly profitable. Denise and Chuck recognized the potential of creating a large company around a similar business model and decided to go for it.

Chuck and Denise had been playing the CASHFLOW 101 board game for several years and had read all of the Rich Dad books. They credit the Rich Dad education as having enabled them to recognize the business opportunity for their furniture business as well as giving them the courage to take action. Through building a successful business, they have truly learned the difference between an S and a B business owner as described in *Rich Dad's*

CASHFLOW Quadrant. They are now able to leave their business and it still makes money, a true B business. They have even started branching out into new states through joint ventures to create more assets instead of trying to do everything themselves.

Ironically Chuck and Denise used to judge their success on the number and quality of the doodads they owned. By understanding the Rich Dad definition of assets, they have now focused on buying, or building, assets and not liabilities or doodads. If they want doodads, they first buy assets that will generate the cash flow to pay for the doodads. After they pay for the doodad they still own the asset, generating additional cash flow each month. This was a big distinction for them and helped them set their own investment rules.

They have taken an idea, a business opportunity, and built a very successful multimillion-dollar business in just a couple of years. They have taken control of their financial ark and are filling it with assets.

Chapter 16

Control #4:
Control over Your Vision

> "In the Industrial Age, big was better.
> In the Information Age, invisible is best."
>
> — ROBERT KIYOSAKI

In the 1970s, poor dad would often drive by a shopping center near Waikiki and say, "When I was in college, I could have bought all that land for $5 an acre." Or the next time we would drive by it he would say, "Did I tell you about the time a salesman offered me that land for $5 an acre?"

The kids would reply, "Yes, Dad, you told us many times."

My dad was in college in the 1940s. At that time, the land he pointed to was a swamp. By the 1960s that same piece of land was one of the largest shopping centers in the world. I estimate that a $500 investment in the 1940s is today worth at least $500 million. The person who did purchase the land was the same age as my dad. The difference between their personal fortunes is a difference in vision.

Paraphrasing something Warren Buffett once said, if history made you rich, then librarians would be billionaires.

Rich dad said, "Many people go through life driving their car by looking in the rearview mirror." He also said, "These are the people that are often heard saying, 'I would of, I should of, and I could of.'"

Recently I was looking at a small house that was listed for $160,000. A person who lived next door came forward and said, "I've lived here for twenty years. I remember when that house was $11,000."

"You should have bought it back then," I said.

"Oh no," the neighbor said. "Eleven thousand dollars was too much money back then. It wasn't worth the price."

"Maybe you should buy it now," I replied.

"Oh no," the neighbor said. "A hundred sixty thousand dollars is way too much money for this house. It isn't worth the price."

Lower Mind Thinking

In control number two, the chapter on control over your emotions, I quoted rich dad when he said, "When it comes to money, many people are financial hypochondriacs." Financial hypochondria is thinking that often comes from the lower mind. If a person thinks only from their lower mind, their vision of the future is often blurred. These are the people that are often found driving their car by looking into the rearview mirror. It is often their fear of losing that causes them to not take action when once-in-a-lifetime opportunities are placed right in front of their eyes. Later as they drive down the highway of life, you hear them saying, "I would of, I should of, I could of." As many wise people have said, "Hindsight is 20/20." Rich dad said, "If you want to be rich, it is best to be farsighted."

A Very Bright Future

When I caution people about the coming stock market crash, I am not pessimistic about the future. I am very optimistic about the future. Warning people about the coming stock market crash is the same as warning a friend about a road up ahead that is washed out. If the person will take another route, they can still get to their destination safe, sound, and on time.

As captain of your own ark one essential skill is to develop your vision, which rich dad defined as seeing with your *mind* rather than your *eyes*. In order to develop this vision, it is important to first train your middle mind and then go out in the real world and allow your higher mind to develop its natural wisdom, often called intuition and instinct.

The Future Will Be Different

Warren Buffett's comment—about how if history made you rich then librarians would be billionaires—is important because the future will be different. Things are changing far too quickly to attempt to see the future through your rearview mirror. Regardless of how old you are, all you need do is stop for a moment and think of all the changes that have happened in the last few years. Thinking back upon my life, I remember when a golf club called a *wood* really was made out of *wood*. Today, the new *woods* are made out of new composite materials I have never heard of. In other words, the game remains the same, but the tools used to play the game have changed dramatically . . . and that is true in many areas of life. Today when someone says, "Let's stay in touch," it could be via foot, car, bus, plane, telephone, fax, regular mail, or e-mail.

If you go further back in time, you will see that just a hundred years ago, not even kings, queens, or the richest people in the world were flying on planes because there weren't any. Almost anyone can afford to fly today. A hundred years ago, only the rich had cars. Today, cars are everywhere. A hundred years ago, you needed to know Morse code to communicate over the telegraph. Today, people all over the world carry cell phones. I do not know too many people who know Morse code. In 1990, the world did not know what the World Wide Web was. Today, the Internet is changing the future of the world faster than any other invention in history.

How Do You See the Future?

In August of 1981, I traveled to a ski resort in the mountains between California and Nevada. I went to attend a conference entitled "The Future of Business" with Dr. R. Buckminster Fuller. At the time, Dr. Fuller was considered one of the world's leading futurists. Even though I knew a little of his fame and reputation, I was still somewhat skeptical that anyone could teach you to see the future without a crystal ball. As such, I went with a large amount of doubt.

But that week with Dr. Fuller was a turning point in my life. It was not an easy turning point, but I believe it was a turn for the better. There was a lot to learn on how to see the future, far more than the scope of this chapter.

Yet, since this chapter is on vision, I thought I would pass on the method Dr. Fuller used to predict the future. The process I shall describe is a principle Dr. Fuller referred to as *ephemeralization*. Without getting into too much mind-numbing detail, I will use the story of the *Titanic* as a simple example of ephemeralization.

In the beginning, centuries before the *Titanic* was built, humans first learned about the possibility of ships by clinging to a log and floating downstream. Soon, humans dug the log out and created a dugout canoe. Next came lighter boats using planks and rib construction. The wooden ships got larger and larger until the battle of the *Monitor* and *Merrimac,* the first iron-clad warships. Once steel construction was introduced, ships grew into giants of the seas, carrying passengers, freight, and armaments throughout the world. Businesspeople began investing in bigger and bigger ships until the *Titanic* disaster. Soon after the *Titanic* sank, the golden age of ships ended. That is an overly simplified example of ephemeralization, one of the principles which Fuller used to predict the future.

Simply put, ephemeralization is the process of starting small, growing bigger, becoming too big, then small again, suddenly disappearing, or becoming invisible, as in the case of wireless communications. On occasion, the end of growth is marked by a disaster as in the case of the *Titanic* and the giant airship the *Hindenburg.* Fuller would say that the technology simply grew too large. In the case of the *Titanic,* and similar ships of that size, they grew too large to maneuver, men operating the ships believed they were unsinkable, and a new technology was on its way . . . and that new technology was the airplane. The airplane was in its infancy stage, starting small, growing bigger and bigger.

Think of It as a Hotel

I was in New York soon after the World Trade Center disaster. Walking down Fifth Avenue, I stopped to purchase a news magazine with the picture of the burning World Trade Center towers on the cover. Two things hit me from that magazine. One was how the two twin towers of the World Trade Center stood out, especially looking at them across the water from the shores of New Jersey. Although I had been to New York many times, it never occurred to me how much those towers dwarfed the other buildings.

The second item that caught my attention in the magazine was a full two-page ad for a new aircraft. The headline for this aircraft ad read, "Don't think of it as an aircraft. Think of it as a hotel." The double-page ad showed the interior of the aircraft having hotel suites instead of seats, a shopping center, and a small bar and restaurant. In many ways it looked like a set from the movie *Titanic*.

Standing on the New York street corner, my mind drifted back in time to 1981, at the ski resort on a warm summer's day listening to Dr. Fuller talk about the symbolism of the *Titanic*. Did the attack on the World Trade Center signal the end of the golden era of airlines? Had giant skyscrapers, symbols of the Industrial Age, suddenly become dinosaurs? Had big business become too big? Did the attack on the Pentagon represent the end of American economic and military leadership? And if the attack symbolized all those things, the question is, What comes next? Could anyone now see the future?

During the 1981 event, Dr. Fuller mentioned that after 1957, the year the Russians launched the first satellite, all new technological breakthroughs would be invisible, not visible to the unaided human eye. Explaining further, Fuller mentioned that after the *Titanic* disaster, we could still see the new technology that would replace the old technology, in this case, the airplane, with our eyes. After 1957, the new technology that would replace the airplane would be invisible. That is why, while standing on that street corner in New York, gazing into the future, I was reminded to begin seeing the changes with my mind, not with my eyes.

Long before September 11, 2001, Buffett advised investors to join AA, which stood for Airlines Anonymous. Buffett said that ever since the Wright brothers, the airlines had never been a very profitable industry. After 9/11, the airline industry and all the businesses that support that industry, like hotels and rental cars, could be industries in decline. While there will be airlines, hotels, and rental cars for years to come, a new technology is about to change things for all of us.

Although Buffett did not invest in major airlines, he did invest in a company that operated small private corporate aircraft, again prior to September 11. I seriously doubt if Buffett ever met Fuller, yet the two men followed very similar principles. Fuller added that if the technology did not disappear and go invisible, the technology would get smaller, as it did in the case of the smaller business jets.

Instead of the example of smaller business jets, Fuller used the example of computers. Not very long ago, computers were physical monsters, requiring a large dedicated room, many people to run it, massive amounts of electric power, and limited computing capacity. Today, computers are smaller, much less expensive, and have much more computing power than the larger mainframes of old. That is another example of ephemeralization, the ability to do so much more with so much less.

Again, these examples are overly simplified. Dr. Fuller went into much more depth with his explanation of this important principle, one of the principles he used to predict the future. The main points are that things start out small, grow, and soon become big . . . maybe too big. The other point is that after 1957, the new technology would be invisible. Today, not only do we have the business of smaller business jets booming, but video conferencing is also finally beginning to be accepted. Video conferencing is the growth industry that is taking away business from the larger airline industry. Video conferencing is one of the invisible technologies of the Information Age that are replacing the need for giant aircraft.

Mutual Funds Are Too Big

Since the late 1980s, the mutual fund industry took off. There are more mutual fund companies than public companies. Some mutual fund companies are even larger than many of the companies they invest in. The question is, Have some mutual fund companies become too big? I'll leave that answer for you to decide. The fact remains that more and more people are becoming independent stock market investors because a little investor can be far more maneuverable than a large mutual fund. Also, there has been an explosion in people investing in hedge funds rather than mutual funds. Again, the reason is the same reason Warren Buffett would invest in a small jet company rather than in the major airlines. The reason is, when things become too big, they are less maneuverable and often think they are unsinkable.

How to Improve Your Vision to See the Future

One way for you to see the future is by watching things getting too big. Then watch for something small or invisible to replace it. For example, soon after the attack on the World Trade Center, Chevron and Texaco, two giant companies, announced that they were merging to become a giant of an oil company. On the same page of the business section, a smaller company announced a breakthrough in fuel cell technology, a new technology that has the potential of taking a lot of business away from big oil companies.

Bill Gates and Steven Jobs became very rich young men by seeing what big companies could not see. Bill Gates got the software contract for IBM's PCs because IBM did not see the spread of powerful and smaller computers. Steve Jobs became a rich man by using a technology that Xerox did not know how to market, a technology that helped create the Macintosh computer.

Invisible Skyscrapers

In early November, I returned to New York for the second time after September 11. On this trip I met a friend who had moved his office from the Empire State Building to a smaller office building. He said, "My staff were quitting because they did not want to sit in the next target." After he made that comment, I realized that we had officially entered into the Information Age . . . the age where being invisible is better.

The network marketing industry is an Information Age business because it is an invisible business. Because it is an invisible business, it is often hard to describe the business's benefits to people who think with Industrial Age minds and who still try to see the business with their eyes, rather than their minds.

It would be hard for a terrorist to attack the network marketing industry simply because the business offices are also invisible. Most network marketing offices are hidden in homes throughout the world. There are people who are running massive businesses from their homes that are invisible. But if you could see their business, it would look like invisible skyscrapers rising from neighborhoods all over the world.

The Invisible Economy Is Strong and Growing

Dr. Fuller predicted that we would soon witness the death of the Industrial Age. He also predicted that it might be difficult for people to see the dawn of the Information Age simply because the changes would be invisible. Dr. Fuller died in 1983 and did not live to see many of his predictions come true, but they did.

Just look at the Internet and you will see that the world of the invisible is here. This invisible economy presents a growing problem for governments because governments are by-products of the Industrial Age. The government is trying to collect taxes and define borders for the invisible economy of the Information Age. This problem for governments will grow if the invisible economy becomes too big and government cannot collect taxes or define borders. If this happens, the currency of the country will eventually weaken simply because the power of a country's currency is linked to its ability to collect taxes. So have governments gotten too big too? Will there still be government, as we know it, in the Information Age? Can government become invisible?

Dr. Fuller believed governments were obsolete. He believed that humanity was about to evolve or disappear because of government's diminishing powers. Fuller believed that humans had to choose between utopian worlds of greater personal integrity and bigger government, or humanity, as we know it, would disappear. In other words, we as individual human beings needed to solve more problems rather than turn those problems over to the government.

Lookouts on the Bow

For centuries, captains of ships have always posted a lookout on the bow of the ship as well as one in the crow's nest or on the bridge. As captain of your own ark, you too will need to post lookouts on your bow and in the crow's nest. Metaphorically that may mean:

1. **Keep your word.** Dr. Fuller said that we were entering the age of integrity. Integrity simply means whole or complete. That means that your thoughts, your words, and your actions need to be the same. If you will do that, the future is yours.

2. **Keep an open mind and your ears tuned for change.** Since changes are now invisible, you will have to see more with your mind than your eyes.

3. **Learn to read financial statements.** Regardless if you invest in companies, stocks, real estate, government securities, or yourself, a financial statement allows the mind to see the true financial condition of the investment, government, or person in question. Always remember that a banker wants to see neat and complete financial statements. Many times a banker decides to

lend or not to lend you money in the first three minutes. If you do not have neat and complete financial statements, are not articulate in explaining your financial position, then the chances are that the only kind of debt you will be granted is bad debt at high interest rates.

4. Use technology. There are now computer programs that allow the individual to see what before only the rich or powerful could see. I have friends who trade stocks or options. They now have charts and software that give them the same power to see and search for investments that giant investment firms have. The individual investors have the same power as the big firms because of these new tools of the trade. Similar advances in technology are available for businesses and real estate. As stated earlier, the game of golf remains the same; just the tools have changed.

5. Watch for bigness. There is a saying in the investment world that when someone becomes famous enough for the front cover of national magazines, their career is over. Not long ago, in the Industrial Age, a blue chip company may have been a leading company for sixty years or more. Today, with advances in technology, the life expectancy of a company is much shorter. In other words, the moment something or someone becomes too big, they are about to decline and be replaced by something or someone new. That same observation tends to be true for mutual fund companies, real estate, and careers. There is always something or someone new coming along to take the place of the leader. Your job is to be aware of people or things becoming too big and then watch for the replacement.

6. Watch for changes in the laws. Rich dad was forever watching for changes in the laws and the effect the laws had upon our future . . . ERISA and its subsequent amendments are an example. The law that created Social Security has created a problem that will have to be solved one way or the other. I suggest you watch how government ultimately decides to handle this massive mess. As rich dad said, "Changes in the law change our future."

7. Watch out for inflation. Just as markets go up and down, so does inflation. Right after September 11, 2001, the Federal Reserve Bank flooded the world with U.S. dollars to provide economic stability and liquidity. The long-term effect of all this printed money may lead to inflation, which means the U.S. dollar goes down in value. If inflation sets in, anything of questionable value will lose value, while things of value, assets such as real estate, gold, silver, and utility stocks, may greatly increase in value.

Governments do five basic economic things:

1. Print money
2. Collect taxes
3. Spend money
4. Push problems they cannot solve forward into the future
5. Control the economy through interest rates

During the 1990s, two more reasons stock prices went so high were low inflation and low interest rates. When inflation goes up, the government often counters it by raising interest rates. When interest rates go up, stock markets usually come down. That means during periods of high inflation, mutual funds generally take a beating or fail to increase in value.

Those of us old enough to remember the late 1970s may remember when inflation went through the roof. When inflation went through the roof, interest rates hit all-time highs, and the stock market went down. I am not saying that such a time will come again, but I would be vigilant. If we enter a period of high inflation and high interest rates, people counting on their DC pension plans and mutual funds may find themselves in serious financial trouble. If inflation rears its ugly head, savers will be punished and debtors will be rewarded just as in the late 1970s.

8. Pay close attention to government's handling of its social programs. It is not news that Social Security, Medicare, Medicaid, and other government programs are in trouble and the problem is getting worse. As stated earlier, government is not solving these problems . . . it is pushing these problems forward onto future generations. The problem is, sometime around 2016, all this pushing the string forward is about to come to a head. Pay close attention as to how the growing problem is handled. If governments begin raising taxes excessively, be prepared for anything, and be prepared to act quickly. Today, money can literally move at the speed of light.

A 2002 report from the National Conference of State Legislatures detailed how serious the problem is becoming. Twenty-eight states have spending overruns and lower than expected revenues.

The report also shows the specific programs the states are overbudget on. Medicaid is the leading reason for overspending. The problem is only going to get worse as more and more people grow old and need medical care they cannot afford. This is why we all need to watch how the handling of this growing problem unfolds.

The future will be different. It is more important than ever to see what others cannot or do not want to see.

Build Your Ark

Get together with friends who encourage you in your efforts in building your ark. Discuss the following goals as outlined in this chapter:

1. Keep your word.
2. Keep an open mind and your ears tuned for change.
3. Learn to read financial statements.
4. Use technology.
5. Watch for bigness.
6. Watch for changes in the law.
7. Watch out for inflation.
8. Pay close attention to government's handling of its social programs.

Next, with these eight concepts in mind, review the eight changes listed in Chapter 9, "The Perfect Storm," with your group. How can you turn these negatives into business opportunities?

1. Millions will be left destitute in old age.
2. Medical care will get even more expensive.
3. Terrorism will increase.
4. Japan, currently the world's second largest economy, is on the brink of financial collapse and depression.
5. China will become the world's largest economy.
6. The world population will continue to age.
7. Wall Street is obsolete.
8. Big corporations are losing the public trust and failing.

By reviewing these items regularly and brainstorming the possibilities for business opportunities, your financial awareness will improve dramatically. If you can do it with a group you can challenge each other to set and achieve goals.

Chapter 17

Control #5: Control over the Rules

"As ship's officers, you will need to be very aware of the rules. Always remember that the rules of the sea are not the same as the rules of the land."

— ADMIRALTY LAW INSTRUCTOR,
U.S. MERCHANT MARINE ACADEMY,
KINGS POINT, NEW YORK

As students at the academy, we spent a lot of time learning about driving ships, loading cargo, and tying knots. We also spent a lot of time studying the different laws a ship's officer needed to be aware of. Although we were not being trained to be lawyers, we needed to be familiar with the different laws that affected the running of a ship on the water. The laws we studied in depth were admiralty law, which is the law of the seas, business law, which involved contracts and other legal documents used in the business of shipping, labor law, how to deal with crews that were members of labor unions, and the rules of the road, which are the laws that govern the safe operation of a ship upon the water.

There were also classes on the laws involving war as well as how to deal with pirates, a problem that is growing in the twenty-first century.

We needed to know that the rules for navigating on rivers were different from the rules on the ocean. There was also extensive study of channel markers such as buoys that ships from all over the world are required to abide by. There were also classes on the different laws of the different ports of call in different countries. For example, we needed to know the difference between the rules for bringing a ship into New York versus bringing a ship into Hong Kong.

One of the more extensive and toughest sets of rules we were required to study were the rules of the road. These were the international rules of ships on the shipping lanes throughout the world. The reason I say this was one of the toughest sets of rules to study was because many of the rules were required to be memorized and written verbatim for the U.S. Coast Guard licensing exam. The rules were fascinating because they were written to amalgamate the changes in technology upon the high seas. For example, Rule #16 had to do with the advent of radar being introduced to the world of shipping. The rule states that a ship which detects the presence of another ship without visually sighting it must stop its engines. In other words, if you could see a ship via radar but not with your eyes, and a danger of collision existed, the rules had to be followed to the letter. There were many times at sea, our ship could see small fishing boats ahead of us on our radar, but we could not see them through the fog with our eyes. Immediately, we stopped our engines. After we stopped our engines, we were then directed by the rules to guide our ship cautiously until danger of collision was over. All ships are still required to follow that rule.

Another set of rules created because of change of technology are the rules between a sailing ship and a ship powered by an engine. Upon the high seas, a ship powered by an engine must always give way to a ship powered by sail. The exception is if the ships meet in a restricted channel or harbor. Then the ship that is more maneuverable must give way to the less maneuverable and often large ship, regardless if sail or engine propels it. These rules were required to be committed to memory because there was often not enough time to call an admiralty attorney and ask for an opinion. A ship's officer had to know the rules and the rules were different for different situations.

Rules of Engagement

As military pilots we were also trained to be very aware of the rules. When flying from one country to another, we were briefed as to distance and altitudes over beaches, altitudes over cities, rules for different airports, and many other rules. In war zones, we were also taught the rules of engagement. Even though we may have been coming under enemy fire, we were still required to follow the rules before firing back.

Rich Dad's Rules

Rich dad was also very aware of the rules. He too required his son and me to know that there were different rules for different people and different situations.

When he drew his CASHFLOW Quadrant for Mike and me, much of his discussion of the differences between each quadrant was a discussion of the different rules that guided the different quadrants. For example:

In 1943, the Current Tax Payment Act was passed. This law basically made it possible for the government to get paid before any employee got paid. When people say, "Pay yourself first," that statement technically does not apply to anyone in the E quadrant because in the E quadrant the government always gets paid first. My tax strategist, Diane Kennedy, says, "If you are in the E quadrant, there is nothing I can do to help you." In other words, there is very little an accountant can do to help you with paying less in taxes.

Up until 1986, the people in the S quadrant enjoyed many of the same tax loopholes the people in the B quadrant enjoyed. But after the 1986 Tax

Reform Act, anyone who was a licensed professional, such as a doctor, lawyer, engineer, accountant, or architect, as well as some employees, could no longer use the same loopholes as those in the B quadrant and I quadrants continue to use. That 1986 change in the law led to the crash of the real estate market, the stock market, and the end of many savings and loans. Banks, big business, and well-advised businesspeople and investors gained while many others lost tax advantages because of this law change.

In 1933, Joseph P. Kennedy, head of the newly founded Securities and Exchange Commission, and father of President John F. Kennedy, supported a law that in essence keeps the poor and middle class from investing in the same paper asset investments of the rich. As a result people who are not millionaires or people who earn less than $200,000 individually or $300,000 as a couple, which is less than 5 percent of the U.S. population, are often unable to invest in some of the best investments in the world.

When you look at the game board of CASHFLOW 101, you see two different tracks:

The CASHFLOW 101 game board reflects the 1933 SEC ruling. The smaller circular track is the rat race. That is where the poor and middle class invest. The larger track, the track known as the fast track, is where the rich invest. The point is that not only is the game different on the different tracks, the rules are different as well. Rich dad insisted that Mike and I know the differences between the games and the rules.

Rules of the Quadrants

I want as little money as possible coming to me from the E quadrant. I do not have nor do I ever want any income as a specialist such as a doctor, lawyer, or accountant from the S quadrant. Today, 90 percent of my income comes from the B and I quadrants. Why? The answer is because the rules for getting rich are better in those quadrants.

If you are to become the captain of your own ark, you may need to be very aware of the different rules for the different quadrants. Now that does not mean going back to school to become an accountant or attorney. It simply means you will need control over competent advisors, a subject covered in the next chapter. The reason you want to be aware of the different rules for the different quadrants is simply because as skipper of your ship, you need to know the differences.

At the academy, a very important course of study was labor law. The reason we had to study labor law was because as ship's officers, we had to deal with unions, union labor, and union rules. If we as ship's officers were not aware of those rules, we would not have been effective leaders. So that is why we studied labor law.

On a similar note, rich dad had his son and me pay particular attention to the rules of the E quadrant. Once we understood the rules that govern workers in the E quadrant, Mike and I knew which quadrants we wanted to be in. The following are a few simple examples of some of the differences and the reasons why, as captain of your ark, you too want to know the differences.

1. Saving money versus borrowing. As covered earlier, most people think that saving money is smart. Yet, if you look at the tax laws governing each quadrant, you will see that saving money in the E quadrant is a losing proposition. For a person to save a dollar in the E quadrant requires that the worker earn nearly $2 since taxes take nearly 50 percent of a worker's earnings. When looking at the taxes a person in the E quadrant pays on the interest from those savings and the loss of value to inflation, saving may be a good habit but it is not a financially smart way to drive a ship.

In the I quadrant, I would rather *borrow* money than *save* money. In fact, the more money I borrow and the less of my own money I put into the real estate investment, the higher my ROI (return on investment). In other words, the more I borrow, the harder my own money works, and the higher my returns . . . if the investment is a good investment. Using an overly simplified example to make a point, if I purchase a $100,000 property and put 20 percent, or $20,000, down and borrow $80,000 at 8 percent interest and net $200 a month income after all expenses, my return on investment, or ROI, is roughly 12 percent.

If all things stay the same, and I only put $10,000 down, or 10 percent, borrow 90 percent, or $90,000, at 8 percent interest, my monthly net income drops to approximately $130 a month but my return on my $10,000 investment jumps to approximately 15 percent. That 3 percent difference is more than the interest rate banks are paying savers today.

If all things could be held equal, and I could find a similar investment, I would be better off buying two properties, putting less down, and earning more money by borrowing more money. If there were capital appreciation on both properties, then my return on capital would be even greater.

Again this is an overly simplified example. But the point is, if the investment is a sound investment, the more I borrow, the higher my returns. That is why I would rather borrow than save, while most people think it smart to save and get out of debt. The difference is a difference of quadrants, rules, a difference in basic financial education, and a difference of experience.

Taking this example further, if you compute in depreciation, the returns go even higher; depending upon which quadrant you are in. If you are a doctor or lawyer in the S quadrant, or an employee in the E quadrant, the following example may not work for you.

There are many times when Kim and I will earn a 15 percent return on our cash just from rental income. Because of the rules, we can also earn an additional 30 percent or more from depreciation, which is also known as phantom cash flow. So what appears on the surface as a 15 percent return may really be a 45 percent return. For example, on a $10,000 down payment on a rental property that returns $1,500 in net rental income, there can be an additional $3,000 in reduced taxes from depreciation, or a total of $4,500 cash flow per year from the $10,000 down payment. And if you structure your corporate entities, in which you hold title to your properties, correctly, that $4,500 in real money can stay virtually tax free as long as you follow the rules. Try getting that kind of return from $10,000 in savings from your bank. At the bank down the street from me, if I had $10,000 in savings, I would be earning $200 a year and would be paying approximately $100 in taxes, netting me $100 instead of $4,500 per year on the same amount of money. That is why I do not save money and would rather borrow.

Years ago, rich dad taught me that investing in real estate through a business generates the investor four types of income. They are:

1. Rental income
2. Depreciation
3. Appreciation
4. Tax advantages

That is why he played the game of Monopoly with his son and me for hours and hours. It went far beyond simply making money. One of the main reasons was to teach his son and me the rules of the B and I quadrants. When all four types of income are factored into the simple example above, the $100 received from the bank is losing value, as is the $10,000 due to inflation. The $4,500 has a good chance of increasing due to rental increases, and the chances of additional capital appreciation of not only your $10,000 but also the bank's $90,000 is good, if the investment is a sound investment.

In other words, if the property increases in value, the bank continues to receive only 8 percent on the $90,000 and you get the rest. If the property goes up in value, let's say from $100,000 to $200,000, I can go back to the bank and borrow an additional $75,000 or more tax free or I can sell the property through an exchange, putting the additional $100,000 to work without having to pay taxes on the capital gains at that moment. In other words, the more financial education you have and the more you know about the rules of the quadrants, the more money you can make.

This simplified example just scratches the surface of what is possible if you understand the rules of the B and I quadrants. In other words, the actual returns can be even greater if you know what you are doing and have competent advisors. I will not go into the more technical information because I do not want to go beyond the scope of this book. If you have questions on the above example, you may want to talk to an accountant or a real estate agent who specializes in investment real estate. They may give you greater insight into the different rules of the I quadrant.

A caution: For these numbers to work, a person should have several years of real estate investing under his or her belt. If a person does not have that experience, I would not recommend using your banker's money to get ahead financially. Debt as leverage can be very dangerous on a ship with a green captain. Warren Buffett says, "When you combine ignorance and borrowed money, the consequences can get interesting."

If you are interested in learning more about what my rich dad taught me about the six steps of real estate investing, you can read about a new product we have created with Time Life at richdad.com.

2. Owner of a business rather than an employee of a business. As the captain of your ark, you will need to know the differences between an owner of a business and an employee of a business. When you compare the financial statements of an employee versus those of a business owner, the differences speak for themselves:

Employee

Income
Expense   Taxes

Assets	Liabilities

Business Owner

Income
Expense   **Taxes**

Assets	Liabilities

I realize many of you have seen this diagram before and understand its importance. It reinforces the differences in the rules of the different quadrants. As an employee, all expenses are after-tax expenses. As a business owner, you have some degree of control of what you spend with pre-tax dollars versus the employee's after-tax expense dollars. Again, the issue is a difference in rules . . . and there are many other differences in the rules. As captain of your ark, you want maximum control over the use of the different rules of the quadrants. An ark consists of all four quadrants and that is why you need to know the rules.

Taking Control of the Rules

One of the reasons I want as little income as possible from the E quadrant is simply because I have the least control over the rules. In the E quadrant, the government controls the rules. Even when it comes to an employee's so-called tax free retirement plan, the government still makes the rules.

In America, the government allows an employee to place a limited amount of money into their DC pension plan but when it is pulled out, in many instances the income is pulled out at the highest tax rate possible, the tax rate of the E quadrant. In other words, even though employees today are investing, in many ways, ERISA forces them to invest into the rules of the E quadrant rather than the rules of the I quadrant. I do not like the rules of E quadrant because the rules of the E quadrant limit the amount I can invest and often limit me to savings, mutual funds, and stocks, which are the investment vehicles of choice for the middle class. People who invest in only these investments often have small arks. If you want to have a large ark, you need to invest in the investments of the rich. To do that, you first need to take control of the rules.

The diagram below appeared earlier in this chapter.

When you look at the I quadrant, you see the date 1933. That was the year the 1933 act required that all offers and sale of securities be registered, unless they fell within certain exemptions. This resulted in a difference between paper asset investments for the rich and for everyone else.

Rich dad said to me, "One of the problems of ERISA is that it confined investors to the paper asset investments of the middle class. Those are the riskiest investments with the lowest level of returns." The reason he said they were the riskiest is because the investor has very little control over the ups and downs of the markets. The reason he said they provided the lowest level of returns is because most mutual funds are diversified. To that point he said, "When you diversify your mutual funds, you are diversifying something that is already diversified. Diversifying mutual funds is like taking a high-octane gasoline and adding water and then adding orange juice to it. Why would you advise someone to diversify something that is already diversified? Why not just tell them to keep their money in the bank? The net return will be about the same in the long run and it's probably less risky." As a side comment rich dad said, "Diversification keeps the stock market floating at unrealistic values. Because a mutual fund is a diversified fund, many stocks are purchased instead of just one good stock. That gives the less valuable companies a higher than realistic valuation." In other words, mutual funds inflate the stock prices of average companies, which causes a bubble . . . a bubble that will eventually burst.

If you will look deeper into the I quadrant, you may notice that there are more investments than just paper assets. In the world of investing, the three main asset classes are businesses, real estate, and paper assets. Again, by investing in paper assets through your retirement plan, by law, you can only invest in the paper assets of the middle class. But if you invest in the other assets, assets such as businesses and real estate, you can use the same rules the rich use and gain the same advantages of the rich. To me, that makes more sense.

Using the Rules of the Rich

When a person realizes that their DC pension plan is not going to carry them the distance, and they ask me what to do, I say the same thing rich dad would say, which is, "Stop using the rules of the middle class and start using the rules of the rich." I then offer the following suggestions and remind the person that they are only suggestions. I would not force anyone to do what I recommend unless they really wanted to do it and they were willing to invest time into study and real-life experience.

Build Your Own Ark

SUGGESTION #1: KEEP YOUR DAYTIME JOB AND
START A PART-TIME BUSINESS

This activity immediately gives you the following advantages:

1. The tax advantages of the rich. The diagram comparing the income statement and balance sheet of an employee and a business owner explains this advantage.

2. Allows you time to practice learning the skills and the rules required for the B quadrant. You have to start preparing now because the years of greatest change are still coming. Starting a part-time business now will give you a number of valuable years to gain priceless experience.

3. More control over your life. Rather than dreading being downsized or forced to retire before you can afford to, starting a business gives you a certain degree of control over your future.

4. When the stock market crashes, business goes on. In 1950, the economy was booming while the stock market stayed depressed. It was only when Charles Merrill, one of the founders of Merrill Lynch, introduced store-front retailing of stocks that the stock market took off again. The reason you want your own business is because if your business is part of the legitimate economy, business and trade will continue even if the market stays down.

Warren Buffett says, "I never attempt to make money in the stock market. I buy on the assumption that they could close the market the next day and not reopen it for five years."

The stock market is not really attached to the smaller but real economy. The economy may be depressed but the economy will go on. Businesses such as food stores, dry cleaners, gasoline stations, insurance agents, real estate sales, pest control, retail stores, professional services will continue on. Big business may be hurt but small legitimate real businesses will do okay.

5. Small businesses can grow into large assets. For example, let's say someone starts XYZ Small Juice Company with a $10,000 initial investment. Ten years later, the company has no debt and nets $100,000 in earnings. Using a ten times earnings formula, if that company were sold, it would be worth $1 million to the owner.

If ABC Big Juice Company comes along and licenses the use of XYZ Small Juice Company's secret formula, that license alone could possibly be worth millions of dollars in royalty payments if ABC Big Juice Company markets XYZ Small Juice Company's products worldwide. That licensing transaction is invisible but very profitable. It is also intellectual property.

Every successful business has intellectual property. Intellectual property includes patents, trademarks, copyrights, trade dress, reputation, licenses, goodwill (reputation), and much more. As the future becomes more invisible, intellectual property has never been more important. It is the *key* to great wealth now and in the future. Educate yourself on intellectual property by reading *Protecting Your #1 Asset: Creating Fortunes from Your Ideas* by Michael Lechter, a Rich Dad's advisor.

6. A higher rate of return. The DC plans are forecasts based on an average 8 percent to 9 percent gain. Small business owners, if they are good, can get a significantly higher rate of return. So rather than investing a dollar into a DC retirement plan, a dollar invested back into your own business could easily get you a 40 percent to 100 percent return, with tax advantages, again if you are a good business operator.

Quoting Warren Buffett: "A lot of great fortunes in the world have been made by owning a single wonderful business. If you understand the business, you don't need to own very many of them."

7. Getting started. So you have decided to buy or build a business. There are many decisions to make. The following is adapted from *You Can Choose to Be Rich* (available at richdad.com):

Build it. Of all the business options, starting your own company is the most difficult because you'll be developing every system on your own. However, it is also potentially the most rewarding. In choosing a business it is always best to solve a problem or serve a need. When you have decided on the type of business, here is a partial list of the next steps to follow:

Name your business.

Begin to seek funding sources.

Search for outside advisors.

Select your business entity and form it.

Obtain any necessary licenses and permits.

Set up a relationship with your banker.

Protect proprietary information (intellectual property).

Write a business plan.

Select your location.

Form your manufacturing or procurement or service procedures—i.e., how you will manufacture and deliver your goods or services.

Plan ahead for bookkeeping, accounting, and office systems.

Decide on pricing strategies.

Determine employee needs.

Prepare your marketing plan.

Seek insurance coverage.

Address legal issues.

Fine-tune your cash flow budget.

Set up your office.

Hire employees.

Announce your business.

Buy it. If you want to avoid the headaches of starting a business from scratch, you may decide you want to buy an existing business. Here are some pros and cons to consider:

PROS

No long risky start-up period

All systems in place

Existing customer base

Faster route to profitability than with a start-up

Existing goodwill of the business

CONS

The danger of buying a lemon

Skeletons in the closet

Sticky personnel issues due to the transition

Potential competition from the seller

Existing ill will of the business

Buy a franchise. You may want to buy a ready-made business system that offers a support structure to you as well. If so you may want to consider a franchise.

PROS

Tried and proven business systems

Licensed trademark and recognition of brand

Training program

Operations manual

Specifications, quality standards, and blueprints

Ongoing assistance in systems and operations

CONS

Expensive

Restrictive, as you must conform to the operations manual

Join network marketing. You may want to join a network marketing company where the entry cost is low and there are training programs to help you succeed. The companies are typically based on direct sales with home-business opportunities.

PROS

Minimal start-up costs

Comprehensive training

Can be either full- or part-time

Can work at home

Work with a national or international brand

Build passive and residual income

Develop communication and leadership skills

Automated order-processing, distribution, and accounting systems prevent many of the headaches associated with traditional start-ups

CONS

Low start-up fees can mean low commitment

Need self-discipline

Need to deal with rejection

SUGGESTION #2: INVEST IN SMALL REAL ESTATE PROPERTIES

This activity gives you:

1. The ability to use your banker's money to invest. Instead of trying to save money for retirement, if you learn to invest in real estate, you can borrow money to become richer faster.

In an earlier illustration, I used the example of a 15 percent return using 90 percent borrowed money. On top of that, if you know what you are doing, you can gain an additional 30 percent in real phantom cash flow. While this sounds easier than it really is, it is also not that hard. One of the reasons I am excited about the joint venture product with Time Life on real estate investing is because this product goes into great detail on my rich dad's six steps to becoming a better real estate investor. The six steps are important, regardless of where you live, because if one or more of the steps is missing, the real estate investment will go sour. That is why all six steps are important.

1. Decide to become a real estate investor: You have to make a commitment and set your goals.
2. Find an area to concentrate on: If you're just starting out, stick with an area you're familiar with or that is nearby.
3. Find properties that meet your criteria: By learning how to analyze properties, you'll be able to tell good deals from bad ones.
4. Negotiate the deal: After analyzing the numbers, you are ready to make offers, negotiate, and reach an agreement.
5. Put the deal together: From due diligence to financing and settlement, it's important to keep on top of all the technical details.
6. Manage the property: It is not as much hassle as you think—and it is one of the best ways to make the most of your investment and get the cash flowing.

(This was adapted from *Rich Dad's Roads to Riches: 6 Steps to Becoming a Successful Real Estate Investor,* available at richdad.com.)

2. The awareness that real estate is real business. When you look at the financial statement of your tenant, you will see why the property you rent to him is so important.

Tenant's Financial Statement

Income

Expense
Taxes
Rent
Food
Clothes
Transportation

Assets	Liabilities

Looking at the financial statement you can easily see that rent is a high-priority expense for your tenant. Rent for many people is more important than their DC pension plan.

For those of you who are concerned about the management of your real estate investment, the real estate investment product created with Time Life goes into how to find good tenants, keep them happy, and keep your cash flowing in.

I often hear people say, "Many people have lost a lot of money in real estate." To them I reply, "That is true. But the facts are, more people have lost a lot more money in the stock market through their retirement plans."

Another comment I hear is, "Real estate is not as liquid as stocks and mutual funds." To them I reply, "Every month, Kim and I receive tens of thousands of dollars in rental income as well as income from tax advantages. That is the kind of real liquidity we want."

If you are concerned about your DC retirement plan, and do not want to make a large commitment to real estate, you may want to consider owning four houses. You have one house to live in, and three houses to provide you income when the stock market crashes.

John Maynard Keynes, the famous economist, once said, "The markets can remain irrational longer than you can remain liquid." Small real estate properties can provide you the liquidity until the market crash is over, regardless of how long the recovery takes.

SUGGESTION #3: PLAN ON BECOMING RICH RATHER THAN BECOMING A HIGH-INCOME PERSON WITH A LOT OF MONEY

In other words, use the rules of the rich, which are the rules of the B and I quadrants. Many people who are high-income people, people such as doctors, lawyers, and high paid executives, are severely penalized for their high income. By utilizing the rules of the rich, a high-income person can gain more control over their money and become rich faster, safer, and more efficiently.

In other words, a DC pension plan, a Roth IRA, Keogh, and other plans really do not help the high-income wage earner. (To further understand how the rich get their money and keep their money safer, you may want to read *Loopholes of the Rich* by Diane Kennedy, CPA, *Own Your Own Corporation* by Garrett Sutton, attorney, and *Real Estate Riches* by Dr. Dolf de Roos. These three Rich Dad's Advisors books can help high-income people become rich people.)

SUGGESTION #4: UNDERSTAND HOW PROFESSIONAL INVESTORS PROTECT THEMSELVES FROM MARKET CRASHES

When I purchase a piece of real estate, my banker requires me to insure my investment. The same is true for my businesses. When professional investors invest in stocks, many use insurance to protect their assets. But most people with DC pension plans have no insurance from catastrophic loss. When the market crashes, they find out they have no control. As captain of your own ark, anything you invest in must be insured.

In *Retire Young Retire Rich* I wrote about how to use options to insure your paper assets. Find out how to use options as insurance, and you will find out how experienced options traders make fortunes with very little risk and much higher returns. Once you know how options work, you may never want to purchase a share of stock or mutual funds again. The advanced game CASHFLOW 202 teaches technical trading in a fun and risk-free environment. However, you must master CASHFLOW 101 before you tackle the advanced version.

SUGGESTION #5: DON'T DE-WORSIFY . . . DIVERSIFY

When I hear people say they are diversifying, I ask them what they mean. Many simply diversify into more paper assets such as sector funds, large cap funds, bond funds, and money funds. This is not diversifying . . . this is de-worsifying. All a person is investing in is more and more paper assets, often more mutual funds. Instead, I recommend investing in different types of asset classes and truly spreading the risk . . . but also improving your chances of higher returns.

My rich dad taught me to build businesses and then invest the profits from the business in real estate. I have followed this formula over and over again.

Case Study

Scott is a dentist and real estate investor in Seattle, Washington. He became a dentist because his father, a life-long employee, encouraged him to be his own boss. A couple of years ago, he took the time to analyze where he was in designing and building his financial ark. He owned two practices as well as the buildings for both practices. Even with this setup, he realized he would still have to work for the rest of his life. The major portion of his income was still from his physical labor as a dentist. He also knew he did not want to join the typical rat race of buying a big house and bigger car, supporting wife and kids, and so on.

At this point Scott read *Rich Dad Poor Dad* and realized that while he had built a successful practice, he needed to diversify more into real estate.

Following the Rich Dad philosophy, Scott developed and took control of his own set of investment *rules*. He started saving 20 percent of the dental revenues weekly and put it toward real estate investing. After starting with small properties, he used his time and discipline to invest in bigger and bigger deals. He has now invested in warehouses, gas stations, strip malls, and other commercial properties. In fact, he owns one warehouse that generates $17,000 every month in cash flow. He also invests in real estate contracts, which are paper assets that pay him 14%. He attributes his success in moving to the right side of the CASHFLOW Quadrant to the lessons he learned from *Rich Dad*. Today, he even passes out copies of the book to his friends.

Scott has built a financial ark full of business assets, paper assets, and real estate assets and has prepared himself to be able to profit during the next down as well as up market.

Chapter 18

Control #6: Control over Your Advisors

"You are the captain of your ship . . . not your advisors."

— RICH DAD

One of the most painful, costly, yet priceless mistakes I made early in my business career was to think that my accountant knew more than me. You may recall at the start of this book, my rich dad said that my business had financial cancer. One of the reasons the business had financial cancer was because the three of us thought our accountant knew what he was doing.

After the nylon and Velcro wallet business got into trouble, the first thing the accountant did was cut back on our sales and marketing budget. He said, "We need to trim our expenses and pay our creditors." Not knowing any better, we let him do that. After the company had crashed, I discovered that the creditors he paid off were his friends who invested in our little company. In other words, he left the company without any debt to his friends and the rest of us were left holding the bag.

After this learning experience rich dad said, "Always remember that you are the entrepreneur, the visionary, and the leader. Never let your advisors run your business. When business begins to slow down, spend money . . . spend a lot of money on promotion. After business has picked up, then you can cut back and pay off some of the bills that came from the promotion." He also said, "Too many people cut back on promotion when business slows, rather than spend on promotion. When business picks up they *spend* instead of *cut back*. That is one reason why so many small businesses stay small. They *cut back* when they should *spend* and *spend* when they should *cut back*. This is also true of big businesses."

After September 11, I noticed many companies begin to cut back on their sales, marketing, and promotion budgets. That is a sign that the company is run by the accountants and advisors rather than the captain of the ship.

The Betrayed Investor

The February 25, 2002, issue of *Business Week,* with the cover that read "The Betrayed Investor," interviewed three people in their cover story article. Two of the betrayed investors interviewed were attorneys and one was an accountant.

The story of the accountant reads like this:

James J. Houlihan Jr.'s plan to retire at 50 is gone. In the last two years, he lost about 30% of a portfolio invested in such stocks as EMC, Lucent Technologies, and WorldCom. Now, the 41-year-old must work harder to rebuild his four children's college funds. "I just don't understand how a business can appear to be so strong and in six months become a fraction of its value," laments Houlihan. "There are people who know what's going on, and then there's the rest of us." He'll save more and spend less—but he's not counting on stocks to make up for what's lost. He and his brother run an accounting firm in Fort Wayne, Ind., so it's not as if he doesn't understand analyst reports. But now, he says, "I don't pay them any credence. It's complete B.S. It's gotten to the point where you don't know who you can rely on."

The story of one of the attorneys reads like this:

Until three years ago, 31-year-old Manhattan attorney Heather E. Barr had no interest in the stock market or planning for retirement. She finally signed up for one of three Salomon Smith Barney Inc. funds offered by her company's 401(k) plan at the urging of a co-worker. It also happened to be at the peak of the market. For a while, the ac-

CONTROL #6: CONTROL OVER YOUR ADVISORS

count did fairly well, but by last year, she had lost a third of her money. The last time she looked, the account was worth less than $2,000. She has since stopped opening her statements. While she still puts an automatic $50 a month into the plan, she's not holding out hope for a rebound. "I don't have any faith in the stock market," she says. "Everyone says you have to ride it out and be in for the long haul. Maybe that's true, but putting money in a shoe box would have landed me more."

You're the Captain

The point is not to put down accountants, attorneys, or any other highly educated professional. The article's choice of an accountant and two attorneys illustrated the point that there is more to being the captain of an ark than having the financial literacy of an accountant and being well versed on the rules like an attorney. Accountants and attorneys are highly specialized professionals, and more often than not from the E or S quadrants. Being the captain of your ark requires you to operate in the B and I quadrants, which requires you to be far more *generalized* than *specialized*. In other words, a specialist knows a lot about a little and a generalist knows a little about a lot.

One of the hardest lessons I had to learn is to listen to my advisors, trust my instincts, and live with my decision, right or wrong, good or bad. As rich dad said, "You are the captain of your ship . . . not your advisors."

A Lesson Relearned

Recently, I had to painfully relearn the lesson that I am still the captain of my own ark and financial statement. Kim and I had purchased a property in December of 2001. After our accountant and tax advisors had blessed the investment, we then turned the finalization of the agreement over to the seller's attorney and our attorney. Two months later and thousands of dollars in attorney's fees, the investment fell apart. What seemed like a simple transaction had turned into an expensive nightmare.

Stepping back into the negotiations, I found out that the two attorneys were now personally at war with each other, rather than professionally and objectively putting the deal together. The negotiation broke down over points that did not matter. All the attorneys could do was focus on what was wrong with each other rather than what was right for the deal. The strong positive points of the investment had been forgotten. The investment objectives, i.e., cash flow, appreciation, depreciation, and tax free gains, were not important to the attorneys. Being right was. Two months of time and tens of thousands of dollars were lost because I let my advisor run the ship. I could hear rich dad saying, "Just because someone is smart and went to a good school does not mean they know anything about the real world of business or investing."

Rich dad surrounded himself with very smart people. He was an active listener and treated each advisor with respect. Yet at the end of the day, he always remembered that he was still the captain of his ship. The final decision was still up to him.

Be the Captain

Many of the recent losses in the stock market were caused simply because too many people let advisors run their arks. If you are going to be the captain of your ship, you need to be in control of your advisors.

Again quoting Warren Buffett: "You don't need to be a rocket scientist. Investing is not a game where a guy with the 160 IQ beats the guy with a 130 IQ. Rationality is essential."

Build Your Ark

Do you have a team of advisors?
Business and investing are team sports and you need competent advisors.
Meet regularly (monthly) with your advisors.
The only silly question is the one you don't ask.
Make the final decision.
Forgive yourself for making a mistake.
Learn from your mistake.

Additional Resources

Genius comes in all forms. The following are two books I have enjoyed reading and have learned a lot from and recommend that people read. The first book, *When Genius Failed,* offers brilliant insight into what happens when people forget that geniuses are human. *When Genius Failed* is about how a group of approximately one hundred people nearly bankrupted the U.S. in the late 1990s. The second book, *At Work with Thomas Edison,* is about America's first high-tech entrepreneur. Both books will give you potent insights into the world of two different types of genius.

These books are important because the two different types of genius are for two different types of eras of history. *When Genius Failed* is about the type of genius that was respected during the era of corporate America's dominance in the world. The book on Edison is about the world prior to corporate America's rise and possibly the new world of business we are entering into now. In other words, in different periods of time, different types of genius are required.

1. *When Genius Failed: The Rise and Fall of Long-Term Capital Management*

> by Roger Lowenstein
> Publisher: Random House

2. *At Work with Thomas Edison: 10 Business Lessons from America's Greatest Innovator*

> by Blaine McCormick and John P. Keegan
> Publisher: Entrepreneur Media, Inc.

Chapter 19

Control #7: Control over Your Time

"I don't have enough time."
"Who does?"

Rich dad said, "One of your greatest assets is time. One of the reasons most people do not become rich is because they do not make good use of their time. Most people work hard making the rich richer but fail to work hard making themselves rich."

In 1974, I began working at the Xerox Corporation in downtown Honolulu. For those of you who have read my other books, you already know that I chose the Xerox Corporation because the company had an excellent sales training program. Rich dad recommended I learn to sell if I was going to become an entrepreneur in the B quadrant. He said, "The number one skill of a business owner is the ability to sell." He also said, "When I find a business that is struggling financially, it is often because the owner cannot sell."

But by mid-1975, I was on probation with the Honolulu branch of Xerox. The reason was because I could not sell. My shyness and fear of rejection had me at the bottom of the list of new sales trainees. If my sales performance did not come up, I was going to be fired. Again I turned to rich dad for advice.

On a hot summer day, I met rich dad at a restaurant near his office, and he re-reminded me of one of his core philosophies. After listening to my tale of woe, my poor sales performance, and my fear of rejection, he said, "So what are you going to do about it? How many times do I have to remind you that you do not get rich at work? How many times do I have to remind you that you get rich in your spare time?"

Getting Rich Faster

A few weeks later, after leaving my office at Xerox, I walked up the street to a nonprofit charity and sat on their phone bank dialing for dollars. The reason I did this was to gain more sales experience . . . faster. Three to five nights a week, I would make ten to thirty phone sales pitches, asking people to donate money to this worthy cause. In a three-hour period, I was making as many sales presentations as I was making in a month pounding the streets for Xerox. In other words, I was getting rich faster. I was getting rich because I was gaining a skill that would enrich my life forever. By late 1975, I was no longer on probation at Xerox, my sales were improving, and so was my income. By 1976, I was one of the top sales reps. When asked by my sales manager what the secret to my success was, I simply said, "I made more sales calls faster." He smiled and I never told him I made my sales calls for a charity, and did them in my spare time.

At about the same time, rich dad encouraged me to begin investing in real estate. That is why I took a real estate investment course before I got out of the Marine Corps. Rich dad always said, "I make my money in my business—and I keep my money in real estate."

When I reflect on my life, I appreciate rich dad's wisdom of getting rich in my spare time. Today I am financially free because of what I did in my spare time, rather than what I did at work. Today, if you are working hard on somebody else's ark, you may want to set aside some spare time to build your own ark.

I Love My Work!

People often say to me, "I love my work. I love what I do." To those statements I reply, "Congratulations. Loving what you do is very important." Yet silently, I ask this question: "Is what you love doing providing everything you need?" The point is, many people love their work but their work will not provide for their long-term needs. For example, Kim and I have a friend who is a great interior designer and her husband is an executive in a manufacturing company. They both love their work, both make a lot of money, but neither of them has anything to fall back on. When they asked for advice, one of the first questions I asked them was, "How much can you sell your job for?"

Both replied, "Nothing. We cannot sell our jobs."

Saying nothing, I simply sat there in the silence and let them listen to their own words. Finally, the silence became deafening. "So what are you saying?" asked the wife. "Quit our jobs?"

Again, I said nothing and the squirm factor became higher. "Look we've come to ask for help. The least you can do is say something. Are you saying quit our jobs? Is that what you're saying?"

Once again I sat quietly smiling, letting them respond to the silence.

My silence was met by their silence. Finally the husband took a deep breath and rocked back in his chair as I sat at my desk. His wife, our friend the interior decorator, was still leaning forward, hoping for an answer from me. After about thirty seconds of silence, she too rocked back in her chair and sat there in silence.

"How much can we sell our jobs for?" said the husband as he rocked back and forth, listening to the question I asked initially, but he was now asking in his own words. "How much can I sell my job for?" he suddenly asked, but this time in a much louder voice. I could tell he was hearing his own question, not my question.

"Well the answer is nothing," he said, answering himself. "Absolutely nothing."

"But it provides us income," said his wife in a defensive tone. "We earn money to put a roof over our heads, feed the kids, and provide for the future."

"I know, I know," said the husband. "I know all that. But that is not the question being asked. The question is, 'How much can we sell our jobs for?'"

"So you say we're working for nothing?" asked the wife.

"No," I replied, breaking my silence. "I just asked a question . . . a question I wanted you to ask yourself."

"So we're working at something we cannot sell," said the husband. "What do you suggest?"

"Well, how about investing time to work for yourself? Why not work just as hard to make yourself rich as you do to make someone else rich?"

"So invest some time in ourselves," said the wife.

I went on to tell the story of my dialing for dollars for the charity and investing in real estate. "When I look back upon those years, my job did not make me rich. What made me rich was what I did after I did my job. What are you doing?"

"Truthfully nothing," said the husband. "We work hard for our clients, we work hard to pay bills, we work hard to set a few dollars aside for our retirement, and we work hard for our kids and their future education."

"So you invest in your kids' future?" I asked.

"I know, I know," said the husband. "I got the message. It's time we invested some time in *our* future."

Investing in Becoming Investors

Today it is no longer enough to be professionally competent. We all need to be professionally and financially competent. Earlier, I wrote that many people today are investing, but very few are becoming investors. The couple I just mentioned fell into that category. After the market crash in March of 2000, they realized that they might be better off becoming investors rather than trusting their money to people they hoped and prayed were investors.

The couple attended some of the courses richdad.com offers. Their comments after leaving the courses were, "I cannot believe how fast a person can make money from their investments. Why would anyone want to put money in mutual funds and hope for a 10 percent per year taxable return? Why would anyone want to take the risk of having his or her mutual funds wiped out in a market crash? Why not learn how to make money when the market is going up as well as coming down?

Richdad.com offers seminars for business owners and investors. I mention this because the comment most people have after leaving the courses is what they learned about how fast money could be made. The point is that you can gain more control over your time if your money can work at a higher rate of return. For example, many participants in our stock options classes are shocked to find out how relatively simple it is to trade options. Participants in our real estate classes find out how relatively simple it is to use your banker's money rather than your own money to generate 50 percent or more in returns per year.

Rich dad taught his son and me that if you can increase the velocity of your money, you could gain valuable time. For example if you earn 5 percent per year on your investment, it takes you approximately twenty years to get your initial investment back. If your money earns 50 percent per year, you get your investment back in two years. If you can earn 100 percent per month, you get your money back in one month, or twelve times a year. These returns are possible with the appropriate financial investment education. In other words, a small investment in your financial education can gain you massive amounts of financial time.

Health and Wealth

Rich dad often said there was a strong correlation between health and wealth. In earlier books, I defined wealth as the number of days you could survive without working, while still maintaining your standard of living. More specifically, wealth is measured in time more than money. For example, if you had $5,000 in savings and your monthly expenses were $1,000 a month, your wealth would be 5 months. The same is true with health. If you are healthy, you have years ahead of you. But if your health begins to deteriorate, then your time on this earth diminishes. So health and wealth can be measured relative to time.

Another measurement of health and wealth is recovery time. For example, if you go for a physical examination, the medical examiner may ask to take your resting heart rate and then put you on a treadmill to get your heart rate up. After attaining an elevated heart rate, the examiner then measures how fast it takes your body to recover to the resting heart rate. That is called recovery time. The same is true with surgery. If a person is healthy, the recovery time is short. If the person is physically weak, the recovery time may take longer.

Wealth can be measured in the same way, relative to time. If a person is a true investor with the proper education and experience, if they lose everything, their recovery time can be quick. But if a person is like the fifty-eight-year-old Enron employee on the front page of the "Money" section of *USA Today*, the financial recovery time may take longer than that person has years of work left. He may be healthy but his wealth is anemic.

Rich dad encouraged his son and me to learn to build businesses and become investors. That is why I went to sales training and learned about property. Today I make my money in business and store my money in real estate. Ever since 1994, I have been studying how to use stock options such as puts, calls, and other derivatives. There are several reasons why I study options and options trading. They are:

1. I have the financial stability to trade them. My businesses and my real estate allow me the luxury to learn the profession.

2. Trading options is fun and fast. I love the speed at which a trade can be executed. Building a business can take years. Buying a piece of real estate can take months. But trading options takes seconds.

3. I am preparing for the next market boom and bust. When the market goes up I will be using *call options*. When the market comes down I will be using *put options*. Earlier in this book I stated that most mutual fund investors were playing Russian roulette with a three-chambered gun with two chambers loaded. Options give me control over the ups and downs of the market. Mutual funds do not. That means during the next market crash, millions will be losing while options traders will be winning.

4. If I get wiped out, being skilled at options trading gives me a faster recovery time, if I am good at the profession. Of course, if I am not good, my recovery time could take longer.

5. By investing time now, I gain time in the future.

Four Kinds of People

Our Rich Dad's advisor on real estate, Dr. Dolf de Roos's wife, Renie Cavallari, a respected corporate strategist, says there are four kinds of people. They are:

1. People who must be right
2. People who must win
3. People who must be liked
4. People who must be comfortable

Right after Renie mentioned these four different types of people, I immediately could place friends and family into each of the four categories. I would say Kim and I are definitely in the category that needs to win. One of the reasons we could retire young and retire rich is because winning was more important than any of the other three categories. By having the return on our money pick up speed we could retire far earlier than most people and win our private race to financial freedom . . . and financial freedom means having more free time.

As captain of your own ark, one of the ways you can increase the speed of your ark and gain more time is by investing some time in your financial education. Earlier in this book, I wrote about educating the middle mind. As captain of your ark, after you gain that education, it is still up to you to turn that middle mind education into higher mind wisdom. One of the more frustrating things about learning is investing the time to convert knowledge into wisdom. When I was struggling financially in the 1980s the hard part of life was knowing what to do mentally but not being able to do what I knew I had to do. The benefit of investing the time first into education and then into live practice is that a person begins to learn to love the game. For example, I did not like building a business when I was failing at it. Today, I love the process. When I was losing at investing in real estate, I hated real estate. Today I love the game of real estate and the properties Kim and I own. When investing in options, the frustration is often very high and profits are low, but I know I am making progress because I am learning to love the game.

As captain of your ark, I strongly urge you to learn to love your cargo. Today, I love my businesses, my real estate, and my options trading. I learned to love these assets and skills because I first invested time into educating my middle mind and then invested time in teaching my higher mind to love the assets.

A Little Education Means Less Time, Less Money, Less Risk, and a Higher Standard of Living

A friend of mind just told me that his 401(k) lost over $350,000 between 2000 and 2002. At fifty-three years old, he is now concerned that he can never retire. He realizes that diversification will not deliver the returns he wants or the long-term protection he needs. When he asked me for some advice, I said, "Why don't you take $30,000, buy three rental houses for $100,000 each, and let your tenants pay down your mortgage as well as give you income. By the time you're sixty-five, you should have a steady stream of income, if you have invested wisely."

His response was, "All I need is $30,000?"

Nodding, I said, "Really all you need is $15,000 to buy three rental properties. The federal government has loan programs, if you qualify, that allow individuals to only put 5 percent down on certain properties."

"So are you saying I could retire with only $15,000? And the bank will lend me the rest?"

"I believe so," I replied. "If market conditions remained the same, and I had five to ten years before retiring, I am quite certain that I could retire with only $15,000 invested."

"What about people who live in expensive cities such as New York or San Francisco? Won't they find it hard finding inexpensive rental properties?"

"In the heart of the city . . . yes, they would. But if you go an hour out of most cities, you can find affordable properties. All you have to do is find an area that is going up in value and over time your property should appreciate. If inflation hits, you can raise your rents. By the time you retire, those three houses should be paying you a steady income, a far more secure income than income from mutual funds."

"And with far less money," he added.

"That's correct," I replied. "With a little education and experience, you can retire using less money, less risk, higher returns, and contribute to society by providing much needed housing."

"But what if everyone begins to invest in rental real estate?" he asked.

"Then we help the government provide housing at lower prices and hopefully raise the standard of living of those who cannot afford to buy a house. If there is more supply, then rents come down. If there are more owners competing for tenants, then competition will improve the quality of housing."

"How long do you hold your property before you sell?" he asked.

My reply was to quote Warren Buffett: "My time frame for holding a stock is forever."

"So you hold forever?"

"Most of the time," I said. "But every now and then I sell. I usually sell when I made a bad investment and I just want to get rid of it. But generally I follow Warren Buffett's idea of investing in what I love and holding on forever. I love the real estate and the businesses in my asset column."

"And I do not have to stop with three houses?"

"No you don't," I replied. "It's just like playing Monopoly. If you have four green houses you can then buy a red hotel. The government loves you, your banker loves you, and your future is more secure. One reason you feel more secure is because real estate can protect you from one of life's greatest financial threats, which is the threat of inflation.

"By owning rental property, as inflation increases due to taxes, excess government spending, the government's printing of money, increasing costs of materials, rising interest rates, and the rising cost of insurance, those increases are passed on to the tenant. Mutual funds often lose value during periods of high inflation and high interest rates and a good property can increase in value during the same period. If you have purchased your real estate early enough and have a fixed interest rate, you have greater control over your investments as long as you do not invest in cities with rent control. As long as the rents are allowed to increase, inflation can actually be your friend. The same is true if you understand how stock options work. If inflation goes up, and stock prices fall, you can make more money on the way down, while those in most mutual funds will be losing money and losing time."

"So I have a lot more control," said my friend. "By investing a little time, I gain more time, I take greater control over my assets, use less of my hard-earned money, control my income for life, improve my returns, and lower my risk . . . all with a little education."

Agreeing, I said, "All with a little education."

Invest in Yourself

One of the ways to gain more control of the time in your life is to invest some time in learning to create assets that return your money at a higher rate of speed. But just as a race car driver must increase their training if they want to handle higher speeds, so does an investor need to invest in their education if they want to handle investments that return more money in less time and at higher speeds.

Most of us know that education requires three steps and all three require an investment of time. The three steps are:

1. Invest some time finding the long- and short-term reasons why you want to learn something. You may want to sit down and write down your goals and the reasons you want to achieve your goals. It is the reasons that get you energy to move forward.

2. Invest some time in learning the technical knowledge required to achieve your goals. For example, I still invest time going to classes on how to build businesses, invest in real estate, and how to trade options. The investment in technical knowledge saves me time because it gives me guidance, tells me what I must learn once class is over, and gives priceless insights from the instructor.

3. Invest some time learning via real-life trial and error. Right after your technical classes are over, it is important to go out and gain some of your own experience and wisdom. The reason I recommend starting small and using a small amount of money is simply because you will make mistakes. In the real world, humans learn by making mistakes. In traditional schools, humans are punished for making mistakes. That is why you may need to forget some of the bad habits school teaches you and go out and make mistakes and learn from them. The more wisdom you gain, the greater financial challenges you can take on.

If you follow this three-step process, you may find that your wealth goes up as your confidence and experience increase. When wealth and experience increase, you gain greater control over your future and expend less time getting richer.

Why a DC Retirement Plan Is a Waste of Time

To me, the great waste of time with pension reform was that it failed to encourage people to learn to manage their own money and their own investments. The plan basically said, "Turn your money over to people who are smarter than you are." The problem is, you may notice that many of the people you thought were financially smarter than you were not.

Warren Buffett says this about students coming out of our current MBA and finance programs:

> "It has been helpful to me to have tens of thousands [of students] turned out of business schools taught that it didn't do any good to think."

In other words, one the reasons he does well in the markets is because graduates of business schools run most of the large fund companies, but they are not good investors. To which he adds, "Current finance classes can help you do average."

Simply put, the biggest problem with saving money and investing in mutual funds is that you do not gain much real-world investing experience. To me, that is a massive waste of time and money. Without real-world investing experience, it takes a lot of time, greater risk, tons of money, and constant financial insecurity all for a small financial return that may not be there when you need it. And as I stated earlier, if you're over forty-five years of age and have been wiped out or are just starting out, investing in a diversified DC pension plan will probably not work. In most cases, for a person over forty-five, time is a real challenge.

So there are many ways to gain greater control over your time. One way is via education.

The reason richdad.com puts out different products in different formats is because people learn differently. For example, some people learn by reading, yet many others do not. Some people learn well in traditional schools, but unfortunately, traditional schools teach little about the game of investing. Some people learn by doing, which is why we have created games for people to learn by playing. And still others learn by attending intensive seminars, seminars that concentrate the learning process in a short period of time.

In addition to our regular products such as books, audiotapes and videotapes, and games, some of the live intensive seminars we offer have covered the following subjects:

1. Stock options investing
2. Sales and sales training
3. Real estate investing
4. Building a business
5. Raising capital

Our courses are designed for people who are looking for real-world investing education, rather than getting an education for a college degree. Real-world investors teach our seminars, and they don't have the time to waste your time. There is too much money to be made and too much fun to have in the real world of business and investing. (If you want to stay abreast of our seminars, simply check in periodically with richdad.com and find out what seminars are being offered.)

Build Your Ark

Go back to Chapter 10 and review your answers:

How many years before you reach sixty-five?
How many years before 2016?

Have you committed the minimum five hours per week?
Make a commitment to a business or real estate investment today. Write
it here:

_____

Case Study

Allen is an attorney and was a partner in one of the premier international law
firms. The more successful he became the less time he had to spend with his
family and friends. He was paid exceptionally well but his income was still
based on the hours he physically invested in each project.

After reading *Rich Dad Poor Dad* and *Rich Dad's CASHFLOW Quadrant*,
Allen realized he was a "Super S" on the left side of the CASHFLOW Quadrant.
After practicing law for over twenty-five years and seeing an ever-increasing
demand for his time from his clients, he knew he had to make a change. Even
though Allen had accumulated a significant amount of wealth in savings, he
realized the bulk of his time was still being spent making others rich.

Allen changed his association with the law firm so he could be more flex-
ible in the way he did business with his clients. Now he can choose the
clients he wants to work with and he has the ability to exchange services for
equity. Instead of just working for an hourly rate, which would keep him in
the S quadrant, he can now invest his time in exchange for ownership in the
companies he advises and has shifted to the B quadrant. He is using his time
to build equity for himself, an asset in the B quadrant of the CASHFLOW
Quadrant.

While Allen had already filled his financial ark with paper assets through
savings plans and 401(k) plans, his wealth was closely tied to the stock market and out of his direct control. He realized just how out of control he was
when he saw the value of his paper assets decline significantly during 2001.

By changing control over how he spends his time, Allen is now building business assets and real estate over which he has more control to add stability to his financial ark and make it less susceptible to fluctuations in the stock market. He currently owns an equity interest in a number of different types of companies including an Internet marketing company, a medical imaging company, an environmental company, a gold company, and oil and gas companies. Some he has invested money in directly while with others he has exchanged his services for stock.

His financial statements now include all three asset categories: paper, businesses, and real estate. Through focusing on moving to the right side of the quadrant, Allen has succeeded in escaping the rat race while also building stability for his financial ark.

Chapter 20

Control #8: Control over Your Destiny

"Inside each of you is a rich person, a poor person, and a middle-class person. It is up to you to decide which person you become."

— RICH DAD

Drawing Out the Rich Person in You

According to *Webster's*, the word *education* comes from the Latin *educo* or *educe*, which means to draw out or lead out. By choosing to attend the U.S. Merchant Marine Academy in New York, I was choosing to have the sailor in me come out. By attending the U.S. Navy Flight School in Florida, I was choosing to have the pilot in me brought out. By deciding to follow in my rich dad's footsteps rather than my poor dad's, I was choosing to have the rich person in me come out.

In 1974, I had to make a decision as to which dad I would follow. I knew that if I followed my own dad's advice of "Go back to school, get your master's degree, and then get a secure job" I would wind up like him. I also knew that if I followed in my rich dad's footsteps, there were no guarantees as to where I would wind up. By 1974, I was old enough to know that rich dad's path had no guarantees. I could wind up broke and destitute just as well as wind up rich. By this time, I had seen many of rich dad's friends who had started on the journey with rich dad but had not made it to their destination. In 1974, I knew I had to make a choice between a guaranteed destiny or an uncertain destiny. As you know I chose the destiny that was uncertain.

My decision to choose an uncertain destiny—to build my own ark rather than build one for someone else—had little to do with the destination and everything to do with the process . . . the road to the destination. Many of us have heard the saying "The easy road becomes hard and the hard road becomes easy." In 1974, I decided to take the hard road, the road without guarantees. In 1974, the decision was easy . . . it was taking that first step that was hard. Five years later, in 1979, I had to make that decision again. Pulling myself up and out of a giant hole I had dug for myself was one of the most difficult things I have ever done, yet it was one of the best things I have ever done. I can honestly say that I have learned more from my failures than my successes . . . and I have learned more from my stupidity than my intelligence.

I recommend people keep their daytime job and start a part-time business, or start investing in a small piece of income real estate, simply because it takes a few years to learn the basics. The journey out of the chicken coop only begins with the first step. There are many steps that follow.

If rich dad's prophecy comes true, and I believe it will, the next few years will be boom years in the stock market. It will be the big boom before the big bust. The baby boomers will be pouring money into their last chance for retirement. Happy days will be here again. But instead of acting like drunken sailors on shore leave during this period of financial euphoria, I suggest you begin to methodically build your ark. Invest your time and some money in education and in experience. Be willing to make mistakes but make sure they are small . . . and then learn from them. After learning from each mistake, congratulate yourself and step forward again. Although you may not necessarily be gaining financially, you will be gaining priceless experience, personal self-confidence, more control over your destiny, and most importantly, you will be calling more and more for that rich person inside of you to come out.

Sir Isaac Newton once said, "I can measure the motion of celestial bodies but I cannot measure human folly." He said this after personally losing a fortune during a period of financial euphoria known as the South Sea Bubble, a bubble that burst in 1720. Even a genius became a fool once he lost control of himself, his emotions, his excuses, his vision, his rules, his advisors, and his fortunes.

I am quite certain that once the stock market recovers and begins its climb, sometime around 2004 to 2007, people will once again forget the past and be heard once again saying, "This time it's different!" But sometime after 2008 to 2012, things really will be different. Things will be different because this time, the past will catch up with the future. So prepare yourself and your ark to do well during the good times and to do even better during the bad times. Study, read, attend classes, and practice as if your life depends upon your ability to invest—because it does. If you can do that, you will have called out the rich person inside you and made him or her the captain of your ark.

Rich Dad Was a Tough Dad

Both my dads were tough men. Maybe that is why I found the discipline at the academy and in the Marine Corps easy. Rich dad was especially tough on Mike and me when it came to money, business, and investing; after all, he was turning over his fortune to his son and he was training me to acquire my own fortune.

Warren Buffett is also tough on his children. His partner has this to say about how Buffett treats his kids: "Warren is just as tough on his children as he is on his employees. He doesn't believe that if you love somebody the way to do him good is to give him something he's not entitled to."

Warren Buffett calls inherited wealth "food stamps for the rich." He goes on to say, "All these people who think that food stamps are debilitating and lead to a cycle of poverty, they're the same ones who go out and want to leave a ton of money to their kids."

When his son Howard ran for county commissioner in Omaha, voters falsely assumed that with his surname, his campaign would be well financed. That was not the case. Buffett senior explained: "I asked him to spell his name in lower case letters so that everyone would realize that he was the Buffett without the capital."

Money Does Not Make You Rich

The other day I was in a store buying some clothes. The clerk asked me what I did, to which I replied, "I'm an investor."

As he rang up my purchase he said, "That takes a lot of money, doesn't it?"

Shaking my head, I replied by saying, "No it doesn't. In fact money has very little to do with investing. Like many other people, I started with nothing."

"But you went to a good school then, didn't you?"

"I went to a good school but what I learned had very little to do with investing or becoming rich," I replied. "And besides, money does not make you rich."

"So how did you become rich?" asked the clerk. "How did you find the money to invest?"

"I studied, I read a lot, I started small and made many mistakes, and I have good advisors and mentors. It's what I learned on the streets that made me rich," I replied as I signed my credit card receipt.

"That sounds like a lot of work," said the young man.

"It is," I replied. "But so is what you are doing."

Not Having Money Makes You Richer

As you already know, rich dad never did finish school and, because of this, his speaking and writing skills were limited. Yet because he had to face the real world at the age of thirteen, his financial adversity caused him to develop his financial abilities and caused him to become one of the smartest persons I have ever known. When his son, Mike, and I get together these days, we continually discuss what we learned about business, investing, money, and life from his dad, my rich dad. We often comment, "Because he had no money he became rich. Because he had no education he became a genius. And because he had no security to fall back on, he found freedom."

What Do You Want to Be When You Grow Up?

One of the more important words to rich dad was the word *fiduciary*. *Webster's* defines fiduciary as *held in trust*, generally referring to financial matters. Rich dad said, "Regardless whether you wind up rich or poor, I always want you to be a person people can trust. Your word is your bond. If you wind up as a poor man and find yourself flat broke, you and your family haven't eaten in days, and there is a $100 bill sitting on someone's desk, you are trustworthy enough to let it sit there. If you are poor, when you are at home, you are a person who can be trusted to protect your family and your wealth, allowing both to grow with safety. If you are poor, I want you to be generous with your time, your wealth, and your wisdom. If you wind up rich men, you are to do the same things as a trustworthy poor man. That is what I want you to grow up to be. Regardless whether you grow up to be rich or poor, I want you to grow up to be people who can be trusted."

Inside each of you is a rich, poor, and middle-class person. Living in a free country means we all have the choice to decide which person we want to be. Start today by taking control of your education and your destiny.

Build Your Ark

Are you in the middle of self-doubt?

Do you want a recipe or quick-fix answers?

Reevaluate which level of thought you are in about money.

To be in charge of your own ark, you must design it with your personal goal in mind. Take action and start building it today.

Review the "Build Your Ark" section at the end of each chapter.

What is holding you back?

A Prophet's Hope Is to Be Wrong

Rich dad often said, "I hope I'm wrong."

He believed that by giving his son and me enough of a warning, we would have the time to prepare just in case he was right. He said, "The question is not whether I am right or wrong. The question is, Are you prepared just in case I am right?"

The good news was that rich dad's prophecy motivated me to prepare rather than remain complacent. In preparation, Kim and I built our ark. Building our ark led to increased financial education, experience, and financial freedom. So even if the great flood never comes and rich dad was wrong, our preparation has led us to a more financially secure position in life.

A giant stock market crash is coming . . . but the market crash is not the problem. Predicting a market crash is not a big deal. All financial markets go up and all financial markets go down. Market cycles are a part of life. Predicting a market crash is like predicting the coming of winter. The issue is the problems the next market crash will reveal. The next crash will be especially hard because three generations have pushed a bigger problem forward . . . the problem of how a person supports him- or herself once their working days are over. That is an unprecedented problem that grows bigger every day.

Warren Buffett says, "It's only when the tide goes out that you learn who's been swimming naked."

The next market crash will reveal who has been swimming naked, and one of those groups could be the government itself. For too long now, the government has made promises it knows it cannot keep. But broken promises are not really the problem. The real problem is a society that is naive enough to actually believe the promises. Too many people believe the government is responsible for saving them from their own inadequacies. Many people believe the government is like their fairy godmother, a mythical person who can wave a magic wand and all their financial problems will disappear. A society that believes in fairy tales is not a mature society.

In the real world of business and investing, the fairy godmother is the Federal Reserve Board and her older sister is the government. In financial terms, they are called the *lenders of last resort*. Right after September 11, 2001, the Federal Reserve flooded the economy with money as any grandparent would, hoping to ease the pain of their grandkids. When airlines got in trouble after the attack, the federal government stepped forward as the lender of last resort to save some of these airlines. This was like the kindly old grandpa stepping forward to rescue one of his adult children who also happens to have kids. My question and concern is whether the federal and state governments can afford to be the lender of last resort for much longer.

Like it or not, within a few years millions of baby boomers in America will start turning seventy years old. The question is, How many of them will have enough to afford to live for the rest of their lives? How many will look to the state and federal governments to be the fairy godparents?

The message of this book is that sometime soon people will begin to realize that neither the government nor the stock market can save them.

The Bad News

The bad news is that the next stock market crash will reveal a level of poverty in America that will shock the world. The world will ask how the richest country of all time can suddenly have so many poor people.

Even worse, economic anger and frustration are on the rise worldwide, which means we will need to solve these problems both globally as well as nationally.

As Warren Buffett says, "In the event of nuclear war, disregard this message."

The Good News

The good news is that when times are bad, people are often at their best. Right after the September 11 attack, millions of people found it in their hearts to do something positive and find the hero within themselves. I believe that the coming financial disaster will also bring out the best in people. Rather than complacency, despair, and depression, I believe people will rise up and work to solve this "problem of poverty" in a rich land. The even better news is that through the power of electronic communications, we can also work to end poverty throughout the world.

Earlier in this book, I wrote that there were three types of education. They are:

1. Academic
2. Professional
3. Financial

In America today, I would grade our ability to teach the basics of reading and writing as a C. I would rate our ability to train people professionally an A. America has great professional schools. But when it comes to financial education, I would give the American school system an F. This deficiency needs to be corrected immediately, if we are to continue as a world power.

In the Industrial Age, all a person needed was academic and professional education. In the Information Age, those two levels of education are no longer enough. In the Information Age, a person needs to be financially competent as well as academically and professionally competent. A high paying job is not enough. We need to know how to survive when our working days are over and that will require financial education on a large scale.

Two Professions

In the Industrial Age, all we needed was a good job or profession. In the Information Age, we will need two professions. One profession is how we make our money and the second profession is how we invest our money. In order to have the second profession, financial literacy is mandatory.

It's Your Choice

Noah could see the future and he prepared for it. If you see a future similar to the one rich dad did, you too may want to prepare while there is time to prepare. Hopefully, of course, the giant stock market crash will not come. Maybe someone will wave a magic wand and we will live happily ever after. But I do not think a stock market crash can be averted. Nor do I think that millions of baby boomers will suddenly save enough money to care for themselves for as long as they live. I think we will face an emergency, and out of this crisis, a new financial world will emerge. Of that I am confident, and I look forward to it. The coming stock market crash will reveal problems that we, as a society, have been pushing under the rug for too long. The good news is that once these problems are exposed and the truths are told, we have a chance of solving them once and for all . . . not just for ourselves, but also for the world.

Beyond the Bulls and the Bears

With the promotion of the 401(k) plans, the U.S. government, and by similar means other governments throughout the world, required millions of people to invest without first requiring them to become investors. As noninvestors entered the market, most were simply told that on average the stock market goes up. With that assumption, the boom in mutual funds was on.

The truth is that real-world investors know that all markets—regardless of whether they are stocks, bonds, real estate, heating oil, pork bellies, crude oil, mutual funds, or interest rates—move up, down, and sideways. A real-world investor would not invest in an asset that only did well in one direction or in a program that did not allow you to exit when prudent to. But that is just what the 401(k) did. It pushed people into assets that they had no control over, only did well in one market, and they could not exit without some sort of penalty. That is like handcuffing a swimmer and throwing him into the deep end of the pool.

Due to their lack of education, most DC pension plan investors have had to buy into the optimistic, Pollyanna point of view, the point of view of an eternal bull market. Real-world investors know that each market is made up of both bulls and bears. For those of you who want to take greater control over your financial destiny, you may want to go beyond just being a bull or a bear. If you want to be a real-world investor, you may want to develop your financial education, experience, and instincts in order to become a person who can see beyond the ups and downs of any market and always see the brighter future that lies ahead.

Noah knew that he had to take action because a catastrophe was about to take place. Being a man of vision, he could see beyond the darkness and see a brand-new world at the end of the flood. Although he knew he could not save everyone, he knew he could bring life to the new world. In other words, he took action not only because of the impending disaster but he also took action for a brighter future he knew lay ahead.

Being a real-world investor means being in tune with the real world. Optimists love the idea of buying, holding, diversifying, and praying. But if you plan on taking control of your future, you need to have real-world skills to see the better world beyond the storm clouds. If you become a real-world investor, you will not care if markets go up or markets go down because you will do well in all markets. You will not get caught in the debate of who is in control, the bulls or the bears . . . a debate that most short-term investors get caught up in, buying or selling with every turn of the market. If you become a real-world investor you will simply see the ups and downs of markets as one of the games of life.

Obviously, we are living in very chaotic times. Obviously, we as a global society have many challenges ahead. One of the challenges is the growing poverty not only in the third world but also in first-world countries such as America. The gap between the haves and have-nots must be narrowed. The reason this book has been dedicated to a teacher, Dave Stephens, and visionary teachers like him is because teachers hold the key to the future. Teachers hold the key because they are the people that prepare our children for the future. My poor dad, also a teacher, often worried that schools focused too much on ancient history rather than the future. He would say, "If I could see the future, I would know what to teach our kids." So that is why this book is dedicated to teachers like Dave Stephens and teachers who have the courage to offer their students the educational skills required for the future. If we have more teachers and more students teaching these financial skills, my Rich Dad's prophecy can be proven wrong. And that is the job of a prophet . . . a prophet's job is to provide enough of a warning so that his prophecy will be wrong and the actions taken will lead to a better world for us all.

This book is not meant to be a doom and gloom book. This book is written to inspire you to gain the skills you need to see the bigger and brighter picture of life . . . life beyond the storm clouds that are brewing. The future will be very bright for those who are prepared. But being prepared also means having faith as Noah did, the faith to see a better world beyond the storm.

Rich dad often used the saying "The darkest hour is the hour just before dawn." That was his way of reminding us to continue to improve our skills, to keep our faith strong, especially in the darkest of hours, and have the courage to step forward while others are running backward.

You have the opportunity to take control of your financial life. By building your own ark full of assets that work for you, you can prepare yourself to prosper no matter how the stock market performs.

In closing, I leave you with this quotation from Warren Buffett, America's richest and most successful investor, who says that he likes to buy stocks when "the bears are giving them away."

Thank you for reading this book.

ERISA

The Employee Retirement Income Security Act of 1974 (ERISA), which was signed by President Ford on September 2, 1974, adopted a sweeping overhaul of the existing employee pension and welfare benefit rules (both non-tax related and tax-related). It affected almost every employee benefit plan in the United States. ERISA has been amended subsequently on numerous occasions and has developed into an enormous, complex set of rules and regulations. The major acts that have amended the various titles of ERISA since 1974 are set forth below:

1974	ERISA enacted
1975	Tax Reduction Act of 1975
1976	Tax Reform Act of 1976
1977	Technical Corrections Act of 1977
1978	Revenue Act of 1978
1980	Multiemployer Pension Plan Amendments Act of 1980
1981	Economic Recovery Tax Act
1982	Tax Equity and Fiscal Responsibility Act of 1982
1984	Deficit Reduction Act
	Requirement Equity Act of 1984
1986	Consolidated Omnibus Budget Reconciliation Act of 1986
	Single-Employer Pension Plan Amendments Act of 1986
	Tax Reform Act of 1986
1987	Omnibus Budget Reconciliation Act of 1987

1988	Technical and Miscellaneous Revenue Act of 1988
1989	Omnibus Budget Reconciliation Act of 1990
1990	Older Workers Benefit Protection Act of 1990
	Omnibus Budget Reconciliation Act of 1990
1992	Unemployment Compensation Amendments of 1992
1993	Omnibus Budget Reconciliation Act of 1993
1994	Retirement Protection Act of 1994
1996	Small Business Job Protection Act of 1986
	Health Insurance Portability and Accountability Act
1997	Taxpayer Relief Act of 1997
1998	Transportation Equity Act of the Twenty-first Century
	Child Support Performance and Incentive Act of 1998
	Internal Revenue Service Restructuring and Reform Act of 1998
	Tax and Trade Relief Extension Act of 1998
1999	Tax Relief Extension Act of 1999
2000	Consolidated Appropriations Act of 2001
2001	Economic Growth and Tax Relief Reconciliation Act of 2001

401(k) Plans

Cash or deferred arrangements (CODAs), which are currently permitted under Section 401(k) of the Internal Revenue Code were a popular feature in profit sharing plans in the early 1950s. Under such an arrangement, an eligible employee could elect to receive a portion of the employer profit-sharing contribution in cash or defer it under a profit-sharing plan, which had to meet certain IRS requirements with respect to the timing of elections and the eligible participant group. Such type of CODA was not particularly popular—less than 1,000 were in existence in the early 1970s. In 1972, the Internal Revenue Service issued proposed regulations regarding the taxation of salary reduction contributions and created issues and uncertainties with respect to CODAs. Then on June 27, 1974, ERISA temporarily froze the tax status of plans with CODA features that were in existence until the end of 1976. Such date was subsequently extended until December 31, 1979. The Revenue Act of 1978 added Section 401(k) to the Code and in 1981, the IRS issued proposed regulations that permitted salary reduction contributions

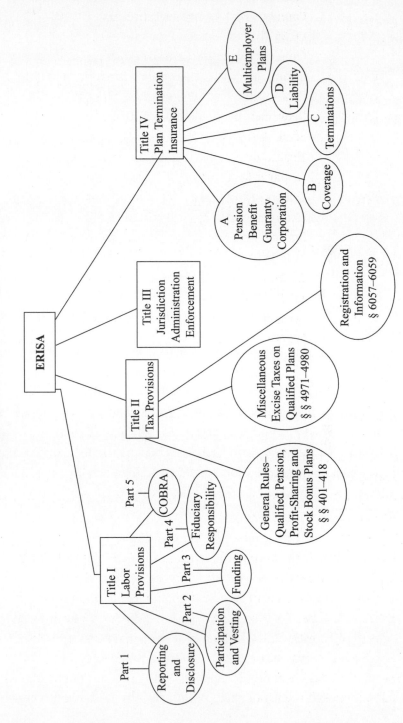

Statutory Framework of ERISA

to be made to 401(k) plans. Thereafter, employers began adopting 401(k) plans and converting after-tax contributions to existing profit sharing plans to pre-tax contributions.

The Tax Reform Act of 1984 made changes to the requirements of 401(k) plans by imposing mandatory nondiscrimination rules that were subsequently modified by the Tax Reform Act of 1986. More recently, EGTRRA (Economic Growth and Tax Relief Reconciliation Act of 2001) has made additional changes to 401(k) plans by permitting increased contributions and raising compensation limits for plan purposes.

Statutory Framework of ERISA

Title I of ERISA provides rules for the structuring of plans, sets standards of conduct for plan fiduciaries, and prohibits certain plan transactions. This is the "Labor" title.

Title II of ERISA sets forth the provisions of the Internal Revenue Code regarding employee benefit plans and excise taxes applicable to certain plan transactions. This is the "Tax" title.

Title III of ERISA sets forth provisions relating to procedures regarding (1) the issuance of determination letters for plans, (2) continued compliance with participation, vesting and funding standards, and (3) prohibited transactions as well as coordination of the function relating to ERISA between the Treasury Department and the Department of Labor.

Title IV of ERISA sets forth provisions relating to the termination of defined benefit plans, the Pension Benefit Guaranty Corporation (PBGC), and multiemployer plans.

About Dave Stephens's Program in Schools

Dave Stephens is a teacher at Warren Central/Warren Career Center in Indianapolis, Indiana. He discovered the CASHFLOW 101 and CASHFLOW for Kids games in 1998. "I am always visiting book stores . . . looking at tons of financial books, always looking at the ways in which material is presented. I saw the Rich Dad books, saw the way they presented the concepts of 'cash flow' and key elements of finance like balance sheets and income statements, and said: 'Finally, someone has put together financial information in a way that reflects how most people learn.'"

After reading *Rich Dad Poor Dad*, Dave ordered CASHFLOW 101 and gave it to his students for evaluation. "The students gave the game rave reviews," says Stephens. "They said it was absolutely a fantastic game." That prompted Stephens to incorporate it into his curriculum for high school juniors and seniors.

After seeing the success of the game as a teaching tool, he launched a pilot program in which his high school seniors who had mastered of the concepts of finance in the CASHFLOW game, would—literally—become the "teachers" who took these games and concepts into elementary schools within their communities.

"I could go on in superlatives forever," says Stephens. "CASHFLOW 101 is a game that has, literally, changed the lives of students. They have a new enthusiasm for education from seeing that, financially, they *can* succeed."

Stephens's work and enthusiasm has spread. In Indiana alone, nearly forty schools have incorporated the CASHFLOW games into their finance curriculum. Two of Dave's students have carried his program into the colleges they now attend. Michael Slate, a student at Purdue, and David Hosei a student at Indiana University have started similar programs for college students.

"Dave Stephens has changed my life," says Slate. Not only has Slate started Stephens's program at his university, he has recently purchased a $270,000 four-plex with only $2,000 down. It will be owner-occupied with other college students and Slate's mortgage payments are less than what he would have been paying in rent. "When I leave college," he said, "the property will continue to be an asset that generates positive cashflow."

David Hosei credits Stephens for teaching him how to apply what he learned in school to real life. "He helps you understand the connections . . . then guides and supports you as you discover your answers," said Hosei. "After playing CASHFLOW 101, I learned to see opportunities everywhere." His goal is to share what Stephens has taught him with his family and his community.

Slate and Hosei are founders of HELP (Helping Educate Lots of People), a nonprofit organization dedicated to carrying on the mission of financial literacy and community service. The members of the organization, nearly one hundred at Purdue and Indiana University alone, take the CASHFLOW for Kids game into Boys and Girls Clubs and schools in their communities to teach the concepts of money, finance, and investing. "These college students in HELP continue to learn by teaching others and they learn to contribute to their communities," says Slate.

This story of Michael Slate and Dave Hosei is one of many stories reflecting the impact of one teacher, Dave Stephens, on the lives of many people for generations to come.

Robert Kiyosaki

Born and raised in Hawaii, Robert Kiyosaki is a fourth-generation Japanese-American. After graduating from college in New York, Robert joined the Marine Corps and served in Vietnam as an officer and helicopter gunship pilot. Following the war, Robert worked for the Xerox Corporation in sales. In 1977, he started a company that brought the first nylon Velcro 'surfer wallets' to market. And in 1985 he founded an international education company that taught business and investing to tens of thousands of students throughout the world.

In 1994 Robert sold his business and retired at the age of forty-seven.

During his short-lived retirement, Robert, in collaboration with co-author Sharon Lechter, his CPA and business partner, wrote the book *Rich Dad Poor Dad*. Soon after he wrote *Rich Dad's Cashflow Quadrant, Rich Dad's Guide to Investing, Rich Kid Smart Kid*, and *Retire Young Retire Rich*—all of which earned spots on the bestseller lists of the *Wall Street Journal, Business Week, New York Times*, E-Trade.com, Amazon.com and others.

Prior to becoming a best-selling author, Robert created an educational board game— CASHFLOW 101—to teach individuals the financial strategies that his Rich Dad spent years teaching him. It was those financial strategies that allowed Robert to retire at the age of forty-seven.

In 2001, the first of the series of Rich Dad's Advisors books was launched. This team of professionals supports Robert's belief that "business and investing are team sports."

In Robert's words: "We go to school to learn to work hard for money. I write books and create products that teach people how to have money work hard for them. Then they can enjoy the luxuries of this great world we live in."

Rich Dad's Organization is the collaborative effort of Robert and Kim Kiyosaki and Sharon Lechter, who, in 1996, embarked on a journey that would afford them the opportunity to impact the financial literacy of people everywhere and carry the Rich Dad mission to every corner of the world.

Sharon Lechter

CPA, co-author of the Rich Dad series of books and CEO of the Rich Dad Organization, Sharon Lechter had dedicated her professional efforts to the field of education. She graduated with honors from Florida State University with a degree in accounting, then joined the ranks of Coopers & Lybrand, a Big Eight accounting firm. Sharon held various management positions with computer, insurance, and publishing companies while maintaining her professional credentials as a CPA.

Sharon and husband, Michael Lechter, have been married for over twenty years and are parents to three children, Phillip, Shelly and William. As her children grew, she became actively involved in their education and served in leadership positions in their schools. She became a vocal activist in the areas of mathematics, computers, reading, and writing education.

In 1989 she joined forces with the inventor of the first electronic "talking book" and helped him expand the electronic book industry to a multimillion dollar international market.

Today she remains a pioneer in developing new technologies to bring education into children's lives in ways that are innovative, challenging, and fun. As co-author of the Rich Dad books and CEO of that company, she focuses her efforts in the arena of financial education.

"Our current educational system has not been able to keep pace with the global and technological changes in the world today," Sharon states. "We must teach our young people the skills—both scholastic and financial—that they need to not only survive but to flourish in the world."

A committed philanthropist, Sharon "gives back" to the world communities as both a volunteer and a benefactor. She directs the Foundation for Financial Literacy and is a strong advocate of education and the need for improved financial literacy.

Sharon and Michael were honored by Childhelp USA, a national organization founded to eradicate child abuse in the United States, as recipients of the 2002 "Spirit of the Children" Award. And, in May of 2002, Sharon was named chairman of the board for the Phoenix chapter of Childhelp USA.

As an active member of Women's Presidents Organization, she enjoys networking with other professional women across the country.

Robert Kiyosaki, her business partner and friend, says "Sharon is one of the few natural entrepreneurs I have ever met. My respect for her continues to grow every day that we work together."

Rich Dad's Organization is the collaborative effort of Robert and Kim Kiyosaki and Sharon Lechter, who, in 1996, embarked on a journey that would afford them the opportunity to impact the financial literacy of people everywhere and carry the Rich Dad mission to every corner of the world.

**Robert Kiyosaki's Edumercial—
An Educational Commercial**

The Three Incomes

In the world of accounting, there are three different types of income—earned, passive and portfolio. When my real dad said to me, "Go to school, get good grades, and find a safe secure job." He was recommending I work for earned income. When my rich dad said, "The rich don't work for money, they have their money work for them," he was talking about passive income and portfolio income. Passive income, in most cases is derived from real estate investments. Portfolio income is income derived from paper assets, such as stocks, bonds, and mutual funds.

Rich dad used to say, "The key to becoming wealthy is the ability to convert earned income into passive income and/or portfolio income as quickly as possible." He would say, "The taxes are highest on earned income. The least taxed income is passive income. That is another reason why you want your money working hard for you. The government taxes the income you work hard for more than the income your money works hard for."

The Key to Financial Freedom

The key to financial freedom and great wealth is a person's ability or skill to convert earned income into passive income and/or portfolio income. That is the skill that my rich dad spent a lot of time teaching Mike and me. Having that skill is the reason my wife Kim and I are financially free, never needing to work again. We continue to work because we choose to. Today we own a real estate investment company for passive income and participate in private placements and initial public offerings of stock for portfolio income.

Investing to become rich requires a different set of personal skills, skills essential for financial success as well as low-risk and high-investment returns. In other words, knowing how to create assets that buy other assets. The problem is that gaining the basic education and experience required is often time consuming, frightening, and expensive, especially when you make mistakes with your own money. That is why I created the patented education board games trademarked as CASHFLOW.

CASHFLOW 101

CASHFLOW 101 is an educational program that teaches accounting, finance, and investing at the same time and makes learning fun.

Learn how to get out of the rat race and onto the fast track where your money works hard for you instead of you working hard for your money. The educational program, CASHFLOW 101, includes three audiocassettes that reveal distinctions on CASHFLOW 101 as well as valuable investment information and a video titled "The Secrets of the Rich."

CASHFLOW 101 is recommended for adults and children age ten and older.

CASHFLOW 202

CASHFLOW 202 teaches you the advanced business and investing techniques used by technical investors by adding volatility to the game. It teaches the advanced investment techniques of "short-selling stock," "put-options," "call-options," "straddles" and real estate exchanges.

You must have CASHFLOW 101 in order to play CASHFLOW 202. This package contains new game sheets, new playing cards, and four audiocassettes.

CASHFLOW for KIDS

Give your children the financial head start necessary to thrive in today's fast-paced and changing world. Schools teach children how to work for money. CASHFLOW for Kids teaches children how to have money work for them.

CASHFLOW for Kids is a complete educational package that includes the book and audiocassette titled "Rich Dad's Guide to Raising Your Child's Financial I.Q."

CASHFLOW for Kids is recommended for children ages six and older.

The Rich Dad Series, International Bestsellers

Rich Dad Poor Dad

What the rich teach their kids about money that the poor and middle class do not. Learn how to have your money work for you and why you don't need to earn a high income to be rich.

The book that "rocked" the financial world.

J.P. Morgan declares "Rich Dad Poor Dad a must-read for Millionaires."
The Wall Street Journal

"A starting point for anyone looking to gain control of their financial future."
USA Today

Rich Dad's CASHFLOW Quadrant

Rich Dad's guide to financial freedom. Learn about the four CASHFLOW Quadrants, and you will understand the most important keys to creating wealth.

The sequel to *Rich Dad Poor Dad, Rich Dad's Cashflow Quadrant* describes the four types of people who make up the world of business and the core value differences between them. It discusses the tools an individual needs to become a successful business owner and investor.

Rich Dad's Guide to Investing

What the rich invest in that the poor and middle class do not. Learn how you can apply the techniques of the rich to create your own wealth and have it grow.

This is the third book in the Rich Dad Series. *Rich Dad's Guide to Investing* discusses what the rich invest in that the poor and middle class do not. Robert provides an insider's look into the world of investing, how the rich find the best investments, and how you can apply the techniques of the rich to create your own wealth.

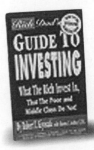

Rich Dad's Rich Kid Smart Kid

Give your child a financial head start. Awaken your child's love of learning how to be financially free. Imagine the results you'll see when they start early!

This book is written for parents who value education, want to give their child a financial and academic head start in life, and are willing to take an active role to make it happen. *Rich Kid Smart Kid* is designed to help you give your child the same inspiring and practical financial knowledge that Robert's rich dad gave him. Learn how to awaken your child's love of learning.

Rich Dad's Retire Young Retire Rich

A powerful personal story about how Robert and Kim Kiyosaki started with nothing, and retired financially free in less than ten years. If you do not plan on working hard all your life, this book is for you.

If you're tired of the same old investment advice—such as "be patient," "invest for the long term," and "diversify"—then this book is for you.

Robert explains in detail the power of leverage. How to leverage your mind, your financial plans, your actions and most importantly, your first steps to becoming financially free.

You will learn Rich Dad's techniques using leverage to first build financial security and ultimately have the life you want.

The Business School For People Who Like Helping People

Learn the Eight Hidden Values of a Network Marketing Business—Other than Making Money! Understand why the word NETWORK is valued by the rich.

The Business School For People Who Like Helping People will reveal:

• The quickest way to build a "B" Quadrant Business.

• Why the word "network" is so powerful to the rich.

Includes a sixty-minute audiocassette free! Tape not sold separately.

My poor dad often said, "What you know is important."
My rich dad said, "If you want to be rich, who you know
is more important than what you know."

Rich dad explained further saying, "Business and investing are team sports." The average
investor or small business person loses financially because they do not have a team.
Instead of a team, they act as individuals who are trampled by very smart teams.

That is why the Rich Dad's Advisors book series was created. Rich Dad's Advisors will offer
guidance to help you know who to look for and what kind of questions to ask so you can
gather your own great team of advisors.

Do you have what it takes to become financially free? When
it comes to money, your greatest asset is financial literacy.

Rich Dad's
STRAIGHT TALK

The first step in taking control of your financial future is
believing that knowledge is power—and applying that
knowledge to the decisions you make about money and investing.

You'll discover the little-known secrets of the rich in Rich Dad's STRAIGHT TALK.
This monthly newsletter created with Time Life is packed full of financial information:

- A Message from Robert Kiyosaki –
  Read Robert's personal message regarding each monthly issue.

- Motivation and Encouragement - Take the leap from job to security to true financial freedom.

- Q&A – Do you have questions for Rich Dad?
  Submit your questions and get personalized answers.

- Advisor's Column – From Real Estate to Taxes, get monthly information
  from Rich Dad's Advisors.

YOU CAN CHOOSE TO BE RICH

Created with Time Life, this powerful home study course will teach
you the three-step plan to riches—Think It—Learn It—Do It.
The program contains a Home Study Course Binder, twelve CD's
or cassettes with specialized lessons from Robert's personal
team of experts, one video that will show you how to stop
living from paycheck to paycheck and enjoy the power of

having money work for you, one bonus audiocassette tape that reveals the six simple obstacles
people face on their path to wealth; and a debt eliminator—a practical tool to help you
eliminate bad debt and build a strong foundation.

FREE Rich Dad's Audio Download

In each of our books we like to provide an audio interview as a bonus with additional insights.
As a thank you for reading this book, you may go to **www.richdadbook6.com**
to download Rich Dad's **FREE** audio. You must first be a member
of the Rich Dad's Community to access this area of the website
and you must also be signed on to the community.

FREE

I appreciate your purchase of my latest book—
Join the Rich Dad's Community at
www.richdad.com
and share your adventure with thousands of others
worldwide. Embarking on Rich Dad's Journey is
the first step to a life free from the fear and worry
of not having enough money. It's the first step in
becoming part of a community of individuals who
are committed to change.

Journey to
financial
freedom

To order books visit: www.twbookmark.com

North America/South America/Europe/Africa:
CASHFLOW Technologies, Inc.
4330 N. Civic Center Plaza, Suite 101
Scottsdale, Arizona 85251
USA
(800) 308-3585 or (480) 998-6971
Fax: (480) 348-1349
e-mail: info@richdad.com

Australia/New Zealand:
CASHFLOW Education Australia
Reply Paid AAA401 (no stamp required)
4-6 Mentmore Avenue
Rosebery NSW 2018 Australia
TEL: 1300 660 020 • FAX: 1300 301 988
email: info@cashfloweducation.com.au